ARAB MASS MEDIA

ARAB MASS MEDIA

NEWSPAPERS, RADIO, AND TELEVISION IN ARAB POLITICS

WILLIAM A. RUGH

Westport, Connecticut
London

Library of Congress Cataloging-in-Publication Data

Rugh, William A.
   Arab mass media : newspapers, radio, and television in Arab politics /
William A. Rugh.
       p.   cm.
   Includes bibliographical references and index.
   ISBN 0-275-98212-2 (alk. paper)
   1. Mass media—Political aspects—Arab countries.   2. Mass media policy—
Arab countries. I. Title.
   P95.82.A65R84 2004
   302.23'0917'0917'4927—dc22   2003062442

British Library Cataloguing in Publication Data is available.

Library of Congress Catalog Card Number: 2003062442
ISBN: 0-275-98212-2

First published in 2004

Praeger Publishers, 88 Post Road West, Westport, CT 06881
An imprint of Greenwood Publishing Group, Inc.
www.praeger.com

Printed in the United States of America

The paper used in this book complies with the
Permanent Paper Standard issued by the National
Information Standards Organization (Z39.48-1984).

10 9 8 7 6 5 4 3 2 1

Contents

Tables

Preface

The flow of information between the United States and the Arab world is overwhelmingly one way, West to East. Arab audiences know much more about America than Americans know about Arabs. Every day, 24 hours a day, Arabs have access to CNN and other American television channels that are relayed to them via satellite. The language barrier is crossed for news going West to East because information from and about the United States is carried almost every day on the front pages of Arab newspapers published in Arabic, and discussed in editorials. Because the United States is the world's only superpower and is involved in many aspects of life in the Middle East and North Africa, and because its foreign policies affect the lives of Arabs in many ways, Arab media editors constantly report on what the United States is doing. Arab television stations typically broadcast reviews of the world's press every morning, and American news is regularly featured. *Newsweek* now appears in an Arabic version that is available throughout the Middle East.

In sharp contrast with the Eastward flow of information, the Westward flow is meager. Americans know relatively little about the Arab world, and almost nothing about Arab media and what newspapers and television are saying. Part of the reason is the language barrier, since most Arab media are in Arabic and probably fewer than one percent of Americans can read that language. There are a few Arab newspapers printed in English, but they are intended for non-Arabs living in the Middle East so their news and editorial content are quite different from the media in Arabic which most Arabs see every day. As a result, Americans have no idea what is being said about the United States or anything else on a daily basis in the Arab mass media, and they have no way of understanding the nature of Arab mass media.

Mass media in any country reflect their particular social, cultural, and political environments. Anyone who wants to understand the Arab world should therefore know its media. After the September 11, 2001 terrorist attacks on the United States, Americans have paid much more attention to the Arab world, trying to understand it better, and they have been puzzled by fragmentary reports of what has appeared in Arab media. Journalists, politicians, and others have talked much more about Arab society and its institutions, including Arab media but most people have little solid information about the subject, and some of their observations have unfortunately been rather superficial. Hopefully this detailed study, which is based on a variety of well-informed sources, will help meet that need.

This book describes and analyzes Arab print media, radio, and television, and is a study of the role that the mass media play in the political process in the Arab world. The mass media are newspapers, magazines, radio, and television that originate from a single source and which are aimed simultaneously at a mass audience. They still have a greater impact than the newer communication media such as Internet, cell phones, and fax, because they reach much larger audiences, especially in the Arab world where access to the newer devices is still limited. Web sites, it is true, are somewhat similar in function to the mass media and may at some time in the future develop into true competitors for print media, radio, and television, but that has not happened yet, certainly not in the Arab world. The Arab audience for Web sites in fact remains very small, and is likely to continue to be small in the near future, for reasons that are discussed in the book.

After an introductory overview, the book analyzes print media. They are not uniform in structure or function across the Arab world, which but can be divided for purposes of analysis of the mass media into a typology of four categories. One is the "mobilization" system to which Syria, the Sudan, Libya, and pre-2003 Iraq belong; another is the "diverse" system to which Lebanon, Kuwait, Morocco, Yemen, and post-2003 Iraq belong; a third is the "loyalist" system to which Saudi Arabia, Bahrain, Qatar, the UAE, Oman, and Palestine belong; and the fourth is the "transitional" system to which Egypt, Algeria, Tunisia, and Jordan belong. This book will describe and explain each of these types of system, giving examples of how they deal with news and commentary, and what role they play in the political process in those countries.

As this book was being completed, a U.S.-led invasion and occupation of Iraq in 2003 was already leading to significant changes in Iraqi media. It will take time for a new structure to settle down, and it will probably contain some characteristics from the past system. The book therefore analyzes the development of Iraqi media in detail up to 2003 in Chapter 2, and developments after that in Chapter 5.

The book also describes and explains a relatively new phenomenon of "offshore" pan-Arab print media, published in Europe and distributed throughout the region, with generally more editorial freedom than local newspapers have.

Finally, the book describes and analyzes Arab television and radio. Since Desert Storm (1991) the most significant change that has taken place in Arab media is the emergence of Arab satellite television. This development has had a significant impact not only on Arab television but also on print media. Americans are aware of al-Jazeera Television that has had a revolutionary impact in the Middle East, but there are other television channels in Arabic which are also important but unknown in America.

The book includes some statistics, for example newspaper circulation data, but because of the great difficulty of obtaining accurate numbers of this kind, they should not be considered to be precise but only rough orders of magnitude for comparison purposes. Also, footnotes have been kept to a minimum, and omitted for some facts that are easily verifiable.

A large number of Arab and American experts in many countries have generously provided advice and information that has been invaluable in the updating of this book. Some are acknowledged in the footnotes while others have preferred to remain anonymous. Any errors of fact or interpretation however are the author's.

Introduction

Why should we study the Arab news media?

The news media have taken on increasing importance in recent years everywhere in the world. The growth of television viewing and radio listening audiences has been dramatic, and newspaper readership has expanded similarly. One cause has been rapid technological innovation, in transistors and then in satellite communications, which have extended the reach of the media. Another has been the population explosion which, together with the trend toward urbanization has resulted in the concentration of large groups of people in places where they have easier access to mass media. Increasing literacy, too, has created a larger newspaper-reading public.

This book is about the mass media as they function in Arab society. Mass media are all the means of transmitting messages or meaning publicly to "large, heterogeneous, and anonymous audiences."[1] The book describes and analyzes the organization of the press and its relationships to the government and the political process. We focus primarily on daily newspapers, radio, and television which reach a mass audience with messages that originate from a single point but reach very large audiences. We will make some references to other printed media such as weekly and monthly magazines. But non-news mass communications media such as motion pictures, and newer electronic means of communication such as the Internet and fax, have been excluded because their role in society is somewhat different, and they do not reach mass audiences in the Arab world. A study treating them in sufficient depth would be a book in itself.

The mass media play a larger role than other forms of communication in the daily lives of people everywhere, but especially in the Arab world. These media are consequently regarded by politicians and governments as having great political importance. In fact, the acquisition and distribution of news has been seen for a long time as a vital political function in society because the news items may have political impact very quickly on large numbers of people. Most societies have wrestled with problems of media controls and freedom, and have dealt seriously with questions of media-government relations. Indeed as the technical means of communication have improved, governments and political leaders have judged these problems as increasingly critical because they think the power of these instruments to affect the political process is growing. Thus the typical news-handling institution has been of great interest to the government and the public because it is a complex organization that involves great expense and because people regard it as politically important. The way government and society deal with this institution is significant for an understanding of that government and society as well as of the mass communication process.

A basic assumption of this book is that news media institutions do not exist independently of their environments but rather take on the "form and coloration of the social and political structures" within which they operate.[2] There is an intimate, organic relationship between media institutions and society in the way that those institutions are organized and controlled. Neither the institution nor the society in which it functions can be understood properly without reference to the other. This is certainly true in the Arab world. The news media there, in fact, are particularly interesting in this regard because of the roles they played since the middle of the twentieth century when most of the Arab countries gained their full independence and developed their own national institutions. Arab media systems have taken on their current institutional forms only recently, and these forms can only be explained by reference to the underlying political realities in the society as a whole.

The spread of communication facilities in the Arab world has been remarkable. By the middle of the 1970s, every Arab country, including even the poorest ones, had built its own television system, and a majority had satellite ground stations capable of transcontinental television transmission. By that time, all Arab countries were active in radio broadcasting for both internal and external audiences, and in many places the programming was extremely varied and rich. Egypt's international radio broadcasting services, for example, were by then designed for many different audiences, and their total hours of air time were the third highest of any country in the world, greater than any Western nation. And all eighteen Arab countries not only published their own newspapers and magazines but each one has its own news agency. The amount of news, commentary, and other information and interpretation turned out by these media every day is enormous.

These media have become quite important in the lives of most of the nearly three hundred million people who live in the Arab world. Growing literacy has given many access to the printed media, but television viewing and especially radio listening have burgeoned as cheaper transistorized receivers became available. The story is told in Saudi Arabia of an American oil-company geologist, crossing a barren expanse of desert in 1969, well before the oil boom and dramatic Arab economic growth, who encountered a lone bedouin tending his flock of camels and stopped to try out his own Arabic. When the bedouin asked where he had come from, the American solemnly pointed to the sky and said, "I've just come from the moon." Without hesitation, the bedouin replied, "Oh, then you must be Neil Armstrong." The story may be apocryphal, but it is certainly true that the details of the American lunar landing became known even by the least educated people in the remotest parts of the Arab world by means of transistorized radios. At the same time, large numbers of Arabs in urban areas enjoyed color television as well as magazines and newspapers printed according to high standards.

Specialists who observe political and other trends in the Arab world follow the Arab media closely. Foreign correspondents reporting on the area use Arab media as a resource for their stories. Foreign embassies in Arab countries depend heavily on the local press for their reporting back to their home governments. The United States government spends millions of dollars annually monitoring Arab radio broadcasts twenty-four hours each day, a service that Washington officials and analysts cull for useful information on Arab policies, ideas, and perceptions. Merely looking at headlines of the daily newspaper, in fact, can often give some indication of local concerns and preoccupations. To cite one example, the Arab press on May 28, 1973, reported on the same meeting of the Organization of African Unity chiefs of state under the following different headlines: "General Gowan Elected President of African Summit Session" (*al-Saba*, Tunisia); "Gowan: We Must Control Our Own Resources to Liberate Africa Economically" (*l'Opinion*, Morocco); "Arab African Split Within OAU Because of Somalia and Ethiopia" (*al-Madinah*, Saudi Arabia); "Soviets Congratulate Sudan on 10th Anniversary of OAU" (*al-Sahafa*, the Sudan); "Africa Concern for Mideast Problem" (*al-Dustur*, Jordan); "New Step to Liberate Palestine" (*al-Sha'b*, Algeria); "Results of Sadat's Contacts Appear in Strengthened African Decision Exposing the Position of Israel" (*al-Akhbar*, Egypt). There is, of course, much more in the press than headlines. Readers look for information, but they also seek nuances in language and even omissions in reporting, which they may detect if they listen to foreign radio broadcasts. In an area of the world where public opinion polls and open parliamentary debates are rare, observers look at media content for indicators of political trends and probable future developments. Journalists, diplomats, and others typically make quick analyses on a daily basis rather than long-term systematic studies, and their conclusions are usually not made public.

This is not a study of media content, although examples of content are provided. This study examines the organization of Arab media institutions which shape that content, and it analyzes the influences that are brought to bear on Arab journalists in writing their news copy, editorials, and other material. The Arab journalist, in order to succeed, must be highly sensitive to the political realities prevailing in his country, which constitute real constraints and incentives on his work. The organization he works for fits into his country's prevailing political system, and he must take that into account, as he must be aware of the ways in which his organization is linked with the government and/or the political system.

In other parts of the world, the relationship of the mass media to the government has been analyzed in detail, and several different types of press system have been described.[3] Do the Arab media fall into any of these categories? The first chapter of this book answers that question in the negative, although there are some characteristics of the so-called authoritarian system which are found in most of the Arab countries. Arab media, however, has some characteristics which set it apart from systems elsewhere, so we have had to describe these with specific reference to the manifestations in the various Arab countries. The first chapter presents those characteristics of the Arab news media which are present in all Arab countries and which seem to be typical of the Arab press as a whole. The book then presents an analysis of the Arab daily newspapers which shows that they can be divided into four fundamental subtypes which have appeared and survived after independence. The Arab countries have organized their daily newspapers according to one or another of these four systems, but the organization is not necessarily static: some countries have gone from one system into another, depending on conditions which are described in Chapters 2 through 7 that discuss these subtypes, and Chapter 8 analyzes the relatively new phenomenon of offshore-based pan-Arab print media.

Chapters 9–11 describe and analyze the organization and function of radio and television institutions in the Arab world. These systems can be dealt with together because they are simpler organizationally and have much more in common than do the newspaper organizations. Finally, Chapter 12 brings together the conclusions of the analyses and offers some generalizations about the conditions under which the various organizational forms have appeared and will probably continue to appear in the Arab world.

NOTES

1. Charles R. Wright, *Mass Communication* (New York: Random House, 1962), pp. 11–16.

2. Fred S. Siebert, Theodore Peterson, and Wilbur Schramm, *Four Theories of the Press* (Urbana: University of Illinois Press, 1963), p. 1.

3. See, for example, Siebert, Peterson, and Schramm, *Four Theories*, op. cit.; Wilbur Schramm, "Two Concepts of Mass Communication," in Bernard Berelson and Morris Janowitz, eds., *Reader in Public Opinion and Communication* (New York: The Free Press, 1966), pp. 206–19.

Arab Information Media: Function and Structure

This is a study of all significant Arab mass media, which are spread across eighteen Arab countries: Algeria, Bahrain, Egypt, Iraq, Jordan, Palestine, Kuwait, Lebanon, Libya, Morocco, Oman, Qatar, Saudi Arabia, Sudan, Syria, Tunisia, the United Arab Emirates, and Yemen. These countries cover an area from the Atlantic Ocean to the Persian Gulf, with a total population of nearly three hundred million people. All are independent, sovereign states except Palestine, which has been promised international recognition but as of 2004 had not yet achieved it.

In some respects, these countries are quite diverse. Economic prosperity measured by per capita Gross National Product (GNP) ranged in 1998 from below $300 in Yemen and the Sudan to a high of over $20,000 in Kuwait. The level of education varies from Oman, where secondary schools were first opened in the 1970s, to Lebanon, which has several long-established institutions of higher learning and a literacy rate of over ninety percent. There are different types of government too—absolute and constitutional monarchies, presidential and one party regimes, and some representational institutions. Even their preindependence political histories varied considerably. To cite two examples, Algeria, for more than a century considered to be an integral part of France, liberated itself in 1962 after a traumatic war, while Saudi Arabia had only minimal experience with colonial rule and achieved full independence and unity well before World War II.

Nevertheless, the peoples of the eighteen Arab states feel bound together by strong cultural and psychological ties. The vast majority of them regard

Arabic as their mother tongue; most of them share a single culture, language, and religion, and their sense of a common destiny is very strong. Nationalism, both in the pan-Arab sense and as felt toward the newer individual nation-states, separate and distinct from Western or any other identity, is a powerful force. And despite the differences in wealth, the Arabs are all living in a developing world environment of rapid economic and political change in which high priority is given to modernization.

What roles do mass communication media play in these Arab societies? A basic assumption of this study is that a media system necessarily responds to and reflects its environment, particularly the existing political realities, but also economic, cultural, and other factors. Mass media facilities, of course, serve the function everywhere of disseminating messages from single originators to mass audiences, and their roles are circumscribed to that degree. But the precise function and structure of the media in a particular country can only be understood within the context of existing political and other factors in that country. Therefore, as there are some common cultural and other elements throughout the Arab world, there are some similarities in Arab media systems; and as there are political, economic, and other differences there are naturally differences among their media systems. In this chapter we will look at some of the general characteristics of Arab mass media, and then in the next ten chapters we will look at factors that make them different. First, how widespread are the mass media in the Arab world?

MASS MEDIA DENSITY IN THE ARAB WORLD

Newspapers and magazines are published in every one of the eighteen Arab countries, some of which have press traditions going back more than a century. The first Arab newspaper, that is the first periodical publication carrying news written by and for Arabs, was apparently *Jurnal al-Iraq* that began appearing in Arabic and Turkish in Baghdad in 1816. Two Arab newspapers were published in Cairo in the 1820s; Algeria followed in 1847, Beirut in 1858, Tunis 1861, Damascus 1865, Tripoli (Libya) in 1866, San'a 1879, Casablanca 1889, Khartoum 1899, and Mecca 1908. The first Arabic daily was published in Beirut in 1873.

Radio listening began in the 1920s, but the size of the audience was small until later decades and only some of the Arab states began their own radio broadcasting in the period before World War II. Television viewing began on a small scale in the late 1950s in Iraq and Lebanon, when those countries established TV transmitters in their capital cities. The only other Arabs who could watch television in the 1950s were those few who happened to be able to see non-Arab television: French TV could be seen by some Arabs in the Maghreb states of North Africa; U.S. military-operated TV could be seen by Libyans living near Wheelus Air Force Base; and telecasts by the Arabian-

American Oil Company could be seen by Saudis living near ARAMCO head-quarters in Dhahran. Indigenous electronic media developed rapidly in some countries, but not until 1970, when Oman opened its radio transmitter, has every Arab state had indigenous radio broadcasting, and not until the fall of 1975 when Yemeni TV went on the air has every Arab state had its own indigenous television capability. Despite the long head start by the print media, the electronic media in the Arab world had by the end of the twenti-eth century spread much farther among the population, as Table 1.1 shows.

In most Arab countries the people have relatively good access to radio and television, while the press remains primarily a medium reaching elite groups. This can be seen, for example, if we match the statistics against the minimum standards used by the United Nations Educational, Scientific and Cultural Organization (UNESCO), which suggested that every country should provide at least the following media facilities per thousand people: fifty radio receivers, twenty television receivers, and a hundred copies of daily newspapers.

TABLE 1.1   Media Density in the Arab World[1]

	A	B	C	D	E	F	G
Algeria	30	244	110	67	1,080	38	53
Bahrain	0.7	580	472	87	67	117	8
Egypt	64	399	189	55	2,400	38	99
Iraq	23	222	83	39	407	20	—
Jordan	4.9	372	84	90	250	42	9
Kuwait	2.0	624	486	82	635	377	38
Lebanon	4.3	687	335	86	435	141	17
Libya	5.3	273	137	80	71	14	—
Morocco	29	243	166	49	704	27	33
Oman	2.4	621	563	72	63	28	16
Qatar	0.6	450	404	81	90	161	15
Saudi Arabia	20	319	260	76	1,105	59	173
Sudan	31	464	273	58	737	27	11
Syria	16	276	67	74	287	20	17
Tunisia	10	158	198	71	280	31	20
UAE	2.9	318	292	76	384	170	49
Yemen	18	65	283	46	230	15	9

Key

A   Population (in millions) for 2000

B   Radio receivers per 1,000 inhabitants for 1997

C   Television receivers per 1,000 inhabitants for 1997

D   Literacy in percent for 2000

E   Total circulation of daily newspapers (in 1,000s) for 1996

F   Copies of daily papers per 1,000 inhabitants for 1996

G   Gross Domestic Product (in $ billions) for 2000

All of the Arab countries have surpassed those minimum standards for both radio and television. Some, such as the Sudan and Yemen, still have low receiver/population ratios, largely for economic reasons, although countries like Jordan, Yemen, and Egypt have surprisingly high ratios in view of their economic problems. Radio listening is nearly universal in most Arab states (assuming five to ten listeners per receiver) because of the availability of inexpensive transistorized receivers, the prevalence of group listening, and the great amount of international medium-wave broadcasting of interest to Arab audiences that takes place especially in the area of the Mediterranean and Fertile Crescent. Television, too, reaches a remarkable number of Arabs, probably well over 100 million, and has grown very rapidly in recent years.

By comparison to other developing areas of the world, the Arabs have kept pace in radio listening but seem to be ahead in the extent of their television viewing.

The wealthy petroleum-exporting states especially have achieved relatively high radio and TV audience densities as their citizens have spent more and more money on receivers to tune in to their own national and some foreign stations (see Chapters 9 and 10). The Arab print media, on the other hand, still reach only a highly select audience. As of 1975, not one Arab country had achieved the UNESCO minimum standard for daily newspaper circulation. By 1998, only five Arab states—Lebanon, Bahrain, Kuwait, Qatar, and the United Arab Emirates—had achieved that standard, and all of them were wealthy states with small populations (the total population for all four was under ten million people), with fairly large numbers of literate, newspaper reading expatriate Arabs living and working there. Low literacy is a major factor in inhibiting Arab newspaper circulation, but there are others, such as distribution problems. Lebanon, for example, has a relatively high literacy rate, and a tradition of producing and consuming print media. But the long civil strife in Lebanon severely affected newspaper distribution in many parts of the country and helped depress circulation figures, while radio and television were able to cross these barriers.

Arab newspapers have always been written for an elite audience. Fifty-five years ago an Egyptian newspaper had the highest circulation of any Arab daily with 7,000 copies, and most dailies did not surpass 2,000. The total number of Arab newspaper readers in the early twenty-first century is still relatively small. Each copy may be read by an average of two to six people, depending on the paper and location, but many readers see more than one paper. Therefore, there are probably not more than thirty million regular newspaper readers in the Arab world, or roughly ten percent of the population. Some of the Arab states have only recently had enough newspaper readers to sustain indigenous papers; Qatar, Bahrain, and Oman did not have successful dailies until 1975, 1976, and 1980, respectively. Only five Arab countries have daily newspapers which distribute over 60,000 copies and some have dailies only in the under-10,000 range. Only Egypt has dailies which distribute more than a half million copies.

CONDITIONS AFFECTING ARAB MASS MEDIA

What special circumstances and conditions have affected the mass media generally in the Arab world?

Weak Economic Base

Arab information media have by and large been established on a weak economic base. Newspapers developed when the national incomes and populations were small, and the literacy rates were low. Thus both advertising revenues and mass-circulation sales, the two main sources of commercial newspaper income elsewhere, were restricted. Even after World War II, as the Arab economies developed, advertising did not become important enough to Arab businessmen, or promising enough in the modest-circulation press, to help newspaper publishers very much. In the following half century, as the Arab states became wealthier, the Arab media remained relatively poor. One Arab editor has calculated that by 2003, well after the oil boom and substantial Arab economic development, the total revenue of all Arab media is less than that of the *New York Times* or *Washington Post,* and that annually the combined incomes of all journalists in wealthy Saudi Arabia add up to less than Peter Jennings' annual salary.[2]

A few publishers, like Cairo's al-Ahram Publishing House, have been able to expand their operations into printing periodicals and books in their own plants, and also advertising and distributing foreign publications, but most daily newspapers have a far more modest financial base. The short supply of newsprint, other printing costs, plus the various limitations on distribution, such as political differences and poor domestic and international transport facilities, work against the publisher who is trying to make a profit from his newspaper. The daily newspaper is no longer an expensive luxury for the middle class throughout the area, as it was in the early 1950s, and in the 1980s newspapers in the Gulf states expanded rapidly as a result of oil wealth there, but price and illiteracy are still limiting circulation figures. High costs are even more restrictive in the case of the electronic media, which are considerably more expensive to operate, and in most cases private Arab entrepreneurs have not been able to afford such an undertaking. This is a major reason why most radio and television stations are monopolies owned by the government.

Politicization

Arab information media have always been closely tied to politics. The first newspapers that appeared in the Arab world were not private but official government publications intended to tell government bureaucrats and the public what the government wanted them to hear. The newspaper Napoleon printed in Egypt on his own presses starting in 1798, *Courier de l'Egypte,* was intended to inform and instruct French expeditionary forces and improve their morale. The first indigenous Egyptian papers, *Jurnal al-Khadyu* and *al-Waqa' al-Masriya,* which began in 1827 and 1828, were published by the Egyptian government. They contained news and entertainment, such as stories from "A Thousand and One Nights," but they also contained official government guidance and authorized editorials. Similarly, the first newspapers that appeared elsewhere in the Arab world at that time also were official organs of the authorities. *Jurnal al-Iraq,* which began in 1816 in Baghdad, was issued by the government for the army, the bureaucracy, and the literate population. *Al-Mubashir* was started in Algeria in 1847 and was an official bi-weekly; *al-Raid al-Tunisi* was begun by the Tunisian authorities in 1861, *Suriya* by the authorities in Damascus in 1865, *Trablus al-Maghrib* by the authorities in Tripoli in 1866, *al-Zura* by the government in Baghdad in 1869, *Sana* by the government in Yemen in 1879, *al-Sudaniya,* by the government in the Sudan in 1899, and *al-Hijaz,* by the Ottoman representatives in Mecca in 1908.

A very few newspapers were published by private individuals or families in the nineteenth century but these appeared only in Egypt, Syria, Lebanon, and Morocco. Khalil Khuri printed *Hadiqat al-Akhbar* in Beirut in 1858; *Wadi al-Nil* and *al-Ahram* appeared in Egypt in 1867 and 1876, respectively, and *al-Maghrib* started in Morocco in 1889. As one student of the press has observed: "We can say that the Arab press [in the nineteenth century] was published officially except for a few places like Lebanon and Morocco, and the press was influenced by this official character in that from the point of view of the reader it expressed the opinion and biases of the government. . . . Arab journalists working under Ottoman rule realized it was a tool for battle and revolution."

Arab governments tended to control the early newspapers, and colonial administrations in the Arab world sought to do the same, also for political reasons. With the growth of Arab nationalism in the twentieth century, Arab newspapers were attracted to this cause in opposition to colonial rule; they were thus drawn into political issues, and the nationalism/anti-imperialism theme has remained strong in Arab media to this day. The fact that the British and French had a tradition of free press at home, in most cases made less of an impact on media development in Arab areas under their control than did the overriding issue of nationalism and politicization of institutions. As radio became technologically feasible for mass broadcasting, most of the governments recognized its importance also, and controlled it as well. In recent years, changing political conditions, differences over policy, changes of regime, and changes of political system have helped to focus attention on the value of the media for political purposes. Periods of tension and instability have made governments especially concerned about the influence of the media and their control. Radio stations and television facilities are prime targets of revolutionaries, who typically seize them first in any move to take power. Consequently, Arab regimes take special care to protect them carefully with military guards against such politically significant eventualities.

Arab governments since World War II have increased their influence and control over the mass media in part with the justification that their newly independent nations face overwhelming external and internal problems requiring unity and purposefulness and a minimum of dissent in the public debate. The country cannot afford, so the argument goes, the luxury of partisan conflict, and the media must further the national interest by supporting governmental policies. This argument is used in connection with economic development and other domestic problems, but the most common focus of such reasoning has been the Arab-Israeli conflict. This conflict has been the single major political preoccupation for the Arab world since the late 1940s. Every Arab government has had to deal with it and has felt compelled to declare its support for the "struggle" against the Israeli enemy, calling upon citizens to sacrifice for the sake of this vital national cause. In this context, Arab governments have been able to justify explicitly and implicitly their influence over the mass media as necessary either while the country is "at war" with Israel, or politically confronting Israel's policies. Because of the degree to which the Arab-Israeli dispute has become the central issue in Arab foreign policy and a matter of Arab patriotism, this justification is difficult to oppose.

Cultural Influence

Historically, the Arab press has had a strong tie to Arab culture. Arab literature, including poetry, tales, and stories, predated mass media by more than a millennium and had developed a very rich tradition by the time the first newspapers appeared. The publishers of these papers, influenced to some extent by the example of the contemporary French newspapers which were heavily cultural in content, quite naturally regarded the Arab press as a proper vehicle for Arab literature.

CONSEQUENCES FOR ARAB MEDIA

Economic, political, and cultural factors have influenced the character and shape of the Arab mass media in several ways.

Political Patronization

The weak economic base of the newspapers has led many of them to seek financial support from a variety of government and private sources, and recognition of the political importance of the press has encouraged patronization. Many private newspapers throughout the Arab world have been able to survive only because they have been subsidized, openly or otherwise, by outside elements. Subsidization may take the form of across-the-board payments by the government to all media, government ads, or material benefits such as low postage rates, contributions to specific publications from political parties, businessmen, or individuals, or secret payments from local or even foreign groups. Because some of this subsidization is kept secret, it is difficult to know the exact magnitude and nature of it, although attempts have been made to get some idea by calculating the budgets of individual newspapers and assuming that those in the red must receive hidden revenues.

Subsidization may, of course, be directly related to media content. Many of the first Arab newspapers in the nineteenth century were financed by government and then political party interests, in order to promote the views of that particular interest. Even private newspaper owners, finding themselves in need of additional financial resources to keep their publication going, "shopped around among elements" in this community with which it agreed politically and philosophically, in order to find backers. Usually like-minded patrons were found, so the newspaper owner did not have to give up his principles and alter editorial policy to obtain funds, but occasionally that happened as well. Many newspapers were able to survive without patronage, and still others were party newspapers and openly labeled as such. The latter tended not only to follow party guidance in editorial policies, but to staff the paper with loyal party types also. Immediately after World War II the Arab press had many more truly "party" newspapers than it does today, and at that time observers compared it to the American press before 1860.[3]

The numerous, small enterprise, highly partisan newspapers that dominated American journalism in the years after the American Revolution were quite similar to those that appeared in the Arab world, as the Arab states emerged from colonial domination and wrestled with the basic questions of national political organization. Partisan journalism in the United States, which emerged after the American Revolution, increased during the thirty years before the Civil War so that every party schism or prominent new political leader brought with it a new newspaper: politicians arranged such newspaper affiliations with care, and considered them essential to success. The Arab world has seen such arrangements also. The proportion of party-affiliated newspapers has decreased over the last forty years, and there has been some increase in the information function of the press, aimed at a mass audience. But the press as a whole, and even more so the electronic media, have not developed in the direction of American big business, mass-oriented media as some observers thought they might. It is still true that "all Arab daily papers are partly business and party politics, but the politics is dominant."[4]

Patronization is still a major feature of the Arab press, but it has become primarily a function of governments. As we will see in subsequent chapters in many countries the regime and its agents have taken over the exclusive right to patronize the politically important newspapers, excluding political parties and other private groups from patronizing them. Radio and television, too, have been sponsored almost without exception by governments, because of their considerably higher cost, the limited number of broadcast frequencies, and broader (mass) political importance they are assumed to have.

In short, all of the media have been susceptible to political influence of one kind or another, particularly in recent years, by strong national governments. It must be remembered, however, that not all of the content of a newspaper or broadcast can be politicized; a large proportion of it, as we shall see below, is cultural and otherwise nonpolitical.

Fragmentation

Second, the factors mentioned above have led to considerable fragmentation in the Arab media. The development of the press in various periods of political conflict and competition, with the support of various political and individual factions, has led to a proliferation of newspapers in most Arab countries beyond the number warranted by literacy rates. Although the overabundance of newspapers was more of a problem in the earlier decades of the twentieth century, when political parties and factions were emerging more rapidly, it is still a problem in Lebanon, for example, and the tendency affects other Arab states as well. There are more newspaper conglomerates than there used to be (such as Cairo's al-Ahram Publishing House), but these are exceptional still, and many governments have attempted to consolidate the press in recent years.

In recent years, a few Arab newspapers based outside the region and aiming at a pan-Arab audience have emerged. Nevertheless, looking at the Arab world as a whole, most daily newspapers are still limited in circulation to one country because of restrictions on importation of papers frequently imposed by governments seeking to keep out hostile ideas, and because of the weakness of transportation and distribution systems throughout the area.

In addition, there have in the past been relatively high birth and death rates for Arab newspapers, although the situation has stabilized somewhat in recent years. It is no longer possible to start an Egyptian paper on a shoestring as it was in the late 1940s, but political change in the Arab countries has and still does bring with it turnovers in newspapers. The Arab states that went through the most political change after World War II experienced the rise and fall of so many newspapers that it would be difficult to chronicle them all. With greater political stability in the 1960s and

1970s came a much greater longevity in newspapers. Radio and television, which grew up in this latter period and which require much greater financial resources, have changed hands very little once established.

Radio and television are less hampered by these barriers, and the development of satellite television in the 1990s is an important phenomenon (see Chapter 10) but most television channels also are closely identified with the country in which they are based, because no Arab government wants these media to be controlled in any way by other countries, so that even two small adjacent states like Bahrain and Qatar have completely separate radio and TV systems. There is no genuine 100 percent pan-Arab broadcasting station, and attempts at cooperation among national systems have not met with much success.

Geographic Concentration

A third consequence of the above mentioned factors is the tendency of the media to concentrate in the more densely populated urban centers of the Arab world. Close ties with both politics and cultural expression, plus such economic factors as low literacy rates, little advertising, and weaknesses in distribution systems, have encouraged Arab newspapers to grow in the cities but not so well in the provincial areas. In most Arab countries, one city serves as the political, economic, and commercial center, and all daily newspapers plus all radio and television broadcasting emanate from that city. The Arab world has no equivalent of New York City, where economic and commercial activity attracted the most press and information facilities from the start, despite the growth of the central government elsewhere, and they stayed in New York. Jidda and Alexandria began that way, but later the national political capitals in Riyadh and Cairo caught up in media development. In these countries and in a few others (Syria, Morocco, Algeria, the United Arab Emirates, and Yemen) a second city is economically important, and they have important daily newspapers, too. There are however no dailies or broadcast programming of national significance outside these two main cities, except in Saudi Arabia and the UAE, where third cities (Dammam and Sharjah, respectively), have nationally important newspapers. Radio listening of course extends throughout the country, but newspaper reading and television viewing tends to be concentrated in a few urban areas.

Media Credibility and Low Prestige of Journalism

As a result of many of these factors, news journalism as a profession has been slow to develop and has not achieved the high status that it has in the West, for example. Political influences on the media, their relative economic weakness, and the absence of an independent "Fourth Estate" concept of the profession have made journalism a less attractive profession than many others in the Arab world. Although there are today many competent Arab professional journalists, the economic and sometimes political risk in entering the profession has to some extent kept talented people away from it. A shortage of trained personnel is a basic problem for all Arab countries, and the economic and political pressures on journalism merely make the situation worse for the media. Schools of journalism are few, so most media staff have learned their trade on the job. Many media personnel, especially in the smaller newspapers, must supplement their incomes by working concurrently at other jobs, and their professionalism suffers. Although media units are generally on a larger scale and more prosperous than they were in the late forties and professionalism has increased, still it remains a problem in many places.

Only a handful of news journalists in the entire Arab world have become famous and respected throughout the area, partly because of the limited distribution of the media, but also because so many journalists are suspected of being merely spokesmen, mouthpieces, or "hired pens" of one political group or another. Muhammad Hassanain Haykal, the most widely read journalist in the Arab world in modern times, gained his popularity not only by his facility with the Arabic language, which was conceded even by his critics, but also because his readers were convinced that he was such a close friend of Egypt's President Nasser that he was in effect speaking for Nasser, the most important leader in the Arab world. In his day, thousands of Arabs read Haykal's weekly column and followed the news in the daily paper he edited, not as much for factual reporting and objective analysis as for clues about what the Egyptian regime was thinking and doing.

There are newspapers which have achieved reputations for relative objectivity in news reporting, although their columnists are known for their various political biases. But typically the news treatment as well as the commentaries of a newspaper or broadcasting station will be regarded by the audience with a large measure of defensive skepticism, akin to that of an American toward a commercial advertisement. Certainly the most sophisticated groups, and to a large extent other people as well, do not accept the news in the mass media entirely at face value, but assume that it may not be completely objective or reliable. They read between the lines, looking for significant omissions and implied meanings. The credibility for the news writers and political columnists in the media tends to be lower than in the West. They are frequently suspected of being politically motivated rather than professionals dedicated solely to accurate, factual reporting and enlightenment of the public. Journalism ranks relatively low in prestige except for the handful of prominent columnists in each country, usually fewer than a half dozen, who write the signed political analyses that appear in the daily press. Most of them are chief editors as well, and their relationship to the regime in power is a very important political factor, as we shall see in subsequent chapters. In the electronic media, the professionals who read the news regularly, or mediate discussion programs, may gain some prominence and prestige, but most reporters are unknown.

Satellite television has in recent years given prominence in the region to a few Arab journalists, but the rank and file of Arab reporters, writers, and copy editors in all the media tend to be unknown to the public, and their profession is not one to which large numbers aspire. In addition to their relatively low prestige (compared to the profession in the United States, for example), Arab journalism suffers from low pay and a shortage of trained personnel prevalent in most Arab societies in this period of rapid economic growth. Moonlighting and part-time journalism is common. Mastery of the Arabic language as such seems to be a sufficient prerequisite for entering the profession, and other necessary skills are learned on the job. In the 1960s and 1970s the profession did increase somewhat in prestige, especially with the spread of the newer electronic media, but it still has not achieved the status that it has in the West.

The quality of journalism varies considerably throughout the Arab world, and local characteristics will be discussed in subsequent chapters. Suffice it to say that the areas where the mass media developed more recently and which are today expanding most quickly, particularly in the small states along the Persian Gulf, these media attracted many Palestinians, Egyptians, and others who have been trained as professional journalists in areas with long press traditions. They went there for the high salaries paid by the oil-rich states that were promoting mass media expansion as fast as possible. Local talent then developed and gained more prominence in the Gulf, but still some non-Gulf personnel are working there. Thus the radio and television stations as well as the newspaper offices in Bahrain, Qatar, Abu Dhabi, Dubai—and to some extent still in Kuwait—even at the beginning of the twenty-first century, have many non-Gulf Arab media professionals, including some of the most qualified in the Arab world. They have in a very short time raised the standards of journalism, at least technically, to compete with the much older media in other parts of the Arab world. The movement of journalists around the Arab world is not new; Egypt's famous *al-Ahram* newspaper was founded, for example, by two Lebanese in 1875. But the direction of movement in the late twentieth century was primarily toward the newly rich states on the Persian Gulf. Consequently, standards of journalism in those areas are rising rapidly.

Continued Importance of Oral Communication

A fifth consequence of the circumstances mentioned above is that despite the widespread and recently quite rapid growth of mass communications media in the Arab world, oral communication channels remain extremely important throughout the area. Arabs seek information through oral communication in a number of forums. First of all, families tend to be close, stay in frequent contact, and discuss a variety of matters among themselves on a regular basis. Secondly, trusted friends supplement the family as a group of people who can also be relied upon to supply useful information. It is common in contemporary Arab society to find informal circles of friends, usually not more than a dozen, who meet regularly and talk frankly about public affairs as well as private concerns. Opinions are formed and information is exchanged in these sessions in ways that the mass media do not and cannot duplicate. In these groups, known as shillas or by various other names, trusted friends talk openly about matters that are politically or otherwise too sensitive to appear in any detail in the press or on the radio, and they depend on these informal gatherings to supplement the mass media.

Thirdly, face-to-face oral communication takes place more broadly in Arab society among acquaintances meeting privately, and among people meeting in semi-public places, such as at work and in the bazaar, the coffeehouse, or the mosque. Information and opinion of apolitical and nonpolitical nature is exchanged in these forums as well. Face-to-face spoken communication has always been very important in Arab society, and the traditional reliance on information from friends and personally known individuals has continued as a strong preference among Arabs. Information from the impersonal mass media is not necessarily trusted more just because it is printed or broadcasted, in fact its credibility is in some cases lower because the source is remote. Trusted friends are believed; they do not have the credibility problems the mass media suffer from. In addition, of course, the mass media do not reach Arabs uniformly, so many must depend quite heavily on oral communication. Literate, urban Arabs who can afford television and radio have access to all mass media channels, but illiteracy, rural residence, and poverty reduce these opportunities for many other Arabs, who consequently must depend more on word of mouth for their information. For these reasons, direct oral communication continues to be important throughout the Arab world as a channel for information which coexists with and supplements the mass media.

Intensification of the flow of information is a sixth and final characteristic of Arab media that has resulted from new technology developments in the 1990s, namely use of the Internet and the cellular phone. The Internet has had several effects on Arab media. It has opened up to journalists new sources of information which are rapidly available, and which they can use in their newspapers or radio and TV reports. Their use of it is still subject to constraints of the local political environment, but they now have much more news to work with. Secondly, the Internet is to some extent competition for the mass media, although access is still confined to elites in most Arab countries. Some newspapers and electronic media in the Arab world, as elsewhere, make their copy available on the Internet. As for cellular phones, these are very widespread everywhere in the Arab world, especially in the wealthier states. The Arab preference for oral communication makes them much more popular than the Internet, which relies on the written word and mostly requires a knowledge of English. Cellular phones have also facilitated the dissemination of information, which helps journalists do their job and also adds an element of competition to the mass media.

Variations among Countries

It must be emphasized that although some characteristics are shared by media throughout the Arab world, there are of course many differences between countries and some within each country. As we shall see in subsequent chapters, the mass communication media have emerged in different ways depending on a variety of factors. The press went through different historical evolutionary patterns; the early development of the press in Lebanon, Egypt, and elsewhere was not, for example, followed until much later in the Arabian Peninsula. For economic reasons, such as the sudden rise of petroleum wealth after World War II in some Arab states, those states accelerated their media expansion, particularly in radio and television which were concurrently coming into use, so that the oil-producing states have acquired some of the most modern equipment and some of the best personnel in the area. Connections and ties with other countries have also affected media development. North Africa's long French connection has, for example, left behind media systems which are still nearly half in French and have only slowly been Arabized. In Algeria, for example, for many years after independence the French language newspapers enjoyed the largest circulations, but because Arabic was the language of instruction after liberation, the younger generation prefers to read Arabic, and French newspaper circulations declined. And political conditions profoundly affect the functioning of the media, so that the latter vary in their operation as do the former.

MEDIA FUNCTIONS

The Arab mass media perform generally the same basic functions as media elsewhere, but in different ways. The basic functions of media can be defined as follows: (1) conveying news and information of general interest; (2) interpreting and commenting on events, providing opinion and perspectives; (3) reinforcing social norms and cultural awareness by transmitting information about the society and its culture; (4) providing specialized information for commercial promotion (advertising) or available services; and (5) entertaining. How do Arab media carry out these functions?

By and large, the Arab media follow the same format as media elsewhere in the world, and there are superficial similarities. Arab radio stations typically broadcast eighteen or twenty hours per day, of which usually less than twenty percent is devoted to news and commentary, either in two or three long newscasts or in shorter ones throughout the day. The Arab radio listener can hear his own country's single national network throughout the day, and after sundown (because signal propagation improves then), the listener usually has a choice of several regional stations from neighboring countries, plus the new satellite television channels (see Chapters 10 and 11). Most Arab television stations are on the air from about six in the evening until midnight, with an additional afternoon program on weekends. News is typically confined to two twenty-minute bulletins, sometimes followed by a comment, but a few stations devote more attention to these topics.

Many Arab daily newspapers average only eight to ten pages in length, but they are much larger in the Gulf and some other countries, where they approach the bulk of a successful Western daily. Many Gulf dailies run to thirty-six or more now, with specialty supplements often doubling this size. Generally the size and printing of Arab dailies are similar to Western papers everywhere except in the poorer countries like Yemen, where smaller, badly printed sheets without photographs are common. Page one is usually devoted to major national, government, regional, and international news and to the lead editorial. Headlines tend to be bolder and longer than in the Western press, and news stories tend to be shorter, with less detail and background, and sourcing is often incomplete. Inside, the Arab newspaper may have several pages of international and regional news and one or two more of local news, plus additional editorials, and a page or two of features on sports, science, women's affairs, and culture. Larger papers carry classified ads. Personal notes on comings and goings of prominent citizens generally appear in a special column with stock photos and are popular with readers in this highly personalized society. Some of the more successful dailies, for example in Lebanon, Egypt, and the Gulf, have regular supplements containing features on the arts, cinema, literature, and history. Most dailies actually publish six times per week and do not appear on either Friday, Saturday, or Sunday.

It is not in format, however, that Arab media differ most from other media elsewhere, but in content. How are each of the five functions mentioned above handled?

News and Commentary Functions

We shall examine the first and second functions, news and commentary, together. News handling and the role of commentaries will be a major theme in all subsequent chapters because they are key manifestations of the relationship between the media and the political environment. Here we will make a few generalizations that seem to apply throughout the Arab world. Since very few systematic content analyses have been made of Arab media, these generalizations are based primarily on the conclusions of qualified observers who have extensive familiarity with the media themselves.

Arab newspapers and radio stations tend to be more obvious in their editorial comment than American papers and radio broadcasts do; Arab television generally carries somewhat less commentary, but total air time is much shorter than in the United States. In their interpretive, or opinion function, Arab media are very active but they perform it somewhat differently from Western media.

Except for some of the new television channels, Arab media rarely meet the ideal expressed for American journalism, of providing "a forum for the exchange of comment and criticism."[5] Specific opinions, attitudes, and articulation of goals which are expressed in Arab media are usually those of a small elite group, but there is two-way exchange only on some television and radio programs. Letters to the editor are published only in some papers. Nongovernmental sentiment is sometimes expressed, but it is filtered through a few editors, so the flow of opinions is rather restricted.

The concept of the watchdog function of the media acting for the public against the government is manifest only in limited ways in the Arab world. However, looking at the Arab world as a whole, an exchange of opinion between groups does take place between Arab countries, whose elites speak to each other, in effect, via radio and television, and to some extent via print media. These elites have differing views, and they are not uncritical of each other.

The content of the news is a complex subject. One professional American journalist, writing about the media in an Arab country, concluded that there was "scarcely any distinction between news and editorial matter" by which he implied that Arab editors do not follow the ideal of contemporary American journalism which is strictly to separate news and commentary. This judgment is a broad generalization that must be qualified and made more specific. It is true that the Arab editor in performing his function of selecting news items, and positioning them in a newspaper or in a broadcast, may from time to time do so in a way that reflects opinions which are also expressed in that medium's commentaries. The editor can do this in many ways, by omitting parts of the story, by emphasizing other parts by putting them in the lead paragraph or headline, by juxtaposing elements of the story to create a certain impression, by printing as unattributed fact information from only one source on a controversial issue, by uncritically publishing information from a doubtful source, or by outright fabricating. Arab editors have at one time or another done all of these. Their reasons vary.

The most common reason is that the editor's perceptions of events, which are determined by his own experience and his cultural, historic, economic, and social environment, cause him to make certain choices in the presentation of news. This cultural bias is the major reason for a given medium's particular slant on the news. It leads to similarities within a given Arab country and also on another level within the Arab world, in the news-handling function of the media.

The second most important factor influencing Arab editors in their news presentation is political bias. That is, in presenting the news they sometimes make choices because of prevailing political factors, such as the policies and preferences of the government in power. The editor may do this in order to support a government he favors or simply to avoid trouble with a government he fears. Political bias is usually a conscious act in which the editor has deliberately compromised the truth as he saw it because of the consequences of presenting the truth. Cultural bias, by contrast, is usually unconscious conformity with accepted norms. The extent of political bias varies greatly in the Arab world; in some places it affects very little of the newspaper or broadcast, in others it permeates all parts of them.

Distortions in news handling also occur, of course, because of error or sloppy journalism, when the reporter or editor fails to do his job properly and does not obtain all the facts or present them strictly according to their merits. Such distortions occur throughout the area, but they are relatively rare in those countries that have had time to develop the profession.

How truthful is the news in Arab media? The answer depends partly on the definition of truthfulness. As we have seen, there may be some inadvertent misstatement of fact resulting from poor journalism, which is not deliberate untruthfulness; and there is cultural bias, which leads Arab editors to make choices different from editors elsewhere simply because of the way they see the world. They are not being deliberately untruthful but rather honestly expressing their different perceptions. If these two types of influence over news selection are put aside, leaving deliberate political bias as the only real type of untruthful news distortion, we see that much of the news in Arab media is basically unaffected by it, and straight.

It is true that many of the major political news stories in many of the Arab countries are affected in some way by political bias, and that Arab readers can in some cases detect that bias by reading the front page of the newspaper or listening to a newscast, provided they have other sources of news for comparison. It is also true that many news stories in Arab media do not entirely measure up to the ideal that some have set for the American press, for example, of a "truthful, comprehensive, and intelligent account of the day's events in a context which gives them meaning."[6] However, the bulk of the material in a given newspaper or on a given broadcast day is factual. The Arab media perform the function of presenting facts about events in order to inform their audiences, and it is probably fair to say that most of these facts conform to reality. The facts are accepted with a degree of skepticism, as noted above, and supplemented by oral communication, but they provide the basis for information exchange for most of the community on a wide range of subjects.

Cultural Reinforcement Function

Arab media also perform the function of reinforcing Arab cultural values, defined broadly as those values learned by an individual because he is an Arab. As noted above, the media present information in ways that are understandable only by reference to local social, historical, and other factors. Thus they help reinforce the attitudes and perceptions of the society, or more precisely of its majority. In addition, although some believe the mass media today are destroying classical Arabic culture by trying to popularize it or by promoting colloquial forms, it can be argued that the media transmit some of those values of Arab culture more narrowly defined as a heritage in creative endeavor and thought. A sophisticated and complex Arab culture was developed hundreds of years before the advent of the mass media. It was logical that the media would be influenced from the beginning by the rich Arab intellectual tradition in literature, religion, philosophy, and music. Communicators in those fields were well established in Arab society, so naturally many of the earliest Arab newspapers in the nineteenth century resembled the political-literary journals being published at the time in Europe. The latter were being imitated in form if not in content, and in this way the Arab writers and poets found outlets in the press for their creativity.

Even today, some of the important content of the Arab media is created not by professional journalists in the modern sense but by educated Arabs who have careers outside the mass media. Intellectuals write op-ed columns. Nonpolitical authors have gained wide prominence and respect by writing poetry and stories for the press and plays for television and radio. Arab newspapers generally carry more literature than do Western ones, and it is not uncommon for prominent local literary figures to write for the newspapers and the electronic media. In Egypt, for example, the noted writer and theological reformer Shaikh Muhammad Abduh first became known through his columns in *al-Ahram* newspaper, and more recently the press has given considerable space to fiction, and to the current affairs comments of literati who are well known throughout the Arab world. Several of these writers are on regular newspaper staff payrolls, and a few have even become chief editors.

By giving considerable time and space to literature, Arab media help to reinforce Arab cultural identity. The same function is performed by the electronic media in carrying a great deal of Arab music as well as dramas on traditional themes. The music is both traditional and modern, and is performed by local artists and artists known throughout the area. In many Arab countries such programs take up hours of prime time on television as well as on radio. Similarly, readings from the Koran are broadcast regularly by stations all over the Arab world, and in some places religious commentaries or advice on proper moral and ethical behavior are featured on radio and TV.

The Arabic Language

The language used in the media also serves the function of communicating cultural identity. Indeed, the Arabic language is an especially crucial element linking the Arabs with each other and with their culture; it is inseparable from Arab culture, history, tradition, and Islam, the religion of the vast majority of Arabs. The best definition of who is an Arab is not in terms of religion or geography but of language and consciousness, that is, one who speaks Arabic and considers himself an Arab. Arabic is extremely important to Arabs; they pay considerable attention to the language, and it shapes their thinking in many ways. There is an "intimate interdependence" between Arabic and the Arab psychology and culture, and, thus, as carriers of the language, the mass media are very important in the communication of Arab cultural commonality. As the historian Philip Hitti said, "no people in the world has such enthusiastic admiration for literary expression and is so moved by the word, spoken or written, as the Arabs."[7]

Language carries special meaning for Arabs, for several reasons. First, Arabic is intimately connected with Islam; the Koran is accepted as the highest linguistic achievement in the language and remains after more than thirteen centuries the standard for good usage today. Secondly, there is a close association between Arabic and an historic past in which Arabs take pride; they are proud to use the language of their illustrious ancestors. Thirdly, Arabic is an essential element today in their very strong concept of an "Arab nation," that is, pan-Arabism to which leaders continuously vow their allegiance. Even the Arabic word for foreigner (ajnabi) is usually used today to mean non-Arab foreigner only. And finally, Arabs love their language because of its intrinsic beauty quite apart from the meaning it conveys. Arabic is filled with what speakers of English would consider exaggeration and repetition.

For all of these reasons, the mass media which use Arabic have a particular impact on their audience, which a literal translation into English cannot convey. The importance of the language itself helps shape the content of the media. Whereas the American journalist seems to have a passion for factual details and statistics, the Arab journalist by contrast seems to give more attention to the correct words, phrasing, and grammar he should use in describing an event. It would be oversimplifying to say that "It is a characteristic of the Arab mind to be swayed more by words than by ideas and more by ideas than by facts"[8] but a tendency in that direction can be seen in the style of the mass media.

Two Levels of Cultural Reinforcement

Arab media may be unique in that they convey sociocultural values on two levels, namely to the large pan-Arab audience and to the smaller nation-state one. A great deal that is of cultural value to an individual Arab is commonly shared with other Arabs throughout the area. Arab media convey such cultural messages. On the other hand, other cultural aspects are strictly local and are shared only with others who live within the borders of a country or region. Arab media also convey effectively these local Arab values. For example, the media in Saudi Arabia rarely carry pictures of adult Saudi women because they are still required to wear the veil in public, but they do carry pictures of women from other Arab countries. Thus all Arab newspapers and radio or TV broadcasts carry sociocultural characteristics of their country of origin, and they also carry sufficient pan-Arab "flavor" to make them familiar to Arabs everywhere.

The duality of this cultural identification function can be seen clearly in the language used by the media. The Arabic language used in newspapers throughout the Arab world is a modified and somewhat modernized form of "classical" or literary Arabic which is universally understood by educated Arabs. Moroccans, Saudis, and Lebanese who can read Arabic are able to read each others' newspapers just as they can all read the Koran, the highest authority for classical Arabic. Similarly radio and television throughout the area generally uses the same slightly modified classical Arabic for all news and other serious programming. There are some minor differences in the accents of professional radio and TV people from country to country, but these are little more than exist in the United States, and they are all understood.

Simultaneously the media use colloquial Arabic for special purposes. Each local dialect, derived originally from the classical, has been modified so much over the years that it is only understood well by the local group that uses it. This colloquial Arabic appears only to a very limited extent in the printed media, for example in some cartoon captions, short stories, and quotations of spoken Arabic—because it is not generally considered appropriate to write it down. However, it is used extensively in radio and television, particularly when dealing with less serious subjects. Some interviews and discussions about local matters, vernacular plays and soap operas, comedy routines, and other programs that are intended for the local audience are usually in colloquial Arabic. And it is not uncommon for a national leader, when making a political speech broadcast on radio and television, to sprinkle his rhetoric with colloquial phrases designed to develop rapport with his audience, although it is considered more correct for the main body of the speech to be in classical Arabic. Egypt's President Nasser, for example, often began formally in classical Arabic but increased his use of Egyptian colloquialisms as he warmed up to his listeners; however, the printed version of his text that appeared in the newspapers the following day did not give that localized flavor.

Thus the media communicate in modified classical Arabic horizontally to educated elite groups throughout the Arab world, and at the same time they communicate vertically to literate and illiterate members of their respective nations. It is also a characteristic of the language that the colloquial varieties, while differing from each other, use words that are quite concrete and tangible in their meaning. The classical, on the other hand, has a great capacity for vagueness, ambiguity, and exaggeration. As a result, it is especially difficult to pin down the precise meaning of newspaper editorials dealing with more abstract subjects. They convey a sense of what the writer is thinking but with far less economy than an editorial by a native English speaker. Such ambiguity and vagueness in the interpretive function is a characteristic of Arab media.

One important complicating factor in Morocco, Algeria, and Tunisia is the extensive use of French due to earlier colonial ties and continued cultural connections with France. In the early years of independence, roughly half or more of the press and the radio and television air time in these countries was in French because so many people especially in the elite groups had learned French in school and used it in their work. The three governments have deliberately promoted Arabization policies, requiring Arabic in schools and in government communication, and the balance has shifted in favor of Arabic, but still a large segment of the media uses French. In Algeria, for example, in the 1980s the highest-circulation daily was still the French-language *el Moudjahid,* but by the twenty-first century the Arabic-language daily *al-Khabar* had by far the highest circulation of any Algerian daily. Nevertheless, half of the top twenty circulation dailies were published in French.

Those Arab media which convey their message in French perform a somewhat different function, because of the added filter of French. The effect is complex, but in general Arabs who communicate in French tend to convey ideas and values that are part Arab and part French, thereby keeping French perceptions alive in the society. To a limited extent this occurs in Lebanon also, where some radio and television broadcasts and an important newspaper are presented in French. In the Eastern Arab world, there are newspapers published in English, primarily for residents (most of them foreign guest workers) who do not know Arabic, and the content of these papers focuses on their interests. In the Gulf, for example, the English-language papers contain a great deal of material related to South Asia. Some countries also have radio and television broadcasts in English for the same foreign audiences. In most of the Arab world, however, almost all the leading mass media are in the Arabic language.[9]

Advertising and Entertainment Functions

The two functions just discussed, namely interpretation and socialization, tend to overlap with and permeate all other functions, even entertainment and advertising. Thus the type and amounts of entertainment and advertising presented are governed by local social and cultural norms and even by political conditions, so their presentation helps reinforce those norms and conditions.

Entertainment per se plays a relatively small role in the Arab press. The few cartoons that appear are usually political, and puzzles and quizzes are rare. The newspapers do print fiction and even poetry, and some newspapers have sizeable supplemental sections, but this can be considered as much cultural as entertaining. The press is regarded primarily as a serious vehicle for news, information, and opinion intended to be read by the literate elites, not as entertainment. In contrast to daily newspapers, radio, and television are mass-oriented media, so they generally devote a majority of their time to entertainment, but the entertainment programs usually do more than just entertain. Popular radio and TV dramas convey ideas about Arab society, and often they are frankly political, communicating themes that relate directly to current political questions such as the Arab-Israeli conflict, anti-imperialism, etc. Popular songs do the same; for example Egypt's famous singer Um Kalthoum broadcast patriotic songs at the time of the 1967 Middle East war which were especially written to exhort Arab soldiers to greater efforts.

As for the advertising function, it, too, is affected by other factors. Commercial advertising plays a relatively small role in the Arab media, as contrasted, for example, with the American media. Whereas the latter is run as a business enterprise in a consumer-oriented advertising dependent system, the Arab media are regarded as having primarily other purposes such as information and interpretation, with advertising clearly a subordinate or even marginal function.

Commercial advertising revenues make up only a minor part of a typical newspaper's budget, although government ads are important in some places. And although most Arab radio and TV stations carry advertising, it is strictly limited and normally a minor part of the station's budget, since most are government-owned stations which receive most of their income from the government. Aside from commercial advertising of consumer goods, the Arab daily press generally serves as a community information source, announcing film shows and other local public events, but this function is limited.

MEDIA SYSTEMS

How should we classify Arab media systems? How are the media structured? Who controls them and for what purpose? What theory, or theories, lie behind Arab media?

To answer those questions it is not enough to look at the legal status of the press and the electronic media. In the Arab world, press and broadcasting laws do not reveal all the details of who decides the content of a newspaper editorial and why. In fact, looking at the laws alone may obscure the real dynamics of the system, because the laws tend to imply that the media are freer than they really are, and they do not mention some essential extralegal influences. In the Arab world, that system cannot be understood without specific reference to political and other conditions prevailing at the time in the country. Such factors as the existence of open political opposition groups and/or parties, the strength and legitimacy of the ruling group, its character (revolutionary or traditional, for example), the stability of the political system, the perception of an external threat, the existence of a tradition of journalism and a Fourth Estate, and the economic strength of the media are all very important influences on the structure of the media. The Arab media system and the "theory" under which it operates tend to grow out of such political, economic, and other realities that prevail in that country. We must therefore look more closely at the individual countries to see how their media systems operate, and we will do that in the following chapters.

Can we make any generalizations about Arab media systems? Can we classify them under any of the categories used by students of other mass media? One standard classification is the four-fold one of (1) authoritarian, (2) libertarian, (3) social responsibility, and (4) totalitarian.[10] The Arab media do not fit neatly and completely into any one of those categories, but there are some elements of all four present in the Arab world. However in most, but not all, of the Arab countries the media operate under variations of the authoritarian theory, and of the four theories, this one comes closest to explaining what is taking place. (These countries tend to have authoritarian governments also, based on the same general theory.)

In the authoritarian system, the media support and advance the policies of the government, which controls the media either directly or indirectly through licensing, legal action, or perhaps financial means. The regime allows the media some discussion of society and the machinery of government, but not of the people in power. This system is based on the theory that truth is "not the product of a great mass of people, but of a few wise men . . . in a position to guide and direct their fellows."[11] Comment and criticism are carefully guided, and articulated goals for the community conform with goals of the regime itself. There are authoritarian features in many of the Arab media systems, even in places where the press is not under government ownership—a common element in authoritarian systems elsewhere. A leading Lebanese journalist and sometime Minister of Information described the philosophy prevalent in the Arab world, attributing it to all developing countries:

In developing societies, truth has always been considered divine in form as well as in content, to whatever god or prophet it is attributed. The knowledge of this truth is therefore considered a privilege, the privilege of one man or of a few men, who henceforth necessarily claim a monopoly of freedom—the freedom of those who know and have alone the right to tell the others what they must know and believe. A phenomenon accentuated by the sacred character of the written word, to be written in the most perishable fashion: in newspapers. . . . In such a context, it is natural and logical that the press should assume a very particular role. Instead of being a "mass medium" in the sense commonly held, it becomes the instrument of transmission of the official truth, the media by which this truth is authoritatively communicated to the masses.[12]

One characteristic of an authoritarian media system is that communication tends to be from the top down, emphasizing messages from the government to the people, and readers are often ignored by editors, who do not welcome feedback. This is especially true of print media, as radio and television recently have included more listener and viewer input.

The libertarian theory, by contrast, holds that the media must be completely free of government controls and provide the consumer with sufficient objective information and variety of opinions so that that consumer can make up his or her own mind. The libertarian media are both an outside check on government (the watchdog function) and a vehicle for what Milton called a "free and open encounter" of ideas which should help reasoning people to distinguish truth from error. The social responsibility theory seems to be a modification of this, developed in recent times when it appeared that a laissez faire approach to media control did not guarantee freedom. The libertarian theorists did not deal with the problems of economic independence or of a party's political influence, both of which are crucial for Arab media, as they were important to the history of the American press.

The Arab response has been different. To be sure, there are examples of such journalistic responsibility in the Arab world, and evidence that some of the Arab media reflect a few features of both the libertarian and social responsibility theories. But these features tend to be in the effects of the system rather than in the underlying philosophy or purpose. The prevailing Arab attitude toward mass communications seems to be more akin to the authoritarian view than to Milton's, and the efforts to publish or broadcast the truth have come under strain from a variety of sources—cultural, social, and especially political. This is, in fact, from a worldwide perspective, more the norm than unique.

The pressures on an Arab newspaper or broadcast editor from his society, which is simultaneously going through the trials of economic development and national self-fulfillment, are enormous. Regional tension and the perception of an external threat tend to exacerbate the situation, and the editor is caught in the middle because of his very public role. On the other hand, looking at the Arab media area as a whole, it seems that a Miltonian clash of views does take place. There is a variety of partisan voices in the Middle East and North Africa, particularly on radio broadcasts and in satellite television programs which can not be contained within national frontiers, which has provided Arab audiences with an open encounter of ideas from which to choose. It is within each country that restrictions are more effective.

Are any totalitarian media Arab? While a few elements of the totalitarian system have appeared at times, none of the Arab media systems can really be classified in this fourth category. Under the totalitarian system, all information media are centrally controlled by the government, whether they are in private or public hands, and unapproved foreign or other competing media may not be distributed at all in the country. Unlike the negative controls of an authoritarian media system, which merely restricts anti-regime content in available media, totalitarian controls are intended to force the media into a positive, active role of agitation and propaganda within an overall scheme to mobilize the population. Most important, while the authoritarian system generally is concerned only about mass media and outward obedience, and allows free speech in private, in the totalitarian system the rulers attempt to control all aspects of a person's life, demanding an individual's positive, active commitment in public and private to their goals. In the Arab world, there are some restrictions on the importation of foreign print media, and even a few cases of jamming of foreign radio broadcasts.

But these restrictions are by no means comprehensive. The media have not been forced, even under one-party regimes, into the completely single-minded agitation and propaganda effort of the kind found in the Soviet or other totalitarian systems. The most restrictive Arab regimes have, in general, been satisfied with outward compliance by press, radio, and television, and they have not invaded the sphere of private, face-to-face oral communication which is still so important in the Arab societies. Thus while there are a few elements of totalitarian thinking behind the controls on Arab media, the systems themselves cannot be put in this overall category.

However, with these four categories, namely authoritarian, libertarian, social responsibility, and totalitarian, we can do no more than put the Arab media systems rather roughly into a worldwide context. These generalizations are not at all sufficient to make the Arab media systems and their dynamics fully comprehensible. Indeed, none of the existing analytical theories helps much in going beneath the surface of the Arab media systems, and in order to explain their real functioning we must devise new theories designed to fit the cases at hand.

Beyond the generalizations in this chapter, which apply to media in all eighteen Arab countries, we have found four major subtypes which we shall examine in this book. One group which we call the "mobilization press" includes the Arab republics which have undergone the most political change in recent years—Syria, Libya, the Sudan, and Iraq until 2003. Each of these states has experienced European colonialism, and their media systems have developed during periods of political turbulence, rising nationalist and anti-imperialist sentiment, and episodes when political parties participated in national life. They have all gone through four identifiable stages in media development, ending in a kind of nationalization by the regime. The regime directly controls the media using legal and extra-legal means. It attempts to mobilize the media, giving them considerable guidance on goals which should be emphasized, on how to interpret events, and even on news presentation.

Media systems in a second group of states—Saudi Arabia, Qatar, the United Arab Emirates, Bahrain, Oman, and Palestine—have experienced a more even, linear development along traditional authoritarian lines, although there have been ups and downs in the degree of freedom. We call this the "loyalist" system. Political parties have played little or no role in media development in these states, and ownership of the press remains largely in private hands, though radio and TV are generally owned by the governments. Like the first group the tenor of the theory behind the media is authoritarian, and the degree of government influence is high, but the system and the style are quite different. Influences and controls over the press, particularly, are quite indirect and subtle, not discernible so much by reading the press laws in search of legal restrictions as by reading the newspapers themselves. In practice they tend to be loyal to the regime in presenting news and commentary on important issues.

The third main category of media systems is considerably less authoritarian in nature than the others, and it exhibits a clear degree of diversity and freedom of expression not found elsewhere in the Arab world. Government influence over the media is limited, and exercized by legal means. The archetype of this group, the Lebanese system, has the freest journalism in the Arab world and is practically a case by itself. However, the press in Kuwait, Morocco, and Yemen have a degree of diversity and independence which puts them, too, in this special category—and for some of the same reasons as exist in Lebanon.

The fourth category of print media types is a new one that has emerged in recent years, in Egypt, Jordan, Tunisia, and Algeria, and seems to be emerging in Iraq since the spring of 2003. The largest circulation print media are controlled by the government directly but smaller publications exist which are owned by parties or private individuals. The government attempts to influence the press but generally uses legal means, especially through the courts. Self-censorship exists but restrictions on press freedom are openly discussed. We call this the "transitional" press system because it is undergoing change, the outcome of which is uncertain, and it contains some characteristics of other systems.

IMPORTANT MAGAZINES

A word must be said about nondaily periodical publications in the Arab world, since they are important but are not discussed in detail in the following chapters, which are limited to the daily press plus radio and television.

Every Arab country has some nondaily publications. Many of them have a variety of different types. The most common are the weekly pictorial current-events magazines such as Egypt's *al-Musawwar* or Lebanon's *al-Hawadith,* and the radio-television magazines. But also there are scholarly journals such as Egypt's *al-Siyasah al-Dawliyah* (International Politics), religious magazines such as Saudi Arabia's *al-Da'wah* (The Call), and another in Egypt by the same name, literary quarterlies, and special publications for women, youth, and the military. Each of these publications reflects, in one way or another, its country of origin and most are unknown outside their borders. But some, particularly a few Lebanese and Egyptian weeklies, and one Kuwaiti monthly, *al-Arabi,* have been successful in developing readerships outside.

We must now look more closely at the individual Arab states. In many ways, each state is unique in the way its media function. But for purposes of analysis we shall examine them grouped into the four subtypes, starting with what we shall call the mobilization press.

NOTES

1. Web site World Bank, "World Development Indicators," worldbank.org (March 2003), and Unesco, website unesco.org (March 2003). Reliable statistics for the West Bank and Gaza (Palestine) are not available. Data are for the year 2000 except for 1996 for newspapers, 1997 for radio and TV data in Oman, UAE, Bahrain and Qatar.

2. Interview with Jihad Khazen, London, January 22, 2003.

3. Tom J. McFadden, *Daily Journalism in the Arab States* (Columbus: Ohio State University Press, 1953), p. 26, 36–37; and Wilton Wynn, "Western Techniques Influence Party Newspapers in Egypt," *Journalism Quarterly* 25 (4): 391.

4. McFadden, pp. 28, 84, 94; Wynn, "Western Techniques," pp. 291–93.

5. The Commission on Freedom of the Press, *A Free and Responsible Press* (Chicago: University of Chicago Press, 1947), pp. 23–28.

6. *A Free and Responsible Press,* p. 21.

7. Philip K. Hitti, *The Arabs, a Short History* (Princeton: Princeton University Press, 1943), p. 21.

8. Edward Atiyeh, *The Arabs* (Baltimore: Penguin, 1955), p. 96.

9. *L'Orient-le Jour* in Beirut is a leading daily newspaper. There are no significant French dailies outside of the four countries mentioned. Several countries have English dailies but they are mostly read by the resident foreign community.

10. Fred S. Siebert, Theodore Peterson, and Wilbur Schramm: *Four Theories of the Press* (Urbana: University of Illinois Press, 1953), pp. 1–37.

11. Siebert, p. 2.

12. Ghassan Tueni, *Freedom of the Press in Developing Societies* (Beirut: al-Nahar Press, 1971), pp. 2–3.

2

The Mobilization Press:
Syria, Libya, the Sudan,
and Pre-2003 Iraq

The daily newspapers in four Arab countries—Syria, Libya, the Sudan, and pre-2003 Iraq—play generally a similar type of role in the political process despite the fact that they vary greatly in age, origin, and history (see Table 2.1). On superficial examination the press appears to have been nationalized in these countries, but this would be an inaccurate and over-simplified term to use. The state does not itself own the newspapers, and the relationship between the government and the journalists is a subtle, complex one which will be dealt with in this chapter. We shall briefly describe journalists' behavior, then analyze the underlying factors, the structure of the press, and the channels of political influence.

PRESS BEHAVIOR

No Criticism of Policy

The mobilization press does not criticize the basic policies of the national government. The government's foreign policies are particularly unassailable, but the major lines of domestic policy, too, are never attacked. The newspapers may carry stories and editorials critical of gov-ernment services on the local level, such as the shortage of electricity or shortcomings of the public sanitation department. In these cases, however, the lower-level bureaucrat rather than the national leadership is held responsible, and the criticism serves a pedagogical purpose for the

TABLE 2.1   The Mobilization Press: Daily Newspapers[1]

	Estimated circulation, 1999	First published
Iraq		
Babil	NA	1991
Al-Thawra (The Revolution)	250,000	1968
Al-Jumhuriya (The Republic)	150,000	1958
Al-Iraq	30,000	1976
*The Baghdad Observer**	22,000	1967
Al-Qadissiya (Sanctity)	20,000	1983
Al-Ba'th	NA	NA
Syria		
Tishrin	50,000	1974
Al-Thawra (Revolution)	40,000	1964
Al-Ba'th	40,000	1964
*The Syrian Times**	15,000	1979
Al-Jamahir (The Masses)	10,000	1966
Ash Shabab (The Youth)	9,000	1960s
Al-Uruba (Arabism)	5,000	1965
Al-Fida' (The Sacrifice)	4,000	1963
Al-Wahda (Unity)		
The Sudan		
Al-Sudani (The Sudanese)	305,000	1980
Al-Ayam (The Days)	200,000	1953
Al-Siyasah (Politics)	60,000	1986
Al-Khartoum	25,000	1988
Al-Ra'y al-Akhir (The Other Opinion)	NA	1980s
Al-Ra'y al-Aam (Public Opinion)	NA	1945
Libya		
Al-Fajr al-Jadid (The New Dawn)	40,000	1969
Al-Shams (The Sun)	40,000	1980s
Al-Ra'i (The Opinion)	24,000	1973
Al-Jihad (The Holy War)	20,000	1973

*Published in English.

leadership as well as providing an outlet for very limited debate. This airing of the views of the "public," dissatisfied with the service and with the bureaucrat who is supposed to provide it, is the only internal political discussion that appears in the press. Otherwise, politically important issues are not treated from various angles but are presented from the one point of view which is acceptable to the government.

Sanctity of Leaders

The mobilization press never criticizes the personalities heading the national government, either in editorials or by unfavorable news play. Negative information about the character, behavior, or personal lives of the top rulers does not find its way into print, no matter how well known by the newsmen or even the public.

Non-Diverse

It follows that there is no significant diversity on important political issues among newspapers in any one of these countries. Since they are all highly respectful of the national leadership and its fundamental policies, their editorials and news stories on these matters tend to be strikingly similar. These three newspaper characteristics can be found not only in the four countries we are dealing with here, but elsewhere in the Arab world as well (see below). What sets the four apart as a group are the following special traits.

Mobilization Tool

The regimes in these four countries regard the press as a very important tool for the mobilization of popular support for its political programs. These regimes tend to adhere to activist domestic and foreign policies that advocate social, economic, and political change, and their ideologies usually include elements of intense struggle against alleged hostile forces ranged against the national welfare. The ruling group seeks to use the press to advance its causes and help fight these battles.

The term "mobilization" has been applied to political systems in which new values are being created and "political leaders are trying to work out a moral system of authority" in order to "establish, as much as possible, different solidarities and identities," so that society will rapidly modernize and industrialize, and the new leadership will acquire legitimacy.[2] This is essentially what was happening in these four states in the third quarter of the twentieth century as they became fully independent. It is appropriate to apply the same term to the press in these four states because the mass media are seen by these regimes as crucial to the mobilization process. Some outside observers have recognized that "the mass media can be used to mobilize the energies of living persons . . . by the rational articulation of new interests. . . . The mass media can simultaneously induce a new process of socialization among the rising generation that will, among other effects, recruit new participants into political life."[3]

This power of the mass media is fully appreciated—perhaps even over-valued—in the four Arab states. The regimes there, seeking revolutionary change and active popular support against obstacles to development and perceived enemies, look to the media for support. Criticism when it occurs is not free speech but part of the mobilization process. As Iraq's ruling Ba'th Party declared in 1965: "The masses [have] the right of constructive criticism within the limits of the nation's progressive line of destiny. Naturally, criticism under the socialist revolutionary regime cannot be an end in itself, nor can it be allowed to proceed unchecked to the limit of undermining the nationalist socialist line itself."[4]

The Sudanese regime has basically the same attitude toward the press, which it expresses in slightly less vigorous terms: "The information media play an important role in the national, political, economic, and social revolution and share in an important strategic line of revolution and change by clarifying the path before the masses."[5]

Similar social, economic, political, and even cultural goals, in similar language, are enunciated by the leadership in all four countries, and it is toward these objectives that the press is supposed to help mobilize public support. The newspapers are expected to help publicize great campaigns launched by the regime against some obstacle to economic development or against a foreign enemy, for example. They are supposed to help announce and explain any new government policies, to convey the idea that all right thinking people are united behind such policies, and that the regime has chosen the goals wisely.

The tone of editorials and headlines is often stridently aggressive, combative, hyperbolic, quick to react to events and to paint black-and-white pictures. The mobilization messages, implied as well as explicit, are intended to generate support for the regime's programs on several levels, mainly philosophical and institutional but also personal. They are addressed primarily to the domestic audience, but occasionally also directed at a foreign target, for example to persuade a foreign government to change its policy while persuading people at home that the foreign government should change its policy.

Many of these characteristics would apply to the press in a totalitarian system. The system in these four countries is not, however, totalitarian. It seeks active support for programs rather than just passive compliance, but it does tolerate some passivity and it does not go so far as to invade the sphere of personal privacy. In the totalitarian system, "the atmosphere of mobilization is one of crisis and attack"—an atmosphere which is developed on some occasions in the press in those Arab countries but tends not to be sustained over long periods of time or on many issues.[6]

How does the government obtain this kind of support from the press? The answer is that a certain type of press structure and journalistic behavior has been established under political conditions particularly conducive to the emergence of this system. Let us look at those factors, starting with the political environment.

POLITICAL CONDITIONS

There are several characteristics common to the political environments of Iraq, Syria, Libya, and the Sudan which seem to be important to the development of the mobilization newspaper. Aside from other political factors that may be important for other purposes, there are four factors which are directly related to the press system. First of all, a small, aggressive ruling group is in authority, effectively in control of all important levers of power. It faces no genuine organized opposition and allows no challenger to its authority to speak out publicly on the domestic scene.

In Syria, the Ba'th Party dominates the political system including the People's Council (parliament). The constitution mandates that the Ba'th Party is the ruling party and is ensured a majority in all political institutions. At least since 1996, six small parties were permitted to function and they are part of the National Progressive Front with the Ba'th, but the NPF is dominated by the Ba'th and is only to give the impression of a multiparty system. The six parties exist in name only and follow the Ba'th line. Since 1990 the Ba'th has allowed non-NPF candidates to run for a limited number of seats in the parliament; in 1999 there were 83 out of 250. The last parliamentary elections were in 1998.

In 2001 the Syrian government did permit the pro-Ba'th faction of the Communist Party to publish its newspaper *Sawt al-Sha'b* (Voice of the People) which had been banned forty-three years earlier, and it also allowed two new weekly newspapers, the satirical *al-Domari* (the Lamplighter) and the pro-Nasserist *al-Wahdawi* (the Unionist) to be published, which were nominally in private hands. But the regime set limits to what they could publish and generally retained control over the press.

Secondly, this ruling group tends to regard itself as a revolutionary vanguard of the people, engaged in a struggle for social change domestically and representing strong nationalistic sentiment in fighting alleged foreign and domestic enemies of the people. It claims to represent the true interests of "the masses" and typically uses revolutionary socialist language to rally support and warn of enemies.

Third, this ruling group is not content with passive acquiescence from the population, but is instead highly conscious of a need to appeal for active support of the people, and it recognizes that this must be done through the mass media.

Finally, the ruling group usually has behind it a single political party which is the only really powerful political organization allowed to function in the country. It is a monopoly "party of solidarity" rather than a representative party of the type found in Western democratic systems which must compete for power against other parties on an equal basis.

Such a political organization is called by different names in the four countries—Arab Socialist Union or National Liberation Front for example.

In Libya and the Sudan, no other legal political organizations exist; in the other two—Syria and Iraq—the additional political organizations that are allowed to function do not espouse policies that are basically different from those of the regime and its party. The regime maintains this party in order to help mobilize popular support, since the style of the leadership is to confront what it perceives to be its enemies in a highly partisan manner, despite the fact that there are no real opposition parties and no real party system exists.

In Iraq, for example, the 1968 provisional constitution said that the Arab Ba'th Socialist Party (ABSP) governed Iraq through the Revolutionary Command Council (RCC) which has both legislative and executive authority. Saddam Hussein is president, prime minister, chairman of the RCC, and Secretary General of the Regional Command of the Ba'th Party. In October 1995 he was re-elected once more president by 99.96 percent, and in October 2002 with allegedly 100 percent of the votes cast, in rigged referenda. Other "elections" are also predetermined, for example for the March 27, 2001 elections, the only candidates running were from the ABSP.

In the Sudan, Lieutenant General Omar Hassan al-Bashir and his National Salvation Revolution Command Council has been in power since the 1989 military coup that overthrew Sudan's democratically elected government. Bashir suspended the 1985 constitution, disbanded all political parties and abrogated press freedom. In 1990 the RCC specifically banned both multiparty and one-party systems. In rigged elections in 1996 Bashir won a new mandate as the opposition boycotted the elections. In January 1999 Sudan reimposed the multiparty system for the first time in nine years. The constitution now allows formation of opposition parties, with certain registration criteria, but within a few weeks the Information Minister Amin Hassan Omer imposed a news blackout on opposition political parties. The government ordered the press not to give publicity to unregistered parties. In June 1999 the government announced a press law amendment which provided for administrative punishment of journalists. In December 1999 Bashir declared a three-month state of emergency, disbanded parliament and dismissed Parliamentary Speaker Dr. Hassan al-Turabi, his rival for power.

In Syria, Hafiz al-Assad consistently won rigged elections for three decades after taking power in 1970. In March 1999 he was elected to a fifth seven-year term in a national referendum with 99.9 % of the vote. But he died in June 2000, ending a thirty-year rule, and was succeeded in July by his son Bashar, continuing Syria's authoritarian rule, as Bashar was elected in a similarly predetermined process.

Political Agents and the Structure of the Press

In such an environment, there are strong incentives for journalists to support the regime and its policies, at least on issues about which the regime is sensitive. Without an organized opposition party or group, there is no public criticism of the regime to report in the newspaper columns, and the psychological atmosphere makes it very difficult for the newspaper columnist independently to voice criticism of the government. In addition to this psychological pressure on journalists, the ruling group in each of these countries had structured the press in such a way that it has clear and legitimate mechanisms to influence journalists' behavior. This has been achieved primarily by taking all newspapers of any consequence out of the hands of private owners and making them the property of political agents and supporters of the regime, most commonly its own party. In all of these countries, the ruling party derives its importance solely from the fact that its leaders hold political power. These parties are fundamentally quite weak institutions, but the ruling groups have built them up as instruments of rule and mass mobilization. It is natural, then, that these parties would be used to control the press. Control is ultimately assured because the head of the ruling group is also leader of the ruling party.

Provisions in the law in these countries support the system.

In pre-2003 Iraq and in Syria, where other parties exist alongside the ruling one, they are controlled by the regime and not independent. Ownership of the press is not exclusively in the hands of the ruling party, but the effect is the same as if it were. In Syria, the constitution provides for free speech but the government restricts it in practice. The government permits no criticism of the president, his family, the Ba'th party or the military, or sectarian issues. The emergency law gives the government broad discretion to determine what is illegal. It prohibits publishing "false information" which opposes the "goals of the revolution." Syrian journalists are in effect employees of the Ba'th Party, with a mission to perpetuate its ideology. Syria has been under a state of emergency almost continuously since 1963, and the government justifies it because of a state of war with Israel. The emergency law allows the government to override constitutional free speech provisions.[7]

In Syria, the government owns all the major publishing houses. After Bashar became president, he opened the door slightly to private ownership. He first allowed a private weekly newspaper *al-Domari* (The Lamplighter) and a private magazine *Black and White* to appear. When *al-Domari* published criticism of government ministers and quickly expanded its readership the government advertising was cut off and it struggled financially; it continued, but showed more restraint. By 2003, aproximately fifteen private newspapers and magazines had been established.[8]

Some foreign papers are allowed entry but they must be cleared by censors. Syrian journalists are in effect employees of the Ba'th Party, with a mission to perpetuate its ideology. Syria has been under a state of emergency almost continuously since 1963, and the government justifies it because of a state of war with Israel. The emergency law allows the government to override constitutional free speech provisions.

Syria since 1963 has been ruled by one or another wing of the Ba'th Party, whose leadership controls the press either through the party or through the governmental machinery. Currently the party itself publishes the largest-circulation daily, *al-Ba'th,* while the Ministry of Information publishes the other major daily, *al-Thawra.* The Ministry also publishes four provincial dailies: *al-Uruba* in Homs, *al-Jamahir* in Aleppo, *al-Fida'* in Hama, and *al-Wahda* in Latakia. The youngest daily, *Tishrin,* was founded to commemorate the October 1973 war.

In Libya, the ruling group's party has been the only legal party in the country and at the same time the owner of all politically significant newspapers. One state-run newspaper, *al-Shams,* has a circulation of 40,000, while local Revolutionary Committees publish smaller papers. The state owns all media. In *The Green Book,* Muammar Qaddafi said, "The press is a means of expression of the society and is not a means of expression of a natural or corporate person. Logically and democratically, the press, therefore, cannot be owned by either of those." He added, "Democratically, a natural person should not be permitted to own any means of publication or information." He is saying that democracy is misapplied, and the media's role is to educate society, so media must belong to the people as represented by the regime.[9]

The Libyan government tolerates some difference of opinion in the General People's Congress and the People's Committees, but not of Qaddafi. The GPC is controlled by Qaddafi. Occasional criticism of officials and policies is used to test public opinion. The regime does not permit publication of opinions contrary to government policy. The government censors incoming foreign publications. The regime prohibits all political activities not officially approved. Laws are so vague that the government can interpret them as it wishes. The government uses a pervasive system of informants that creates a system of mistrust. Libian laws regulating the media are: The General Press Corporation Law of 1972; the Publications Law No. 76 of June 17, 1972; The Public Corporation for Publication, Distribution and Publicity Law of September 25, 1974; the General Corporation for People's Revolution Broadcasting Station Law of 1973. Mass media are run by the People's Committees.[10]

The Sudanese press law since 1989 allows detention of journalists without trial if they are seen to be working against state policy. In June 1999 the government announced a press law amendment which provided for administrative punishment of journalists. The 1999 Sudanese constitution calls for freedom of the press "as regulated by law," but the government regularly suspends newspapers, intimidates journalists and conducts surveillance over them, using networks of informers. Journalists practice self-censorship. The government controls the press primarily through the National Press Council, which applies the press law and reports directly to the president. Seven of its twenty-one members are selected by the president, five by the National Assembly, and nine by journalists. It has the power to suspend a newspaper for two months and a journalist for two weeks. The government and the Press Council regularly suspend newspapers. In 1999, for example, four different newspapers were suspended multiple times each. In 1999 at least three editors were arrested. As a result, they practice self-censorship.

In Iraq, the constitution under Saddam Hussein's regime called for freedom of the press "in compliance with the revolutionary, national and progressive trend." But in practice the regime does not permit freedom of the press. Several laws allow repression. RCC Decree No. 840 of 1986 penalized free expression and stipulates the death penalty for anyone insulting the president or other high officials. The 1968 press act prohibited the writing of articles on twelve specific subjects including those detrimental to the president, the RCC, and the Ba'th Party.[11]

Iraq's Law No. 155, announced over Baghdad Radio on December 3, 1967, abolished all private newspapers and stipulated that no papers could be published subsequently without a license issued by the "General Establishment for Press and Printing" of the Ministry of Information. Therefore it was the practice that the Ministry licenses only those papers that conform to the basic policy line of the ruling group. In the 1980s the Iraqi ruling group controlled the largest daily, *al-Thawra,* through its Ba'th Party organization which owned the paper. It controlled the daily *al-Qadissiya* through the Defense Ministry, and it controlled two other dailies, *al-Jumhuriya* and *The Baghdad Observer,* through the Ministry of Information, which published them.

A 1991 Iraqi law allowed the creation of parties other than the Ba'th. The regime used the law to allow parties that support it and prevent others. No ethnic or religious parties were permitted. Iraq also had a law which prohibits any criticism of the president, the Revolutionary Command Council (RCC), or the Ba'th Party, and those who do may face the death penalty. The RCC's Decree No. 840 of 1986 allowed the death penalty for insulting the president or high government officials, and the 1968 Press Act listed twelve topics which journalists were prohibited to write about, such as negatively portraying the president or the party.[12]

Control Mechanisms

The regime influences the press under this system primarily through its control over personnel. Even though the state does not own the press, the regime is able to assure itself of basic press loyalty because of the people who run it.

First, the head of the national ruling group is usually head of the political party or other agency that owns the press. Journalists working for such newspapers are aware, without being told so explicitly, that they are expected to promote these policies to the extent that they can.

Beyond that, the ruling group can also control the content of the press through its influence over press personnel assignments. It can, and does, see that right-thinking people are appointed to key editorial positions. In addition, it can cause its political party or other owning agent to dismiss a recalcitrant journalist from the newspaper or suspend him from work. Just the threat of being barred from one's profession is a strong incentive to conform. Dismissals or suspensions usually occur on an individual basis.

The ruling group under this system can also use the powers of the state, such as arrest and detention of journalists, to help enforce conformity with the regime's basic policies. This weapon may be available in other countries as well, but it is especially easy to use where the law has put ownership of the press in the hands of an agent that is known to have primarily a political purpose. Serious deviation from basic policy can readily be used as a reason for arrest and punishment of the offender.

By the same token, the rewarding of "helpful" newspapermen by providing them with inside information which enhances their role as journalists is a technique used by regimes in many countries, but it is especially common under this system because of the political affinity between the ruling group and most of the leading journalists.

Finally, the regime usually is able to exercise direct censorship over these newspapers more easily because of the fact that their political agent usually owns the press, and because of the general political climate—especially in a crisis situation. But most of the time a kind of gentleman's agreement is in operation, and the ruling group ordinarily does not have to resort to censorship because of the self-censorship by the newspapermen. Thus the political climate, personnel considerations including both assignments and dismissals or suspensions, plus the stick of legal sanctions and the carrot of access to inside information all are powerful inducements to make the journalist in this system conform to the regime's basic policy line. Whether motivated by true sympathy, loyalty, conformity to the constraints of the environment, fear, or opportunism, the newspaperman supports and actively promotes this line. He will write independent news stories and editorials where he can, but when he touches areas that are sensitive to the regime he will support the official policy.

In Iraq, under the rule of Saddam Hussein's Arab Ba'th Socialist Party (ABSP), journalists were under pressure to join the Ba'th party and must follow directions of the Iraqi Journalists' Union, headed by Uday Hussain, the son of the president. Uday dismissed hundreds of journalists in 1999, for example, who did not praise Saddam enough. The regime arrested many journalists. In Saddam's Iraq, the Ministry of Culture censored all media to use them for guidance and compliance with ABSP party policy and ideology. It banned material contrary to policy or promoting contrary ideas, plus also sexually explicit material. Censorship was direct for all incoming foreign material, and mostly indirect for local media whose editors practiced self-censorship.[13] Most importantly, Saddam's son Uday in effect dominated all media, giving Saddam the most effective control possible.

In Syria, the government controls the media through several means, including licensing, laws, and guidance within a nondiverse political context. The Ministry of Information censors the domestic and foreign press. Censorship is stricter for materials in Arabic. They censor anything on the government's human rights record, the government's role in Lebanon or drug trafficking, material unfavorable to Arab concerns or Syrian religious groups, and graphic sexual material. In 1996–1999, there was some modest relaxation of censorship, for example on regional developments including the peace process, as the media covered some aspects of the peace process factually. In August 1999 the government repealed the ban on import of Jordanian newspapers. The government press in the years after 1996 did publish articles on official corruption and governmental inefficiency. Stories on high-level government corruption were printed in non-Syrian papers allowed in, but these were portrayed as examples of anticorruption efforts. In 2001, the Syrian government under Bashar al-Assad, who had started his regime with some liberalization moves, passed a new press law that imposed additional restrictions on journalists.[14]

In Syria the regime has repeatedly jailed journalists for long prison terms. An offshore Syrian human rights group said in 1996 that there were 2,800 political prisoners in Syrian jails, including Lebanese and Palestinians.[15] In Iraq, for example, in January 2001 Saddam Hussain revoked newspaper editor Hashim Hassan's journalistic credentials and put him under arrest for criticizing Iraqi diplomacy, in May he had two journalists sacked for writing hints about government corruption, and in July he had Shaikh Abdallatif Humayim dismissed as chief editor of a newspaper for indirectly criticizing the government's performance.

The Libyan regime suspends publication, detains journalists, and also journalists periodically disappear.

Guidance Channels

How does the journalist know the policy line on a regular basis? What are the channels for guidance under this system? Censorship is one of the means used to convey the regime's specific views on what should or should not be published. But instructions by the censor generally play an important role only during a period of real crisis, such as wartime. In normal circumstances, and on a daily basis, guidance is transmitted to the press in more subtle ways, and prepublication censorship is not necessary because the editors know their paper will be read carefully and they will hear if they make a mistake. Most of the guidance used by editors and other journalists under this system is not labeled as such, but derives from two open sources. First, they closely watch all of the public statements of policy made by the ruling group and its representatives, in order to keep abreast of current policy initiatives and the regime's official view of events. Whether they are formal declarations, press conference remarks, or explanations of policy in a national assembly, these statements are taken as guidance by the newspapermen.

Secondly, in all of these countries the government controls and operates a national news service which is used as an important source of policy guidance. The Syrian News Agency, the Sudanese News Agency, and Libya's "Arab Revolutionary News Agency," are all controlled by the respective governments, usually through Ministries of Information. (This was also true of the Iraqi News Agency until 2003.) They not only convey news of the regime's activities, which the press is expected to carry, but also provide occasional commentaries or backgrounders which contain the regime's interpretation of events. Transmitted daily to all major newspapers in the country, this regular supply of material is published and is also taken by newspapermen as guidance on what to publish and what interpretations are desired by the regime. In addition to open channels, the ruling groups in these countries have personal ties and informal connections with key newspapermen which they use to convey political guidance from time to time under this system of press organization because of the dependent status of the newspaper and the regime's influence over its personnel. Typically, when the regime wishes to convey specific guidance on a sensitive political subject, an information ministry official, party functionary or aide in the presidency, for example, will telephone a responsible editor in each newspaper to indicate the government's position. This position is not always accepted without discussion and some modification of detail, but the essentials of it will find their way into the press.

These, then, are the guidance channels that the regime uses to convey policy on a daily basis to the mobilization press. It should be kept in mind that the guidance channels, control mechanisms, press structure, and political conditions described in this chapter are characteristic of the model from which individual press systems in these Arab countries may deviate in some details. In the following chapter we will analyze these countries more specifically, looking at the stages of development leading up to this system, but first we will look briefly at one country that has a mobilization system in order to see how individual countries can deviate from the basic characteristics outlined above.

One exception to the system described above was Northern Iraq between 1991 and 2003, when it functioned autonomously from the rest of Iraq, due to restrictions imposed from outside the country. Many independent newspapers appeared there after 1993, and the number increased in 1998. The press in Northern Iraq during that period was free to criticize the government in Baghdad, and also to criticize the Kurdish authorities who governed the North. Most journalists in the North however were affiliated with one of the two Kurdish political parties, KDP and PUK, which effectively controlled different areas, and PUK newspapers rarely circulated in KDP territory and vice versa.[16]

These four countries can therefore be considered to have "mobilization" press systems. They differ from each other somewhat but there are enough similarities to assign them to the same category. Moreover, modifications in the system may occur over time, without altering the basic structure and principles. For example, when Bashar became president in Syria in 1999 upon the death of his father, some observers reported an initial easing of controls and some more liberalization of the press.[17] Yet after he consolidated his power, he saw to it that the Syrian press remained under strict controls and an instrument of the regime.

NOTES

1. Sources: Europa, *The Middle East and North Africa 2000, 46th Edition,* and Editor and Publisher, *Yearbook 1999;* Department of State, *1999 Human Rights Report,* Sudan Section, February 25, 2000; and Web sites.

2. David E. Apter, *The Politics of Modernization,* Chicago: University of Chicago Press, 1965, pp. 36, 240, 359.

3. Daniel Lerner, "Toward a Communication Theory of Modernization," in Lucien Pye, Ed., *Communications and Political Development,* Princeton: Princeton University Press, 1963, p. 344.

4. Program of the Arab Ba'th Socialist Party 1965, cited in Roy E. Thoman, "Iraq Under Ba'thist Rule," *Current History,* January 1972, p. 32.

5. Sudan News Agency, "Revolution, Information and News," Khartoum, 1971.

6. Apter, p. 360.

7. Arvind Singhal and Vijay Krishna, "Syria," in Yahya R. Kamalipour and Hamid Mowlana, *Mass Media in the Middle East,* Westport CT: Greenwood Press 1994, p. 263; and U.S. Department of State, *1994 Country reports on Human Rights Practices,* 1994 and 1999, Syria sections, Washington D.C., March 1995 and February 25, 2000. The annual State Department human rights reports have been used elsewhere in this book, sometimes without specific reference.

8. *Kuwait Times,* May 9, 2002, AP July 22, 2002; BBC World Service Monitoring, "Syria-Media-Overview," July 16, 2003.

9. Qaddafi, *The Green Book,* pp. 38–39, quoted in Karim Mezran, "Libya," chapter 12 in Kamalipour and Mowlana, p. 176.

10. U.S. Department of State, *1999 Human Rights Report,* Libya section, February 25, 2000; Karim Mezran, "Libya," chapter 12 in Kamalipour and Mowlana, p. 183.

11. U.S. State Department, *1999 Human Rights Report,* Iraq section, Washington D.C., February 25, 2000.

12. *2000 World Press Freedom Review,* May 14, 2001.

13. Khalid Serhan Hurrat and Lisa Isabel Leidig, "Iraq," in Kamalipour and Mowlana, op. cit., pp. 104–5.

14. BBC World Service Monitoring, "Syria-Media-Overview," July 16, 2003.

15. *1997 and 1999 World Press Freedom Review,* 1997 and 1999.

16. U.S. State Department, *Human Rights Reports for 1998, 1999, and 2000,* Iraq Section, February 26, 1999, February 25, 2000, and February 2001, respectively.

17. *Al-Sharq al-Awsat* Web site in Arabic, London, June 24, 2000.

3

The Mobilization Press: Development Stages

Four Arab countries fit more or less into the model described in the previous chapter. Now we shall analyze in somewhat more detail how the print media in these countries evolved into this type of system, since the evolution seems to have taken a remarkably similar course in all of the countries. A four-stage development process seems to have repeated itself, with some local variation, in each of the four states. This chapter will describe those stages and the major reasons for their emergence.

In Libya and the Sudan and in Iraq up to 2003, the role of the press in the political process went through four similar stages of development. For convenience we can label the four stages colonial, factional, nonpartisan, and mobilization. In Syria, the press has gone through three of the same stages but has not yet fully entered the fourth, although for all practical purposes the basic system of the press is the same. In Iraq, the press in 2003 has reverted to the factional stage (see Chapter 6 for details). In Table 3.1 we list the dates the press in each of the countries went through these stages. Understanding the complex set of factors behind each stage, however, requires more detailed explanation.

COLONIAL STAGE

Arab newspapers first appeared in all of these countries during a period of foreign colonial rule, usually Ottoman and then either British or French. The papers were established out of literary, commercial, political, or sometimes personal motives, and they tended to grow along with the nationalist

TABLE 3.1   Phases of Press Development in Four Arab Countries

	Colonial	Factional	Nonpartisan	Mobilization
Iraq	before 1932	1932–63 2003	1964–67	1967–2003
Syria	before 1946	1946–58	1958–63	since 1963
The Sudan	1903–53 1964–69	1953–58 1969–70 1985–89	1958–64 1970–85	since 1989
Libya	before 1951	1951–69	1969–72	since 1972

sentiment and the pace of economic life. But the owners and editors had to be careful to keep the colonial administrator as well as the local government in mind. Thus the two major factors of the period were emerging nationalism which promoted the growth of Arab journalism, and colonial rule which tended to restrict it.

As early as the middle of the nineteenth century, an Arab print media, that is newspapers edited and published by and for Arabs, had already emerged in Syria and Iraq, all part of the Ottoman Empire.

Syrian and Iraqi publishers were seriously encumbered until 1908 by strict Ottoman regulations enforced by local authorities, which hampered the free growth of journalism. Pressure from the Young Turks did force a relaxation of these strictures in 1908, so Arab newspapers proliferated in Syria and Iraq during the next decade. Young writers and politicians, with the ideas of nationalism, and many of them educated at colleges in Beirut, Cairo, Alexandria, and Istanbul, started their own organs of Arab consciousness within the Ottoman framework. Nevertheless after World War I, Ottoman rule was replaced by French and British mandates in Syria and Iraq, respectively, and Arab newspapermen had to contend with their publishing restrictions. Journalism in Syria grew somewhat under the French mandate (1920–46), but the French used their mandatory powers to license for publication only those organs which generally supported their policies. Although writers and editors had somewhat more freedom in Iraq under the relatively lighter British mandatory administration (1920–32), they too faced some limits in political discussion beyond which they could not go.[1]

The press in the Sudan and Libya began later primarily because of low literacy rates and an inadequate economic base, but also there it emerged and first developed under colonial rule. The first newspapers to appear in these countries were issued directly by the British colonial administration, usually in English and for resident British citizens.

A biweekly Arab newspaper in Arabic called *al-Sudan* was founded in the Sudan in 1903. Since it was owned by three Syrian journalists who also owned the then-famous Cairo daily *al-Muqattam,* and since the Anglo-Egyptian condominium had been established over the Sudan five years earlier, many Sudanese suspected that the paper was a mouthpiece of foreign interests. Two Greek merchants began publishing an English weekly a few years later, to which they added an Arabic supplement. Only in 1919, as literacy was spreading and the question of union with Egypt had become a live political issue, did the first indigenous Sudanese newspaper appear. *Hadarat al-Sudan* (Sudanese Culture) pleased the British because it opposed union and supported the British administration. Even so, after the prounionist armed uprising of 1924 the colonial administration decided to restrict the scope of political and press activity somewhat.

As a result, for more than a decade, Sudanese publishers turned their attention more to literary efforts. British control over the press was relatively light, however. The Sudan government promulgated its first Press Ordinance in 1930, giving the British administrators licensing authority, but this was in practice very sparingly used. By 1935 the first Sudanese daily, *al-Nil* (The Nile), had started, and the newspapers began to become more politically oriented. They reflected some of the popular discontent with the 1936 Anglo-Egyptian treaty for example. A second daily, *Sawt al-Sudan,* started in 1940 as newspapers proliferated with the growing political consciousness. Political parties were formed after World War II and many of them were able to start their own newspapers. This trend accelerated in 1953 as Sudanese political activity intensified for the February elections and Britain and Egypt declared their intention to end the condominium after a three-year transition period. As far as the press was concerned, the colonial stage ended then.

Press development in Libya was even slower, due primarily to the small size of the literate populations. Libya had no Arab-owned newspapers before independence in 1951, and the only Libyan journalists worked for British-owned papers.

FACTIONAL STAGE

When the press in these countries left the colonial stage, it moved into what we may call the factional stage. Newspapers became more active politically and—more important—the press became considerably diversified and competitive. Newspapers were backed by private individuals, families, political parties, or by government interests, and they could be distinguished from each other in tone, content, and editorial viewpoint. Concomitant with this factionalism was a degree of freedom from governmental restrictions for the press that was greater than in any other stage of its development in these countries. The government did impose restrictions including censorship from time to time, but the newspapers were relatively independent during this period. This stage emerged because of changes in the political environment, and there are several factors which were conducive to the transition.

Lifting of Colonial Restrictions

Lifting of colonial-power restrictions on the press usually corresponded with the achievement of complete national independence from the colonial power, as in the case of the press in Iraq (1932), Syria (1946), and Libya (1951). In the Sudan, the factional press also began to emerge before the British were entirely gone because British colonial administrators stopped exercising rights in the press field.

Competition among Political Groups

The second condition for the emergence of the factional press was a political environment in which several parties and groups were openly competing for power. Individual newspapers were able to align themselves with specific parties or groups with which they sympathized, and in this way gain financial and other support for their publishing efforts. The government usually had affiliations with one or more newspapers, but they by no means controlled all of them since antiregime elements had their spokesmen in the press as well. Some independent papers developed during this period, but many were linked with political factions and known to be editorial apologists for partisan points of view.

During the factional-press phase in Syria (1946–58) the country experienced a high degree of partisan political activity, a rapid turnover in government, and a competition among contenders for power, all of which were reflected in the press. One observer noted that "the press is reorganized every time Syria gets a new regime" during this period.[2] There were many newspapers, virtually every one run by a politically oriented editor who had close ties with a party, interest group, influential family, minister, or even a foreign embassy. These patrons underwrote various interests across a wide spectrum, so there were no truly independent Syrian newspapers.

Similarly in Iraq during this phase (1932–63) there were periods of vigorous, open political discussion, and the press arranged itself along a broad political spectrum. Parties and individuals, competing for power in a relatively unstable political environment, sought support from newspapers in promoting their interests. There was rapid turnover in papers, but diversity remained. In the first decade after World War II approximately half of the papers reflected opposition to the government, and between 1958 and 1963 there was considerable partisan debate in the press, although the framework of the debate shifted to the left in the latter period under Abdal Karim Qasim as Communist writers were given official encouragement.

In 1962 there were twenty newspapers in Baghdad alone, one-third of them Communist backed and the rest of varying shades of political opinion.

The Sudanese press passed through the factional phase three times, 1953–58, 1964–69, and 1985–89. The first phase began when Sudanese party political activity increased in preparation for the February 1953 parliamentary election, and by the time of full independence in 1956 the country had sixteen intensely partisan newspapers, including nine dailies. The National Unionist Party, which controlled the government after gaining a majority in the election, had the support of two leading dailies while the opposition Ummah Party was affiliated with a third. Party newspapers were effectively suppressed during the military regime of General Ibrahim Abboud (1958–64), but after his overthrow a measure of political competition was restored to the Sudan and with it came a revival of diversity in the Sudanese press. This competitive situation among parties and papers lasted until General Jafar Numeiri came to power in 1969.

Party papers, however, reemerged after Numeiri's overthrow in the civilian revolution of April 1985 which brought down the authoritarian regime of Numeiri. It dissolved all of Numeiri's institutions, and passed a new provisional constitution which called for restoration of press freedom. Many new publications appeared and some old ones were revived. An unprecedented number of papers were published between 1985 and 1989; there were ninety-one papers of all types and frequencies including party papers and party-supported "independent" papers. The transitional government abolished the 1973 Press and Publication Act and substituted the 1985 Press and Publication Act, but the latter retained some of the restrictions on press freedom. There were three coalition governments in the 1985–89 period, and their record on press freedom was worse than that of the previous democratic governments. The government imposed restrictions on military news and took other actions. The State of Emergency of 1987 enabled the government new weapons to close down newspapers, which it used against three papers.

During the 1985–89 factional period in the Sudan, however, there was a problem of quality and professionalism because of the long period of authoritarian rule that preceded it, as unqualified people became editors. Many tended to sensationalism, muckraking, and yellow journalism, attacking public personalities. The party papers attacked parties they opposed, and never criticized their own party. Also during the 1985–89 period, financial problems caused the demise of many publications. Of the ninety-one papers which first appeared, twenty folded and twenty-five appeared only irregularly. Financial problems also made the newspapers vulnerable to party, government, and foreign pressure.

In Libya, the press went through a factional stage resembling those described above, but in these two countries the basis was primarily competing individual personalities and informal groups rather than formal political parties.

The Libyan factional phase in the press lasted for eighteen years (1951–69) on the basis of support by diverse private interest groups and a government which restricted but did not suppress them. The government published papers in Tripoli and Benghazi, and various competing private interests that had become politically active after independence found supporters in the press who developed dailies and weeklies in those cities too. The press editorial spectrum ranged from conservative, religious, and anti-Communist to leftist Nasserite sympathies, and it included some criticism of the government.

Governmental Restraint

The third factor behind the factional press was the existence of a national government that was unwilling and/or unable to impose severe restrictions on publications. Typically during the factional stage, direct governmental interference with the press fluctuated; there were short periods of government intervention, but the regime did not maintain or institutionalize it. It may have acted against one newspaper by revoking its license or prosecuting the editor responsible, but it did not permanently change the ground rules for all newspapers. The main reason for this was that there was an element of balance in the political system, so that the government faced political forces beyond its direct control that in effect guaranteed the continuation of critical nongovernmental voices in the press.

The governments did impose restrictions in emergencies such as World War II and the first Arab-Israeli war, and from time to time they attempted to restrict the press for other reasons but without ending its basically factional nature. The governments generally had legal authority, such as temporary suspension of a publication or arrest of an editor, to use against the newspapers, but because of the political situation these were used sparingly. It was the post-colonial political balance of forces and the government's role in that, rather than legal or constitutional guarantees, which was the key factor in maintaining the essential diversity and relative freedom of the press in this phase.

NONPARTISAN STAGE

The third stage of press development in these countries was characterized by a sharp reduction in diversity among newspapers, a muting of criticism, and a greater degree of support for the regime. Thus some of the key trends of the second stage were reversed, although much of the press remained in private hands. This stage was introduced by a zealous new revolutionary leadership group after it seized power. Three major steps brought about the transition.

End of Political Competition

First and most important was the sudden banning of competing political parties and private interest groups by the new leadership shortly after it seized power. Since the ruling group had power but its authority was not yet legitimized or fully established, it banned the parties in order to prevent any real challenge or organized opposition. The group's own political organization, whether pre-existing or created after the coup d'etat, was ordinarily proclaimed the only legal party. Naturally, as a consequence of this political move the party newspapers were banned at the same time, so that members of the outlawed parties would be deprived of their communication channel. This step effectively removed key underpinnings of the diverse and independent press.

Increased Governmental Intervention

Secondly, the new regime increased direct governmental intervention in the press, including its use of censorship of newspapers. The private papers continued to appear, but the government tended to take legal actions against them more frequently in order to make them adhere to the official political line.

Promotion of the Regime's Newspapers

Thirdly, the regime began to promote its own newspapers more as channels of communication and exhortation of the masses in the direction of its goals. Both of these measures were signs that the regime was sensitive to the political role of the press, concerned about evoking support from it, and strong enough to take such steps.

When Syria merged with Egypt into the United Arab Republic (UAR) in 1958, all political parties and their newspapers were banned in Syria as they had been in Egypt, and the regime-sponsored National Union was declared the only legal political organization.

The UAR government also imposed censorship in Syria and sponsored its own newspapers. As one observer described the result, in fact, "the press spoke with one voice" during this period reflecting the lack of open political dissent in Syria.[3] Even after the military coup d'etat in Damascus in December 1961 led to Syria's withdrawal from the UAR, the various and competing political parties did not re-emerge to play their parts in the political system. The new ruling groups and others that came to power by coup d'etat prevented any public activities by political organizations which challenged their authority, so party newspapers also did not revive. The Syrian regimes continued censorship and the practice of sponsoring their own newspapers. After the September 1961 military coup led to withdrawal, some parties tried to resume political activity but boycotted the December elections. They were banned after the next coup in March. The Ba'th coup came a year later, in March 1963, and one wing or another of the Ba'th party has ruled Syria ever since.

Similarly in Iraq, when Colonel Abdul Salam 'Arif seized power on November 18, 1963, he formed the Arab Socialist Union and declared it to be the only authorized political organization in the country, putting an end to the party press which had been active for three decades. Five months later, the Arif regime promulgated Press Law No. 53 which gave the government powers to censor publications critical of the administration, and to revoke licenses of newspapers publishing "whatever contributes a danger to the Republic and the internal and external security of the state."[4]

The press in the Sudan and Libya underwent a transformation of a similar nature, but different in some details.

There were no political parties in Libya when Colonel Muammar Qaddafi and his military group seized power from the monarchy there on September 1, 1969, so he had none to ban and did not need to create his own party. But Qaddafi established a regime similar to the others mentioned above and he did not allow the development of any competing political organizations or party newspapers in the new republic. He did start publishing the regime's own newspaper, *al-Thawra* (The Revolution), to help explain his ideas; the paper disappeared in January 1972, but a new government daily, *al-Fajr al-Jadid* (The New Dawn), began later the same year and carried on the campaign for the regime. Qaddafi also used some of the powers of the government to undermine the effectiveness of the private press. It sharply cut back on subsidies that the monarchy had given the private press, and in January 1970 declared that only *al-Thawra* should receive the lucrative advertisements placed by government ministries. This put the other papers, including the independent dailies, namely *al-Raaid, al-Hurriya,* and *al-Haqiqa,* at a disadvantage.

In the Sudan, General Ibrahim Abboud led a successful military coup d'etat on November 17, 1958; his regime banned all political parties and their official newspapers. Abboud started his own newspaper, *al-Thawra.* The private papers that continued to appear were relatively nonpartisan in content and were kept in line by the strict government censorship which General Abboud imposed and under threat of suspension which encouraged them to follow the official policy line. For example *al-Nil,* Sudan's oldest newspaper, was suspended in February 1960 for disagreeing with Abboud's policy. The October 1964 revolution ousted Abboud and restored some party activity, taking the press temporarily back to the factional stage. But General Jafar Numeiri's coup d'etat of May 25, 1969, led, within a month, to the banning of all political organizations other than his Revolutionary Council, again ending the party-backed press.

Numeiri used some of the powers of the government to influence the private press, which became less outspoken than before his coup, but he did not create his own newspaper to compete directly with them as other leaders had done in similar circumstances.

Thus in all of these countries a revolutionary leadership group was able to use governmental powers to restrict the press more directly than its predecessor regime, and by banning all competing political organizations it undermined one of the essential foundations for a diverse press independent of governmental control. In most places, the ruling group was also able to counter the press competition directly by putting out its own newspaper. By these means, it moved the press into the nonpartisan stage characterized by a greater degree of uniformity and of loyalty to the government.

MOBILIZATION STAGE

In the final stage of development, private newspaper ownership is ended, and all politically important papers are controlled directly by a political agent of the ruling group or its affiliate. They are all supposed to mobilize public support for the regime. This stage has been fully achieved in Libya and the Sudan, and prevailed in Iraq between 1967 and 2003. In the mid-1980s there were signs of liberalization in the Sudan and Iraq as party papers became active, but these lasted only briefly (see below). In Syria, a very similar situation has been brought about without the formal end of private newspaper ownership. What are the conditions that have led to the emergence of the mobilization press?

First, the ruling group, which came to power by means of revolution or coup, has established a reasonably firm hold on the means of coercion (such as military or police). It has also been in power long enough to eliminate all political organizations which openly competed for leadership. Nevertheless the leadership was aware that its authority had not fully been legitimated, and it was sensitive to even slight criticism and the possibility of dissatisfaction with its program. In this situation the leadership regarded the press as an important political tool and was concerned and impatient that the newspapers had not yet more uniformly and enthusiastically promoted the policies and ideas of the regime. The leadership felt that the press should by then have begun to play its part more effectively to help implement important programs.

As President Numeiri said when he announced the end of the private press in the Sudan, one year after seizing power:

Most papers have gone to great lengths to appraise the course of the revolution, giving arbitrary interpretations. . . . They have thus ignored the principles and goals declared by the revolution. . . . Confusion and perplexity have been created according to the different explanations. . . . Certain newspapers have been concentrating on cleverly destroying the positive achievements of the revolution.[5]

Although the opposition party press had disappeared with the abolition of political parties, still the national leadership was disappointed in the remaining private newspapers. Added to this was disappointment that the newspaper published by the ruling group to propagate its ideas had failed to become more successful and popular than the existing private papers despite its advantages over them. *Al-Thawra* in Iraq, *al-Ba'th* in Syria, and *al-Thawra* in Libya, were all daily newspapers published by the revolutionary leadership after it took power, but none of them surpassed the private newspapers with which they had to compete.

The ruling group particularly felt the need for a uniformly supportive press in order to advance its revolutionary program against what it perceived as an unjust resistance.

The transition to the fourth stage of press development, in which the private press was abolished, was usually accomplished by leaders who espoused socialism and perceived themselves as engaged in a struggle for society against vested interests of capitalists. At the same time, these leaders adhered to a strongly nationalistic ideology that put great emphasis on a struggle against foreign influence, imperialism, and Zionism.

In Iraq, for example, the preamble to the 1967 law stated that it was necessary to abolish the private press because of "the current battle the Arab nation is waging against imperialism, Zionism, and reaction, which requires that the Iraqi press be guided on sound national lines to meet the responsibility of the battle, and in order to prevent infiltration of the press . . . [and to] disseminate sound ideas, provide true guidelines, and carry out constructive criticism in a manner that would preserve the state in the present exceptional circumstances."[6]

In the 1970s in Iraq, two small dailies, *Tariq al-Sha'b* and *Taakhi,* were permitted to appear because they were under the auspices of two National Front member parties—the Iraqi Communist Party and the Kurdish Democratic Party, respectively—which were loyal to and did not substantially differ in policy from the Ba'th. *Tariq al-Sha'b,* however, disappeared in 1979, when the Communist Party was banned.

Several Iraqi laws allowed repression. RCC Decree No. 840 of 1986 penalizes free expression and stipulated the death penalty for anyone insulting the president or other high officials. The 1968 press act prohibits the writing of articles on twelve specific subjects including those detrimental to the president, the RCC, and the Ba'th Party.

Saddam Hussain was president, prime minister, chairman of the RCC and Secretary General of the regional command of the Ba'th Party. Other parties existed but they were controlled by the regime and not independent. In Iraq, between 1991 and 2003 the Northern region was an exception because the Saddam government withdrew from the north which came under defacto control of two Kurdish parties. Many independent newspapers appeared there since 1993, with an increase in 1998. The papers even contained some criticism of the Kurdish authorities in the north. But the rival parties, KDP of Massoud Barzani and the PUK of Jalal Talabani, controlled separate sections of the north and each blocks distribution of the other's newspapers in their respective zones. And most journalists are controlled or influenced by various political organizations.[7]

In the Sudan, President Numeiri declared that his takeover of the private press was necessary because some newspapers were "mere tools serving the objectives and goals of British imperialism," and "certain newspapers have become trumpets for saboteurs, publishing the fabricated reports of the imperialist newspapers which have launched a psychological war against the revolution." The press in the Sudan was at first owned by the country's only political party, the Sudanese Socialist Union (SSU). However, Sudanese law also gave the ministries of the government joint control with the SSU. The press law of August 1970 took all publishing out of private hands and turned it over to a public corporation. The successful private dailies *al-Sahafa* and *al-Ayam* were continued but under separate publicly owned publishing houses, which also issued other periodicals.[8]

The following year, a Sudanese republican decree made all newspaper and magazine publishing houses property of the SSU, and the 1973 press law clarified the dual party-ministry control system: "Newspapers shall be the property of the people in whose name and on whose behalf they shall be run by the Sudanese Socialist Union . . . [which has the exclusive right to license publications, while] the Minister [of Culture and Information] shall be responsible for the daily direct control of newspapers in order to ensure harmony with the general information line and commitment to the political plan of the Sudanese Socialist Union."[9] In practice, there were personal connections which made control easier.

The authoritarian Numeiri regime in the Sudan was followed by a short period of civilian rule. When President Jafar Numeiri was ousted in 1985, the SSU was abolished, and the newly elected government of 1986 drafted a new press law that allowed companies, parties, and institutions to own newspapers, but the government retained considerable influence in practice. New publications appeared and some older ones were revived. Political parties published their papers, and in the second half of the eighties, there were over ninety newspapers of all types. Quality in journalism suffered, however, as unprofessional editors and writers joined in, and sensationalist yellow journalism grew. Moreover, financial problems led many of the newspapers to close or to appear irregularly, and these problems made them more vulnerable to party or government pressures on what to publish.

In 1989 the military coup that overthrew Sudan's democratically elected government, brought Lieutenant General Omar Hassan al-Bashir and his National Salvation Revolution Command Council to power. This took the Sudanese press once again into the mobilization stage. The new rulers suspended the 1985 constitution, disbanded all political parties and abrogated press freedom. In 1990 the RCC rejected both multiparty and one-party systems. In 1993 the RCC disbanded itself and appointed Bashir president. In 1996 in rigged elections he won a new mandate as the opposition boycotted the elections. The real power 1989–99 rested with the National Islamic Front headed by Dr. Hassan al-Turabi, renamed itself the National Congress in 1996. Its members held key positions of power. In December 1999, Bashir declared a state of emergency, disbanded parliament and dismissed Parliamentary Speaker Turabi. The Sudanese press has remained under strict control as an instrument of the regime.

The Syrian political system has remained essentially the same for three decades. In March 1999 Hafiz al-Assad was elected to a fifth seven-year term in a national referendum with 99.9% of the vote. He had run for election unopposed since taking power in 1970. When he died in June 2000, ending a thirty-year rule, he was succeeded by his son Bashar. Some observers reported that under Bashar the atmosphere for public debate began to improve. The state-run newspaper began to carry columns of letters to the editor critical of the government policies. In August 2000 three cabinet ministers appeared on television and discussed public finance, fielding tough questions from viewers on job conditions and salaries. For the first time the newspapers conceded that there is an unemployment problem. New Information Minister Adnan Omran passed to the media a directive signed by Bashar ordering them to stop fawning praise and frequent presidential photos in the newspapers. Omran told the press, "Gradually we are trying to change these things." "The idea is to have an information policy that respects citizens and their feelings." "He wants to concentrate on issues, with objectivity. . . . You can talk about anything, without any problem."[10]

Encouraged, groups of Syrian intellectuals began to form and endorsed democratic pluralism and a freer press in public statements. The government tolerated the emergence of these groups and allowed the publication of two new weekly newspapers, and the re-emergence of a third, the pro-Communist *Voice of the People*. But then in 2001 President Bashar began to send signals that he did not want the trend to new freedoms to go beyond strict limits, and the authorities arrested some of the leaders of the new liberalization movement. Discussion of allowing new political parties ceased, as the leadership made clear that they did not welcome major political reforms.[11]

The regimes in these countries, therefore, had firm control over the instruments of coercion but not of persuasion, which they saw—or said they saw—as remaining in the hands of reactionary forces. As long as these regimes had new revolutionary programs to implement, and since the private newspapers did not cooperate enough in that endeavor, they sought to take them over as a useful political tool which would help put their ideas across without interference. Because their countries were not at war and such measures were difficult to justify, these regimes did not wish simply to use broad censorship measures.

Nor did they wish to make their move on the press appear to be the imposition of state control over the newspapers, so they transferred ownership of the private press into the hands of the ruling political organization, which they claimed represented "the people."

In Libya, the government forced the last of the private daily newspapers to close in 1972, and the only dailies which have appeared since that time are the regime's own, primarily *al-Fajr al-Jadid, al-Jihad,* and *al-Ra'y.* In January 1972, Qaddafi's Revolutionary Command Council held "corruption of public opinion" trials which resulted in the suspension of all newspapers and the revocation of publishing licenses for ten papers including *al-Hurriya, al-Yawm, al-Zaman, al-Fajr,* and *al-Haqiqah.* The RCC has also used censorship and other legal means to encourage conformity with its policies. The publications law of June 17, 1972, for example, required that newspaper owners "believe in the Arab revolution and abide by its objectives and the objectives and principles of the ASU."[12]

Until 1972, the Libyan government did not expressly order the privately owned newspapers to shut down but slowly started to cut back on subsidies that the monarchy had given to the private press. In January 1972 following a set of trials held by the Revolutionary Command Council to expiate "corruption of public opinion," the suspension of all newspapers and the revocation of the publishing licenses for the papers were ordered. As a consequence of this policy, all newspapers and periodicals in Libya are published either by the Jamahiriya News Agency, by the government secretariats, by the press services, or by the trade unions.[13]

In Syria, the ruling elite has not formally moved the press into the final stage by legally abolishing the private press. In these cases, however, the loyalty and active support of the press and the *de facto* disappearance of all significant private newspapers has been sufficient to satisfy the regime and it is not necessary to sanctify this situation in law.

The Syrian ruling groups have also not taken this final step to legitimize the government press monopoly that in fact exists. Syrian parties were banned in 1958, but when parties were included again in Syrian cabinets in the 1970s, their newspapers did not reappear. These parties, including the Communists and the Arab Socialists, were in fact not true opposition groups or organizations which in any way threatened and challenged the basic policies of the ruling Ba'th Party leadership. Instead, they were officially members of the so-called National Front, and in fact they followed Ba'th guidelines on all essential issues. Thus the *de facto* creation of a mobilized press, fully loyal and actively supportive of the regime, which had been established in 1963, continued. The Syrian journalist therefore finds himself in the same practical situation as does the Sudanese journalist, for example. He knows he is required to give positive support to the essential policies of his government.

In Iraq, as in Syria, the regime in the last decades of the twentieth century formed National Front governments including parties other than the

Ba'th which were not true opposition parties and thus are not allowed to criticize basic policy. The Communists and the Kurdish Democratic Party participated in the National Front in the 1970s, since they loyally supported essential Ba'th Party tenets. In Iraq, these pseudo-parties were allowed to resume publication of their own newspapers, *Tariq al-Sha'b* (Communist Party organ) and *Taakhi* (KDP organ), but these papers are put out by the government's General Establishment of Press and Printing, just like the Ba'th Party's official organ *al-Thawra* and the government's *al-Jumhuriya*. The Communist paper disappeared in 1979 when the party was banned, and the KDP now publishes the daily *al-Iraq*. The content of all of these papers, and of the government's English-language daily, *Baghdad Observer,* revealed only minor differences in political opinion or in news presentation, and none on sensitive issues.[14] On these sensitive issues, the other parties are in effect agents of the regime, which controls the press ultimately through them. The newspapers published by these parties are therefore very similar in content.

Thus we have seen that in all of these countries, the press has gone through a series of stages leading to the current situation in which it is more or less mobilized in active support of the ruling group. Two key related factors in this evolution were the relative strength of the regime and the existence of organized opposition groups which are able to function openly. Diversity in the press and competition among newspapers did exist during the factional stage following the lifting of colonial restrictions and before the regime acquired sufficient power to take control of the press. During this factional period, representational parties were active and their existence helped create necessary conditions for diversity in the press since some newspapers reflected opposition party views. Where the representational parties and groups independent of the regime were particularly weak, as in Algeria, for example, the factional phase did not last long and did not return once it ended.

Elsewhere, in the Sudan, fissiparous tendencies in the political spectrum reasserted themselves in the mid-sixties, and again in the late eighties, into the re-emergence of political parties, and with them came a revival of a diverse and competing press—although both party and press competition were suspended during subsequent regimes. As these regimes grew stronger, they sought to create a press which was more uniformly and actively supportive, a goal they were able to achieve particularly after representational parties had disappeared. The regime's political organization, a solidarity party, became a favorite agent for newspaper control.

The parties which appeared in Syria and Iraq later as legitimate and legal participants in the political process did not lead to a diverse press in those countries because these were not truly representational parties advocating policies fundamentally at variance with those of the ruling group.

As long as the regimes in these countries remain strong and dominate the political scene, not allowing opposition groups to form and to direct criticism against the government, and as long as the regimes continue to regard the press as important instruments for mobilization of the public the newspapers will probably remain as they are, basically similar in political content and differing only in style. If the political system in these countries evolved so that representational parties emerged and public debate on issues took place, a diverse press less subject to government influence would probably follow. A diverse and criticizing press (which would probably have greater reader credibility, although we have no survey data to prove that) can exist only if there is diversity in the political spectrum that can be expressed publicly. Such a diverse press would, in turn, give opposition groups the open forum they would need to challenge the ruling group in an open system.

We have seen this dynamic at work in the Sudan. President Numeiri, who had created an authoritarian political system and a mobilization press, was overthrown in April 1985, and his successors undertook changes. The al-Dahab regime which first took over allowed political parties to function and the first democratic election in eighteen years to take place a year later. Then the newly elected prime minister, Sadiq al-Mahdi, called for a free press and suspended publication of the two government-owned dailies, *al-Ayam* and *al-Sahafa*. The eleven daily newspapers which began to compete included four independents and seven party papers ranging from Communist and Ba'th to Islamic fundamentalist. Diversity also appeared in the nondaily press. But Sudanese press diversity did not survive because the diversity in the political system disappeared, and the press must function within the prevailing political system.

NOTES

1. See Shams al-Din al-Rifa'i, *Tarikh al-Sahafa al-Suriyah* (Cairo: Dar al-Ma'rif, al-Juz' al-Thani, 1969) pp. 11–15; Adib Mruwa, *al-Sahafa al-Arabiyah* (the Arab Press) Beirut: Dar Maktabit al Hayat, 1961, pp. 216, 322–35.

2. Mruwa, pp. 309 and 319 describing the 1954 law passed by the Syrian regime to abolish the press which cooperated with Shishakli.

3. Ihsan 'Askar, *Tatawwar al-Sahafa al-Suriyah* (Cairo: Dar al-Nahda al-Arabiya, 1973), p. 325.

4. Richard Nyrop, *Area Handbook for Iraq*, Washington D.C.: USGPO, 1979, p. 225.

5. President Ja'far Numeiri, interview with *al-Quwwat al-Musallaha*, August 29, 1970, broadcast on Radio Omdurman on the same day at 6:00 P.M.

6. Preamble to Law No. 155, Baghdad Radio December 3, 1967, 1500 GMT.

7. U.S. State Department, *Human Rights Report*, 1998 and 1999, Iraq section, Washington D.C., and February 26, 1999 and February 25, 2000, respectively.

8. Omdurman Radio, August 26 and 29, 1970, *Sudan News*, September 8, 1970.

9. Sudanese Press and Publications Act of 1973, No. 6 of May 10, 1973.

10. *The Washington Post*, September 20, 2000, p. A29.

11. Najib Ghadbian, "The New Asad: Dynamics of Continuity and Change in Syria," *Middle East Journal,* vol. 55, no. 4, Autumn 2001, pp. 624–40, and *Washington Report on Middle East Affairs,* April 2001, p. 31; *The Economist,* March 24, 2001, p. 53; *Middle East International,* February 23, 2001, p. 11; and *al-Hayat,* July 16, 2000.

12. RCC press law announced on June 18, 1972, Libyan News Agency bulletin, January 18, 1972.

13. Karim Mezran, "Libya" chapter in Yahya R. Kamalipour and Hamid Mowlana, Eds., *Mass Media in the Middle East: A Comprehensive Handbook,* Westport, CT: Greenwood Press, 1994, p. 178.

14. Roy E. Thoman, *Current History,* January 1972: 32–36; *New York Times,* July 13, 1973, and *Christian Science Monitor,* June 8, 1971.

4

The Loyalist Press: Saudi Arabia, Bahrain, Qatar, Oman, the United Arab Emirates, and Palestine

In six Arab countries—Saudi Arabia, Bahrain, Qatar, Oman, the United Arab Emirates, and Palestine—the print media play generally the same kind of role in the political process.[1] We designate this type the loyalist press because its most prominent characteristic is that the newspapers are consistently loyal to and supportive of the regime in power despite the fact that they are privately owned. In this chapter we will discuss that and other characteristics of this type of press, and the major factors that have led to its emergence in these countries. As with the mobilization press we will focus on the daily newspapers and highlight the common features that apply to all six countries, but we will also mention deviations from the model.

In Jidda and Mecca, in the Western (Hijaz) region of Saudi Arabia, newspapers such as *al-Bilad* and *al-Madina* were flourishing as early as the 1930s, and the newspapers *Okaz* and *al-Nadwa* were appearing there by 1960. *Al-Jazira* daily began in Riyadh in 1962. By that time, all five were daily newspapers, and each was owned by an individual family. In 1963, the government asked them to broaden their bases of ownership by creating boards of directors that would include others. In 1965 two more Arabic dailies, *al-Riyadh* and *al-Yawm* appeared in Riyadh and Dammam, respectively. As of 2003, all seven dailies still exist, although four additional dailies, three of them in English, are now being published as well. In the face of competition, *al-Bilad* has run into some financial difficulties, suspending publication in the late 1990s until its owners increased their subsidy, but otherwise Saudi Arabia's relatively small literate Arab population has been able to sustain eleven daily newspapers into the twenty-first century. The strongest papers are published by the two largest publishing enterprises, Saudi Research and Marketing, which puts out an array of publications and the al-Yamama Press.

In the other five countries, daily newspapers emerged later than in Saudi Arabia. Before the UAE, Oman, Qatar and Bahrain became independent in 1971 they generally had only a few small-circulation nondaily papers. In these small Gulf states, the first daily appeared in the UAE in 1970, in Oman in 1971, in Qatar in 1975 and in Bahrain in 1976.

In Bahrain, the weekly paper *Jaridit al-Bahrayn* began in the 1940s, *Sada al-Usbu'* appeared in 1969, and another weekly *al-Mujtama al-Jadid* followed a year later. At independence in 1971 almost no Bahraini print media existed, but by the 1990s there were more than forty-five publications, including three principal dailies (two in Arabic, one in English). The three dailies are *Akhbar al-Khalij* (started 1976), and *Gulf Daily News* (1979), both published by Akhbar al-Khaleej Press, and *al-Ayam* (started 1989), published by al-Ayam Establishment. There are only a few weekly newspapers. The oldest is *al-Adwaa'* (the spotlight) which began in 1965. Other weeklies are *Akhbar BAPCO,* and *Sada al-Usbu'* (weekly echo) which started 1969. In Oman the first newspaper was *al-Watan* which appeared in 1971 as a weekly. Oman's first daily, *'Uman* appeared in 1972, making it the last Arab country to have its own daily newspaper. The *Times of Oman* started in 1975 and the *Oman Daily Observer* in 1981.[2]

Today Qatar has six daily newspapers (four in Arabic, two in English), and several weeklies.[3] The oldest is *al-Arab.* One private company publishes the dailies *al-Raya* and *Gulf Times* and has a ten-man board of directors which includes the oil minister, a former senior official in the Amir's office and several prominent businessmen. Another company jointly owned by the foreign minister and a leading businessman publishes the daily *al-Watan.* The foreign minister also owns another company which publishes the dailies *al-Sharq* and *The Peninsula.* The first newspaper to appear in Qatar was *al-Arab,* but it collapsed because of loss of subsidy. *Gulf Times* was the second paper to be established, and *al-Raya* was the second Arabic paper to appear, but it lost one-third of its circulation when *al-Watan* opened.[4]

In the Trucial States, which in 1971 became the UAE, a number of newspapers such as *al-Ittihad* started as weeklies because there were no local printing presses, and the papers had to be produced in Beirut and transported to the gulf.[5] The weeklies and monthlies *Akhbar Dubai, Ra's al-Khayma, al-Shuruq, Abu Dhabi News, al-Khalij,* and *al-Ittihad,* all appeared in the few years before independence, but only the last two survived. In all of these countries, however, the print media grew rapidly once it began (see Table 4.1).

TABLE 4.1 The Loyalist Press: Major Daily Newspapers[14]

	Circulation estimates, 2003	First published	Location
Saudi Arabia			
Al-Riyadh	170,000	1965	Riyadh
Okaz	147,000	1960	Jidda
Al-Jazira (The Peninsula)	80,000	1962	Riyadh
Al-Youm (Today)	80,000	1965	Dammam
Al-Watan (The Nation)	65,000	1999	Abha
Arab News*	50,000	1975	Jidda
Al-Madina	46,000	1937	Jidda
Al-Bilad (The Country)	35,000	1934	Jidda
Saudi Gazette*	30,000	1976	Jidda
An-Nadwa (The Forum)	30,000	1958	Mecca
Riyadh Daily*	30,000	1967	Riyadh
Bahrain			
Al-Wasat	9,000	2002	Manama
Gulf Daily News*	8,000	1978	Manama
Al-Ayam (The Days)	8,000	1989	Manama
Akhbar al-Khalij (Gulf News)	7,500	1976	Manama
Bahrain Tribune*	2,500	1997	Manama
Khalij News*	1,000	1978	Manama
Qatar			
Al-Watan (The Homeland)	18,000	1995	Doha
Al-Raya (The Banner)	8,000	1979	Doha
Al-Sharq (The Orient)	15,000	1985	Doha
Gulf Times*	15,000	1978	Doha
The Peninsula*	3,000	1980s	Doha
United Arab Emirates			
Al-Khalij (The Gulf)	60,000	1970	Sharjah
Al-Ittihad (Unity)	58,000	1979	Abu Dhabi
Akhbar al-Arab (Arab News)	35,000	2000	Abu Dhabi
Al-Bayan (The Dispatch)	35,000	1980	Dubai
Al-Fajr (The Dawn)	28,000	1975	Abu Dhabi
Al-Wahda (Unity)	20,000	1973	Abu Dhabi
Khalij Times*	45,000	1978	Dubai
Gulf News*	20,000	1978	Dubai
Gulf Today*		1999	Dubai
Oman			
Al-Watan (Homeland)	32,500	1971	Muscat
Oman	25,000	—	Muscat
Oman Daily Observer*	15,560	1981	Muscat
Times of Oman*	5,000	1975	Muscat

(Continued)

TABLE 4.1   Continued

	Circulation estimates, 2003	First published	Location
Palestine			
Al-Hayat al-Jadida (New Life)	—	1995	West Bank
Al-Quds (Jerusalem)	—	1968	Ramallah
Al-Ayam (The Days)	—	1995	West Bank
Al-Hurriya (Liberation)	—	—	West Bank
Al-Istiqlal (Independence)	—	1996	Gaza
Ar-Risala (The Message)	—	—	Gaza
Al-Watan (The Homeland)	—	—	Gaza
*The Jerusalem Times**		1994	Ramallah

*Published in English.

The Palestinian press, which is a special case because of the absence of an independent Palestinian state, has existed continuously only since the 1960s, and has operated under more normal conditions only since the 1990s. The Palestinian press developed under non-Palestinian rule, by Britain, Jordan, Israel, and others. Different Palestinian organizations created their own newspapers. Several papers were licensed by Israel. From 1948 to 1959 the Palestinian press focused on humanitarian and refugee issues, then it stressed national liberation. In 1959 the PFLP founded a monthly *al-Hurriya*. In 1969 a separate PFLP group founded a weekly *al-Hadaf*. In 1969 Fatah started a weekly *al-Fatah* in Beirut. In 1972 the PLO founded *Filastin al-Thawra*. In 1971 the PLO founded a monthly *Shu'un Filastinia*. *Al-Quds* (Jerusalem) was founded in November, 1968, and because it was relatively moderate, the Israelis did not interfere with it much until the *Intifada* (December 1987) when it was more restricted because it had the largest circulation in the West Bank. The daily *al-Fajr* (the Dawn) was founded in April, 1972 and it expressed a leftist view until 1976, when became more pro-Fatah. The owners founded a weekly in English also named *al-Fajr* in 1980, which was distributed in the West Bank and East Jerusalem. Both papers closed in July, 1993 for financial reasons. Hanna Siniora reopened the English edition in 1994 as the *Jerusalem Times,* and it has been left alone by the Palestinian authorities primarily because it is in English.[6]

The Palestinian daily *al-Sha'b* (The People) was founded in July, 1972. It was thought to have ties to Egypt, Syria, and the PLO. Israel deported two of its editors, Ali al-Khatib in 1974 and Akram Haniyeh in 1986. It closed in 1993. Before closure it sold between 1500 and 3000 copies. *Al-Talia* (the Vanguard) was founded in 1978 as a Communist weekly, which appeared in Jerusalem but was otherwise prevented from being distributed in the occupied territories. The daily *al-Nahar* was founded in 1986, a pro-Jordanian paper funded by Jordan and the PLO. Among the underground Palestinian newspapers the most famous was *al-Watan* (the Homeland), which was published by the Communist Party and was active in the early 1970s and continued at least until September 1988. Before the Gulf war there were five Palestinian magazines in the occupied territories, but after the war two were closed and the others adversely affected by lack of funding: *al-Baydar al-Siyasi* started as a monthly in 1976, became *al-Baydar al-Adabi* in 1981, but closed in 1993. *Al-Katib* founded in November 1979 as a monthly with the support of the Communist party, but Israel limited its distribution to Jerusalem until October 1992. *Al-Usbu' al-Jadid,* which was founded in 1978, received permits in the West Bank in 1991 and in Gaza in 1992, but it ceased publication in 1993 when the PLO stopped subsidizing it. The monthly *Huda al-Islam* was founded in 1982, and was funded by the Jordanian government; *al-Liqa',* a Christian quarterly, was founded in 1991.[7]

By 1987, Palestinians had licenses from Israel for publication of twenty-two newspapers, including four Arabic dailies, plus several magazines. Israel closed some of them and restricted others. Then in 1993 after the Gulf states withdrew their financial support of the PLO, the number of dailies declined to two.[8] By 2003, among the older dailies, only *al-Quds* survived, but there were seven other Palestinian daily papers, six in Arabic and one in English, and several weeklies.

PRIVATE OWNERSHIP

Generally speaking, the newspapers in these countries are in private ownership. They have not been taken over by political agents of the regime, as has the mobilization press, nor have they been nationalized directly by the state. Ownership by private individuals, families, and groups is one important structural characteristic of the press in these countries which helps to differentiate it from the press elsewhere in the Arab world. In Saudi Arabia, the print media are by law in private ownership. In the other five countries, private ownership has been the unwritten general rule.[9]

There are exceptions to the basic rule of private ownership in these countries, but the exceptions are few. In Oman, the government owns *Oman* and *Oman Daily Observer; al-Watan* and *Times of Oman* are privately owned.[10] Also, Oman has twenty-three magazines, seventeen owned by the government or government agencies and six private. In 1999 when the Omani Minister of Information was asked about government ownership of the media he said the media are too expensive and generate too little profit for private investors.

In Palestine, most of the newspapers are loyal to the Palestinian Authority; the four major newspapers are owned directly by Fatah or funded by the Authority. Opposition papers exist: *al-Hadaf* is supported by the PFLP, *al-Istiqlal* by the Islamic Jihad and *al-Watan* by Hamas. But the Authority sometimes uses extra legal measures to intimidate them. When the Authority was established, some papers such as *al-Nahar*, which was loyal to Jordan, ceased publication.

In the United Arab Emirates, the government has owned a few newspapers but most are private, and the trend is toward complete privatization. For a number of years, the government-owned UAE newspapers included *al-Bayan, al-Ittihad* and the (now defunct) *Emirates News*. The latter two were established by Abu Dhabi in 1969 and 1970 when it was still a Trucial State but approaching independence and seeking to advocate Abu Dhabi views. These two papers remained in government hands after independence and the formation of the UAE federation in 1971, although in 1976 the government transferred them to a new semi-autonomous publishing house in order to make the government role and responsibility for content less direct. The Dubai government has sponsored *al-Bayan* since 1980; it is the only government paper founded after independence. A number of newspapers in fact appeared in post-independence UAE which were entirely in private hands: Rashid Awaida's daily *al-Wahda* (1973), Muhammad Suwaydi's weeklies *al-Wathba* and *Gulf Times* (1974), Abdul Fattah Said's *Sawt al-Umma,* and Rashid Abdullah's *al-Fajr* (1975). The Taryam family established *al-Khaleej* in Sharjah in 1970 and it became very successful. Two other private UAE dailies, *Gulf News* and *Khalij Times* appeared, and they survived.

As of 2003, in the UAE, nine daily newspapers were being published, of which three were government-sponsored: *al-Ittihad* and *al-Wahda* in Abu Dhabi, and *al-Bayan* in Dubai. The other six were privately sponsored. The Taryam family in Sharjah owned the successful daily *al-Khaleej;* the Galadari family in Dubai owned the English daily *Khaleej News;* the al-Tayer family in Dubai owned the English daily *Gulf News,* and a member of the al-Nahyan ruling family in Abu Dhabi owned the relatively new Arabic daily *Akhbar al-Arab.* The Abu Dhabi government closed its English daily *Emirates News* reportedly for budgetary reasons in the late 1990s.

In 1989, the Abu Dhabi government created a new public corporation, Emirates News Inc., to make the government-owned media including the daily newspaper *al-Ittihad* and radio and television more autonomous. Officials insist that the media owned by this new entity are editorially independent, and that the Information Ministry no longer gives *al-Ittihad* instructions. Although the corporation receives funding from the government, the purpose is to make all of the media it owns financially independent.

The UAE government has in fact encouraged private newspapers. In November 1999, Information Minister Shaikh Abdullah bin Zayid said there was a need for independent and private media institutions.[11] In April

2001 he said that in the age of satellite television, "governments can no longer control the dissemination of information to their citizens. The public will no longer accept media that are seen as being government-controlled and which seek to provide them with a limited and partial view of events. . . . The choice for the Government media, therefore, is often that of either privatization or closure, and the future is clearly for the privately-owned media. . . . Here in the United Arab Emirates, the government has relinquished formal control over the country's largest media group, Emirates Media Inc., which now enjoys editorial and administrative independence. It remains to some extent dependent, however, on government funding, while ownership is still officially vested in the Government.[12] The UAE press is therefore mostly in private hands, and privatization may increase.

In three other countries—Saudi Arabia, Bahrain, and Qatar—the daily press is entirely owned by private persons. In Qatar, four of the ten nondailies had been government-owned, but in 1986 they were suspended for financial reasons. In the 1990s, the predominant characteristic of the Qatari press was private ownership, and commercial (depending on ads, sales, and subscriptions), but it received open government subsidies which some depended on. The government has never owned a political magazine except for the short-lived *al-Khalij al-Jadid* owned by the Information Ministry.[13] In Bahrain, the daily papers *al-Ayam*, *Akhbar al-Khalij* and the *Gulf Daily News* are owned by private individuals, as are the weekly papers *al-Adwaa* and *Sada al-Usbu'*. In December 2001, the Bahraini government licensed a private new pro-reform newspaper, *al-Wasat*, which began appearing in 2002. Two of the five Bahraini dailies, *al-Ayam* and *Bahrain Tribune*, are owned by the Information Ministry, and its chief editor is a former head of the government's news agency.

NEWSPAPER CONTENT

The content of the press in these countries, particularly as it relates to political matters, has some of the attributes found in the mobilization press described in the previous two chapters. Like the latter, the loyalist press in each country tends not to attack the basic tenets of national policy as enunciated by the regime, it eschews criticism of the personalities at the top of the national government, and it exhibits little real diversity of treatment or view on important issues. Editors in these countries admit that their newspapers, in commentaries and in news play, support the official line and the head of government on all essential matters. There are, however, significant differences between the loyalist press and the mobilization press.

The loyalist papers are much more likely to criticize government services that the general public finds deficient, and print stories which put specific government officials in a negative light. This does not happen every day, and the criticism is gentle by Western standards, not in any case casting

doubt on the top leadership. The Saudi press, for example, has criticized
the Pilgrimage Ministry on some details of its handling of the annual pilgrimage, and Saudi papers have criticized the government schools for girls
on their educational policies.

The tone and style of the loyalist press differentiate it from other Arab
newspaper systems. The loyalist press tends to be more passive. On the
whole, it avoids some critical issues, it is slower to react editorially to
events, and it tends to be more muted in its commentaries. It avoids the
language and opinions of aggressive revolutionary journalism which are
characteristic of the mobilization press, in which writers continuously do
battle with enemies and evils, real or imagined, and loudly exhort the public on to victory for the goals of the regime. The loyalist press does take
care to give adequate publicity to government activities and achievements,
and from time to time inveighs against evils, but it does so generally not in
such a strident, combative way; and its news treatment is more likely to be
straightforward or even dull. Thorough and independent investigative
reporting is rare.

The loyalist press in each country lacks essential diversity among newspapers largely as a consequence of the support it gives to the regime on all
fundamental issues. The content of the press on important political issues
is in each country quite similar, despite the fact that nearly all of the newspapers in these countries are privately owned by individuals and groups.

In Saudi Arabia, the press does not publish any criticism of Islam, the ruling family or the government. In the late 1990s, however, the government
began to allow some freedom to criticize governmental bodies and social
policies through editorials and cartoons.[15] Most of the Saudi press is fairly
uniform, but there are stylistic differences among the Saudi dailies.
Observers regard the older dailies, *al-Jazira, al-Nadwa,* and *al-Bilad* as
conservative, restrained, and fairly bland, *al-Riyadh* as semi-offocial, *al-
Madina* as conservative and more Islamist, *Ukaz* as more liberal and
provocative, while *al-Yawm* focuses on Eastern Province news. A relatively
new daily paper, *al-Watan,* which is sponsored by a senior member of the
royal family, Prince Khalid al-Faisal, tends to be more outspoken and
bolder than the others, more sensational and its success has encouraged
some other editors to be more outspoken.[16] Yet even *al-Watan* must respect
basic political realities; in May 2003, its chief editor was fired by order of
Information Minister Prince Naif, apparently because of his columns questioning some of the kingdom's social and political traditions.[17]

In Saudi Arabia the daily newspapers (eight in Arabic, three in English
as of 2003) differ in content from each other primarily in the amount of
space they give to secondary stories and nonpolitical items. For example, if
the king or crown prince makes a public statement or takes a public
action, such as making a trip or receiving an important visitor, that news
will be the top story on most front pages and the treatment will probably

be verbatim from the government-controlled Saudi News Agency. However, the Saudi dailies are slightly dissimilar in the amount of attention they give to particular subjects. Some papers typically carry more news about the Arab world and others carry more international news from outside the Middle East. Some focus on Islamic items, while others are strong on local stories or literary articles and features.

In the late 1990s, Saudi government relaxed restrictions on the press somewhat and it promulgated a new press law. Observers concluded that the royal family decided that a more liberal press was in their interest, in light of rapidly expanding global information from satellite television and the Internet. For example the press in early 2002 covered a fire at a girls' school by reporting negatively on the "mutaween" (religious police), who had always been treated very deferentially in the media. Taboos however remain: members of the royal family are never directly criticized, nor are the fundamental foreign policies of the leadership, such as the Saudi policy toward the Arab-Israeli conflict. Some but not all economic policies have been criticized in the press.

The dailies al-Riyadh and Ukaz are conservative and tend to give greater support to government policies than other papers, while al-Watan, sponsored by Prince Khalid al-Faisal, tends to be critical of the government, for example questioning military spending levels and other sensitive issues. Al-Yawm and al-Jazira are more centrist. The Saudi press occasionally criticizes the police, corruption of government officials, and other such shortcomings, so there is more transparency in government than there used to be in the past. Also, editorials sometimes express criticism of Saudi foreign policy in an indirect way. The most important taboos remaining are related to the royal family and religion, including for example the Imam Muhammad University. The amount of freedom editors have, however, to some extent depends on their perception of their role and how much they want to criticize.

In Oman, the media never criticize the sultan or his policies. Editorials are supportive of government views, but some criticism on foreign affairs does appear occasionally. There is little in-depth reporting on domestic issues. Since 1997, however, foreign publications containing criticism of Oman, even articles criticising the sultan, have begun to enter Oman. Editorials are supportive of government views, but authorities tolerate some criticism on foreign affairs. The government discourages in-depth reporting on domestic issues. In December 1994 the government lifted the Israel boycott, and this led to ending the ban on publications from or about Israel. However, there are limits, for example in August 1999 the government stopped a London-based publication with an interview with the Israeli trade representative.

In the UAE, although the daily newspapers are published in different emirates (see Table 4.1) and reflect local interests to some extent, they all support the most basic policies of the UAE Government and there are no fundamental political differences among them. There is no criticism in the

UAE print media of the ruling families, and any criticism of government officials is limited, for example when the press reports Federal National Council debates. Domestic and foreign publications do not carry any material considered pornographic, violent, derogatory to Islam, supportive of certain Israeli positions, unduly critical of friendly countries, or critical of the government or the ruling families.

The UAE newspapers do show independence of the government in criticizing the work of various ministries, such as health, labor, and education, and they occasionally treat issues such as democracy in a gingerly and muted way, but they never attack the fundamental national policies of the rulers. Many social problems that in the past had been considered taboo are now being discussed and debated in the press. The UAE dailies have different styles. *Al-Ittihad,* although nominally independent of the Abu Dhabi Government, tends to support government policies, as does the new private daily, *Akhbar al-Arab,* which is owned by a member of the Abu Dhabi ruling family. The private Sharjah daily *al-Khalij,* owned by the Taryam family, tended for years to support Arab nationalist causes somewhat more aggressively than other papers although that difference later diminished. The Dubai government's daily *al-Bayan* focuses mostly on Dubai news and business reports. The dailies *al-Wahda* and *al-Fajr,* privately owned by Abu Dhabi businessmen, have smaller circulations and focus on Abu Dhabi local and business interests.

After the 1991 Gulf War there was a modest trend in the UAE toward more open expression of opinion on subjects sensitive to the government, that began during the Gulf war, including articles written by non-UAE Arabs calling for greater democracy in the region. In the 1990s, after Shaikh Abdullah bin Zayid became Information Minister, another increase in free expression took place. Progressive in outlook, he has sent signals to all UAE media that he supports more freedom of expression.

In Palestine the press is lively and outspoken on many issues, but the Palestinian Authority generally does not permit criticism or Chairman Arafat or his policies or style of government. In 2000, for example, *al-Quds, al-Ayam,* and *al-Hayat al-Jadida* tended to support the Palestinian Authority, while *al-Watan* supported Hamas, and *al-Hurriya, al-Istiqlal,* and *al-Risala* were organs, respectively, of the DFLP, Islamic Jihad, and the Islamic Construction and Democracy Party. The PLO subsidizes *al-Hayat al-Jadida.* There is some criticism of official corruption but it is usually quite indirect. Observers regard *al-Ayam* and *al-Quds* as the most responsible newspapers.[18] The Palestinian newspapers which publish in English, however, generally escape official restrictions because they are considered less threatening to the authorities, and are left alone to be critical if they wish.[19]

In Bahrain, the six daily papers differ somewhat in their focus because of their readership. Five of the papers support fundamental government policies and are restrained in their criticism of it. Observers say that the taboos that the Bahraini press respects are the ruler (the Amir), Islam, inciting civil unrest or sectarianism, insulting the head of state of a friendly country, or differing with official policy on the Hiwar island issue. *Al-Ayam,* which is 40 % government owned and has the Information Minister on its board, is the most supportive of the official line. At the other end of the spectrum is *al-Wasat,* a daily which was started in 2002 by a well-known opposition journalist, Mansour al-Jamri, who had spent time in jail. And the paper *Akhbar al-Khalij* is somewhat independent, and historically it has been a rival to *al-Ayam,* which reportedly was created as its counterweight.[20] It criticizes government ministries and services, and it doesn't do celebratory stories like *al-Ayam.* Service ministries can be criticized including attacking ministers by name, but generally not the foreign ministry, defense or interior ministries. However since 1999 now Ali Salih, a Shia columnist, criticizes even the Interior Minister every month on his immigration policy, denouncing his allowing immigration of non-Bahrainis.

In the late 1990s there was some improvement in Bahrain's freedom of speech. After the new amir assumed power on March 6, 1999 the government allowed the press somewhat greater latitude. In his National Day speech in December 1999, the new amir said the press and public have a duty to question the government about developments in the country. Some sensitive issues such as services by the ministries of interior or defense, and discussing the state budget, which were taboo in the past, are being addressed in the local press. In July and August 2000 the press published criticisms of the Interior Ministry's policy toward the bidoon (mostly Persian-origin Shia without citizenship). In August 2000 columnists criticized the Ministry of Finance for not informing the public of the negative impact of oil price increases. Relatively unrestricted subjects in the press in 1999 were international issues and local economic and commercial issues. But the Information Ministry exercises extensive control over the media. Newspapers are privately owned but they use self-censorship. This ministry occasionally revokes credentials of foreign journalists for criticizing Bahrain. When Shaikh Isa was ruler of Bahrain, journalists were arrested and tortured, and newspapers were banned. The government is more liberal now. Bahraini editors believe the new king is responsible for protecting the independent press which others in the government would like to restrict.[21]

In Qatar, the main restrictions that remained after Shaikh Hamad became ruler in 1995, were not offending religious sensibilities, not revealing military information, and not damaging Qatar's relations with friendly states. Newspapers in the late 1990s published critical material, for example about provision of services and treatment of workers which in 1994 would not have been published. The press now criticizes the government for inefficiency, for example for failure to implement copyright laws.

In Qatar there are no serious political differences in content between the publications *al-Raya* and *Gulf Times*. *Al-Raya* is considered the paper most closely reflecting government views, although all of them do that. There are however some stylistic differences among Qatari dailies. *Al-Raya* is rather bland; it tends to simply print press releases and otherwise make minimal effort to gather news, often gives a full page to a minor news story. *Al-Sharq* cares about local issues, and investigates education and health problems. *The Gulf Times* readership is non-Arab: Indians, Pakistanis, Brits, Americans, with deliberate editorial focus on each community.

One observer, says, ". . . freedom of speech and a free press are severely restricted in Qatar. Public criticism of the ruling family or of Islam is forbidden. Even after censorship was lifted [in 1995, see below], newspapers have been shut down . . . [and] some Qatari journalists reportedly were pressured for criticizing officials." Pornography and negative discussion of Islam are prohibited, although newspapers occasionally publish criticism of inadequate government services or maltreatment of workers. Privately, Qataris criticize the lack of democracy but such comments are not published.[22] Another observer says the Qatari papers tend to report only good news, for example the opening of a new factory, ignoring it when a factory burns down.[23]

Press taboos in Qatar today are: anything negative about the ruler (and his family), Islam, or national security. But the press today can criticize any ministry, government services, other countries including Arab countries. After the Information Ministry was abolished in 1995, lawsuits against the newspapers began, because journalists were no longer protected by the Information Ministry, that was the price of freedom. They had depended on the state censors who every night reviewed their copy and approved it.[24]

All English language papers in the Gulf tend to focus much more on news of interest to South Asians and to some extent British and Americans, because they make up the bulk of the readership. For example, in the UAE, the English language papers have heavy coverage of non-UAE news, especially of Asia. A typical issue of Gulf News has thirty-eight pages of which only six carry news of the UAE, while twelve are on other areas: five are on the Indian subcontinent and the Philippines, four on Europe, two in the Middle East and Africa, and one on the United States.

FACTORS RESPONSIBLE FOR PRESS LOYALISM

If the press is basically in private hands in these countries, why are the newspapers so uniform in content and so supportive of the government? How does the government influence the press so much without controlling newspapers through partisan agents or direct ownership? Essentially the government has and uses influence derived from legal authority and its

financial benefits, and this influence is effective because the press is susceptible to it and because of the political environment.

Government Influence Derived from Legal Authority

The governments in these countries have certain rights and powers that
they can use to influence the press even though it is in private hands.

In Saudi Arabia, the 1963 press and publications law moved the press in
a more liberal direction, eliminating prior censorship but maintaining controls as well. The 1963 law was amended by a more liberal press law in
2002 but many of the original restrictive provisions remained, such as
requiring that all newspapers to be licensed. The law declares that the
press is private and the state has no right to interfere with it except for the
sake of the "general welfare." In these cases, which the law says will occur
"rarely" (nadiran), the government has the right to stop a paper from publishing. The law also gives the government influence over personnel selection in the press. The Information Ministry can veto any candidate for the
fifteen-member board of directors each paper must have, and it is the ministry which selects the board chairman and the paper's editor-in-chief from
among a slate of candidates, nominated by the board. All newspapers must
be published by licensed establishments, which are nominally independent
but their heads are appointed by the government.[25] Moreover, a 1982
media policy statement and a 1965 national security law still in effect prohibit dissemination of criticism of the government. The 1982 statement
urges journalists to uphold Islam, oppose atheism, promote Arab interests
and preserve Saudi Arabia's cultural heritage. The Information Ministry
appoints and can remove all chief editors, and it provides guidelines on
controversial issues.

Newspapers publish on sensitive subjects such as crime or terrorism only
after news has been released by the government through the official Saudi
news agency SPA, or from a government official. Saudi censors screen
incoming foreign publications, removing or blackening offending articles
or gluing pages together, to excise sexual or pornographic material. The
Ministry compiles a list of publications not permitted entry. The government tightly restricts entry of foreign journalists into the kingdom. As of
2003, a 1982 Saudi media policy statement and a 1965 national security
law still in effect prohibit dissemination of criticism of the government.

The Saudi press law says the press is private and the government has no
right to interfere except to preserve the "general welfare," which is not
defined, but in 1991 the Information Ministry said it is anything that might
cause friction between the government and citizens, or adversely affect
"each citizen's duty towards his religion, country and community." It says

journalists may not criticize the government or any government body, the royal family, heads of friendly states, or the clergy or offend Islam or Islamic law, or support atheism. All newspapers must be published by licensed establishments, which are nominally independent but their heads are appointed by the government.[26] In March, 2002, for example, the Saudi government ordered the dismissal of *al-Madina's* editor in chief after the paper published a criticism of Islamic judges as being corrupt.[27]

These legal powers to close the newspapers if necessary and to veto or select top personnel are not used very often, but the fact that they are available helps give the government some day-to-day influence over the content of the newspaper. A phone call from the Ministry of Information is usually enough to persuade an editor to emphasize one story or downplay another.

In Oman, the law prohibits criticism of the sultan in any form or medium. The authorities tolerate criticism of government officials but it rarely gets media coverage. The 1984 Press and Publication Law, which is still valid, authorizes the government to censor all domestic and foreign publications. Censors may stop anything politically, culturally, or sexually offensive. But journalists practice self-censorship to avoid government action.

In Qatar, Shaikh Hamad bin Khalifa al-Thani took power from his father on June 27, 1995, and within a few weeks, he withdrew the censors from the newspapers. He announced that he had established "freedom of the press" and to an extent the press became freer. Prior to that, the Qatari press never published any bad news, for example no reports of fires, explosions, or even car crashes. Journalists noticed the change right away when they were allowed to report their first car crash, and then other "bad news" like fires.[28]

Because of Shaikh Hamad, therefore, press freedom has improved substantially. The main restrictions remaining as of 2003 were not offending religious sensibilities, not revealing military information, and not damaging Qatar's relations with friendly states. The Qatari press since 1995 has been free of direct controls but journalists practice self-censorship. In October 1996 the government further reduced restrictions on the press but some restrictions remain and are effective. In 1996 the government abolished the Information Ministry including its censorship office. Customs officials however still screen incoming foreign media, for example blocking pornography and non-Muslim religious items.

Although the Qatari Ministry of Information was abolished, it was replaced with a government-owned corporation which continues to exercise control over the press. The Qatari Press and Publication Law of 1979, still in effect, stipulates that the media should not in any way criticize the amir, not publish anything that could undermine the established order or endanger the political system, and the authorities have the right to impose censorship to ensure media adherence to those rules.[29] As for domestic publications, editors after 1996 have observed self-censorship in not publishing criticism of the ruling family. After the Qatari Information Ministry was abolished, lawsuits against the newspapers began, because they were no longer guided by the censors.

In Bahrain, all media are subject to the Press Law of 1979. The Information Ministry licenses all presses, approves any change in senior editorial staff, and licenses all professional journalists. Violations led to a ban on distribution. The law lists offenses punishable as crimes against the state: critical treatment of Islam, criticism or blame of the amir, agitation to incite civil unrest, provocation of sectarian strife, offense to public morals or privacy or honor of individuals, shaming head of state of a friendly country, and publicizing closed legal proceedings.[30]

In the past, official Bahrainin government censors reviewed domestic and foreign media, but since the 1991 Gulf War there have been no media censors in place and no direct interference in journalism, but self-censorship is prevalent, "not offending sensitivities," and journalists are aware of a line they should not cross. Daily opinion columns are a forum for some exchange of ideas. Print media are the main source of local news. The Bahraini constitution provides for the right to "express and propagate opinions," but citizens cannot. Press criticism of the ruling family, government policy on some sensitive subjects, for example sectarian unrest, dispute with Qatar over Hiwar are prohibited. Press can report on and comment on international issues and local economic and commercial issues. The Information Ministry has extensive control over the press. Newspapers are privately owned but exercise self-censorship on sensitive topics. The Ministry also sometimes deports foreign journalists who write stories the government doesn't like. Daily opinion columns are a forum for the exchange of ideas. Print media are the main source of local news.

In January 2002 the Bahraini government allowed the opening of the first independent newspaper, the Arabic daily *al-Wasat*, published by Shi'a opposition leader Mansoor al-Jamri. He believes his freedom is protected by the ruler himself.[31]

In the UAE, the Publication Law of 1980 said the press cannot criticize the ruling family, or the UAE's allies or friendly countries, or carry the names of crime victims, propagate religion, carry dishonest commercials, one-sided reporting of controversies, promote liquor, sex, or pornography. All published material is also subject to censorship under Federal Law 15 of 1988, which contains a list of prohibited subjects, and journalists practice self-censorship when reporting on government policy, the ruling families, national security, religion, and relations with neighboring states. Censors at the Information Ministry review imported media, and ban any material considered pornographic, violent, derogatory to Islam, supportive of certain Israeli positions, unduly critical of friendly countries, or critical of the government or the ruling families. There is an unwritten but generally recognized ban on criticism of the government.[32]

Starting in the late 1990s, the UAE government indicated more leniency in use of controls, and the UAE press has become more liberal. In practice it does not always respect the strict rules of the 1980 press law. The UAE Information Minister has called for revisions in the 1980 press law, and in the law making it a crime for journalists to raise controversial issues or criticize the performance of public institutions. The Minister has said, "Any attempt to place constraints on the free flow of news is futile." He explained, "There is no point in trying to ignore the changes that have taken place in the international media over the last few decades. The Information Revolution is with us. It is a fact." He said, "We believe our press is not only a source of information, but should also act as the conscience of society, as whistle-blowers, who can help to identify failure, and to celebrate success, within the overall framework, of course, of the unique value system that prevails in each society."[33]

With the encouragement of the Information Ministry in late 1999, *al-Ittihad* printed several articles that were critical of alleged inefficiencies in the delivery of services by the Ministries of Health and Education.[34]

As for Palestinian print media, the legal regulations governing them are somewhat unique. Palestine was ruled by the Ottomans 1517–1917, and the British 1917–1948. After 1948, Palestinian territory was occupied by Israel and Jordan, and then in the June 1967 war Israel also occupied the West Bank, Gaza, and East Jerusalem. Pursuant to the May 1994 Gaza-Jericho agreement and the September 1995 Interim Agreement, Israel transferred most civil government responsibility in Gaza and parts of the West Bank to the Palestinian Authority, but retained responsibility for security and foreign relations. By 1996 the PA had full or partial control over most of the major Palestinian population centers and in 1998 Israel implemented further redeployments. In 1995, just before the January 1996 legislative elections, Chairman Arafat enacted a press law that journalists criticize for not protecting freedoms adequately. Palestinian Authority security forces periodically shut down presses, ban publications or harass or detain journalists. There is widespread self-censorship as a result. One independent source reports that the Palestinian Authority uses pressure, harassment, arrests, and suspensions of journalists to stifle press independence and it said the 1955 law was restrictive because it prohibited criticism of the police. Another says that since Palestinian self-rule began in 1994, there was a "disturbing pattern of harassment by the Palestinian Authority of journalists . . . a number of whom have been detained solely for exercising their internationally guaranteed right to free expression."[35]

The Palestinian Press Law passed in 1995 replaced the press law of 1933 for Gaza and the one of 1967 for the West Bank, and relevant Israeli military orders. The law guarantees freedom of expression, but qualifies that with reference to "public rights and duties" which observers say is an improvement over previous laws but is too vague to provide sufficient protections.

Palestinian newspapers had already focused more attention on human rights abuses under Palestinian rule, and other sensitive issues. Some discussed democracy in general, and even related it to the Palestinian Authority.[36]

In 1996 the Palestinian Authority closed the Gaza newspaper *al-Istiqlal*, because of its association with an Islamist extremist group, but in July 1998 allowed it to reopen. In February and March 1998 the PA closed *al-Watan* and *al-Istiqlal*, the organs of Hamas and the Islamic Jihad, and by end of 1998 had not allowed them to reopen. In September 1998 the PA shut down the weekly independent Jenin because its editor criticized the Jenin municipality. On May 20, 1997, the PA arrested Daoud Kuttab, a Palestinian journalist, director of al-Quds University Modern Media Institute, and a critic of Chairman Arafat. He was not charged, but went on a hunger strike and was freed on May 28 after eight days. He has a private television station at al-Quds University on which he had been carrying live broadcasts of the Palestinian Legislative Council while it was debating charges of PA corruption.[37] In September 1997, the PA closed the Gaza weekly newspaper *al-Risala*, affiliated with the Islamic movement Hamas, after Hamas claimed responsibility for a suicide bombing in Jerusalem in which five Israelis and three bombers were killed.

In Saudi Arabia, the editors in chief of the newspapers are theoretically responsible only to the owners, but in practice the government selects them. The newspaper board submits the names of three candidates to the Information Minister who picks one of them, or he can reject all three and name another person.[38]

In times of national emergencies these governments can and do exercise even greater influence over press content, in the same manner, by asserting to editors that the national interest requires loyal support of the regime and its policies during the crisis. The continuation for over a quarter century of the Arab-Israeli conflict with its intermittent flare-ups of violence and periods of tension, makes this situation not uncommon.

Government Influence Derived from Financial Benefits

The government has another asset that also helps give it practical influence over press content. In all of these countries the government is a major source of revenue to the newspapers, in the form of official government advertisements, subscriptions for government employees, and in some cases direct subsidies. Because the government plays such an important role in the economy in all of these countries, the commercial tenders, personnel notices, and other ads issued regularly by the ministries are voluminous, and typically they are the largest source of a daily newspaper's income. Newspapers in all six of these countries have received government subsidies of one kind or another. Newspapers which encounter financial difficulties are frequently assisted at year's end with subvention payments.

Neither the government ads nor the subsidies are explicitly tied to progovernment newspaper content, and there is usually no discernible discrimination in government distribution of funds. However, editors and publishers are just as aware of the government's carrot as they are of the stick, and the general effect of these financial arrangements is to increase their tendency to make their newspapers loyal to the regime.

In 1993 the predominant characteristic of the Qatari press was private ownership; it received open government subsidies which many depended on, but these stopped in 1996. In Bahrain, all newspapers receive government subsidies, but *al-Ayam* tends to receive more because it is so supportive of the regime.[39]

The Omani government owns two of the four daily newspapers and gives subsidies to the remaining dailies and several private periodicals, subsidizing the private press to influence it.

In Saudi Arabia, most newspapers were originally a family enterprise, published not so much out of financial considerations but as a symbol of family pride. Today the press is largely a business, more market-driven. For example the Hafiz family founded *al-Madina* newspaper in 1932, and although sons and grandsons of the founder are today on the board of the publishing house, it is managed more on a financial basis, and includes investors from the Saudi business community. The government does occasionally provide financial support to various publishing houses through subsidies or encouraging investors to support it.[40]

As for the Palestinian press, it is somewhat different in this respect also because a fair amount of its financing comes from outside. For example, before 1991, the West Bank had four Arabic dailies and two weeklies, one in English, but after the Gulf War, the Gulf states withdrew their financial support of the PLO, and the number of dailies declined to two.[41]

Susceptibility of the Press to Influence

Government influence over the private press in these countries would not be as great as it is, however, if the newspapers themselves did not have some particular characteristics that make them vulnerable. For a variety of reasons, these newspapers have not developed a strong tradition of independent journalism, or an independent financial base, to help them withstand government pressure to conform and be loyal to the regime. Publishers, editors, and other newspaper staff members carry out their tasks not from a position of Fourth Estate strength based on an ethic of independence and a self-sufficient budget, but from a position of relative institutional weakness.

Saudi Arabia has had indigenous journalism almost since the beginning of the twentieth century, but its experience with modern-style newspapers and political reporting and commentary is not very extensive. In December 1925 the al-Sa'ud family unified the country by adding the Western Province

(Hijaz) to the Central and Eastern Provinces which it already controlled. Prior to that, the Hijaz had enjoyed a fairly active press for seventeen years, but virtually all of the newspapers were run by resident foreigners. Then, during the first fifteen years of Saudi rule, the Hijaz press flourished under the leadership of Hijazi intellectuals, but the content of the press was almost entirely literary rather than news or politics. Even the official Saudi government journal *Umm al-Qura* (which today is merely an official gazette of laws and decrees) in the beginning contained primarily literary articles, as did the private *Sawt al-Hijaz* and *al-Madina al-Manawara* which were established in the 1930s. They all had financial difficulties, and all except *Umm al-Qura* were suspended 1941–1946 because of World War II. It was not until the late 1940s that real newspapers began to emerge. Until that time, Saudi Arabia had lacked the economic base, literacy, secular education, commerce with other countries, and interest in the outside world on a scale necessary to bring forth modern newspapers.

Even then, these conditions appeared only in the Western Province, not in the rest of the kingdom. Both *Sawt al-Hijaz,* which began publishing again under the name *al-Bilad al-Sa'udiya* in 1946 and *al-Madina* which resumed in 1947, became news-oriented dailies and were published in Jidda, but there were no such papers elsewhere in the country for some time. It was the growth of the economy, improvement in printing and distribution facilities, and the growth of government ministries with their advertising needs during the 1950s and 1960s which led to the proliferation of daily newspapers at that time.

The individuals or families who founded these papers did so not to become rich, since the economic conditions were not right for that, but generally to participate in public life through this new medium. Editorials became bolder as owner-editors increasingly criticized the government for various shortcomings. When in 1963 the Saudi government issued a new press law, which required that the newspapers be owned by groups of Saudis, individual and family pride in the development of an independent Fourth Estate was considerably diluted. The new groups that formed included mostly businessmen and others who knew little about journalism. Many regarded the paper as a business undertaking, but they soon realized that economic conditions were not right for making a profit. The owners did not invest very much in staff and did not vigorously encourage quality reporting. Employees had to moonlight to make a living and many editors became discouraged with the profession. In this situation, it was often easier to do the minimum effort necessary to put out a paper that relied heavily on wire service copy and government releases, rather than to take chances in dealing with controversial subjects. Aggressive investigative reporting never developed, and editorial criticism became muted. Even Saudi Arabia's increased prosperity, which brought more money to the press in the late 1970s, has not changed this situation very much.

In Bahrain, Qatar, and the United Arab Emirates, too, the press has so far failed to develop into an independent force for some of the same reasons. These are even younger states with even shorter press traditions than Saudi Arabia. They achieved full independence in 1971, and have had little time to develop indigenous journalistic talent. By 1975, five different newspapers (including two dailies) were being published in the UAE by five different UAE citizens, but at four of the five papers the top two editorial positions had to be filled by expatriates, mostly from the Arab world. Similarly, the Bahraini and Qatari press depend heavily on expatriate journalists, especially Arabs. For example in Bahrain, 'Abdulla Mardi, publisher of the weekly paper *Sada al-Usbu'*, attempted in 1971 to bring out a daily, but it failed after a few months because it had a weak staff; then in 1976 when he made his second attempt with the daily *Akhbar al-Khalij*, he took the precaution of bringing in an almost complete staff of trained newspaper people from Egypt, and the venture was an immediate success.

Upheavals in the Jordanian press (see Chapter 6) have been to discourage talented Jordanians from entering the profession, and to help persuade a number of experienced journalists to leave the country, primarily to seek employment in the nascent media of the Arabian Peninsula. They were hired especially by government-owned radio and television there. This movement of skilled personnel from Jordan to the oil-rich Arab states was to an extent because of the weakness of the financial base in Jordan. Saudi Arabia and the UAE could pay good salaries to attract from Jordan the media talent that they lack, but this movement of personnel somewhat adversely affected all the countries involved. The ability of the UAE and Saudi Arabia to afford to import foreign skilled labor, retarded the training of indigenous journalists because the need for them was less urgent. On the other side Jordan, which had developed a small group of qualified journalists, lost some of them to these other states partly because it could not pay them enough, and the general skill level declined. The growing demand for competent journalists in the Arab electronic media has put additional pressure on the small pool of available talent, causing movements and dislocations in several countries.

Political Environment

The most important factor of all behind the status of the press in these countries, however, is that the political environment in which the press must function has been conducive to nondiverse, relatively passive, and politically conformist newspapers.

The nature of the press reflects the facts of political life in these countries. The press has developed along similar lines in these countries because key factors in the political environment are similar enough to have helped create the necessary conditions for it. Differences of course exist among these political systems, but the following characteristics are found in common.

Saudi Arabia, Qatar, Oman, and the UAE have no independent parliament, and no institutionalized political opposition. No fundamental public dissent is expressed publicly in any way. Some of these countries have created "consultative councils" but they are appointed bodies which occasionally express some criticism of the government that is covered in the press, but it is generally very mild. The Palestinian Authority has an elected parliament, since 1996, and Bahrain has had one since November 2002, but even they ordinarily do not express fundamental disagreements with government policy.

Bahrain for example is a hereditary emirate, no political parties or organizations are permitted. The al-Khalifa family has ruled since the late eighteenth century. On March 6, 1999 Isa died after thirty-eight years as emir, and eldest son Hamad bin Isa became ruler, and he subsequently called for elections, but the basic system did not change. Bahrain's elected parliament had been suspended in 1975, but in February 2002, Shaikh Hamad issued a decree amending the constitution making himself king and calling for a bicameral parliament of which one house would be elected, the first elections in nearly thirty years. However political parties are still prohibited. Local elections were held in May and legislature elections in October 2002.

The absence of an elected legislature has helped create an atmosphere in which the people believe they are not free to say what they think in public, so the newspaper editors are generally not anxious to use their papers to violate or even test that prevailing norm.

The governments in these countries are essentially authoritarian, backed by elites who support some reforms but generally favor perpetuation of the political, economic, and social status quo. They are not revolutionary regimes which seek sweeping changes, and they require from the public passive acceptance of their rule more than anything else. They do promote such changes as the expansion of education, improvement of health and welfare services and public works, as well as continued economic prosperity. They expect any public comment on these efforts, including all treatment in the press, to be favorable, and government ministers tend to be sensitive to criticism of their respective spheres of endeavor. But the primary requirement from the public and the press is absence of criticism and at least passive acceptance of whatever the regime does. The ruling elites are not controlled by public opinion, though they consult it privately. Neither the establishment nor the general public insists on the right to free public debate of politically important issues, so there is no such debate in the press.

This environment of public consensus puts considerable pressure on newspaper editors and writers to conform, that is, to support the political status quo and the regime. The government does not need to use censorship with any frequency because the press is sensitive to the political environment and regulates itself to conform with the general consensus and climate of opinion.

In fact, some observers believe that the habits of journalistic conformity to the public consensus are so strong that self-regulation is even stricter than it needs to be, that newspaper editors in these countries conform more than they need to. It is generally acknowledged by journalists in these countries that they exercise self-censorship because of the political environment. It is difficult to know, however, whether or not editors in these countries could be bolder and more critical of the status quo than they are. In any case it is clear that the public consensus acts as a strong restraint on the freedom of the press in these countries. And lest any journalist forget that, the government does usually make certain to remind the press periodically of its responsibilities in furthering the "national interest" at a time when economic development and other major problems must be faced. As the Saudi Minister of Information put it during a visit to the offices of one of his country's leading private daily newspapers, the "common goal" of the government and the press is development of the kingdom, and Saudi journalists are "called upon" to put forward opinions beneficial to this goal.[42] The importance of the public consensus factor becomes particularly clear when one examines earlier periods in these countries when the public consensus and government control were relatively weaker, and the press was more diverse and independent.

In Saudi Arabia, for example, the press was more outspoken and contentious in earlier periods when the political situation was less stable and the government weaker. Between 1909 and 1925, the press was developing in the Western Province (Hijaz) at a time when that area was under the rather loose control of the Hashemite government of Husayn in Mecca acting for a remote Ottoman sultan, and Abd al-Aziz al-Sa'ud was expanding his control over territory to the east. One leading newspaper in Mecca openly criticized Husayn's rule, while another in Jidda defended it. During the next fifteen years, most Hijazi newspapers had partisan political tendencies including Arab nationalist, Hijazi nationalist, and then pro-Saudi after the 1924 capture of Mecca by Abd al-Aziz al-Sa'ud. But this political ferment in the press ended after the al-Sa'ud family captured the Western Province in 1925. The Hijaz became politically stable as it was joined to the al-Sa'ud domain covering most of the Arabian Peninsula. The newspapers that prospered turned away from politics and became preoccupied with literary concerns.

The Saudi press underwent another period of limited political diversity during the late 1950s as the country experienced its first major surge of modernization resulting from oil revenues. The economy and the government administration grew rapidly, and the burgeoning press, especially in the kingdom's commercial center of Jidda, attracted a number of highly respected writers, some of whom began to criticize various aspects of public life. In 1957 the government began to act against newspapers which printed editorials it found objectionable; it closed the newspaper *al-Adwaa'* for openly attacking Aramco and the royal family, and *al-Riyadh* for advocating more rapid development of democratic institutions, for example. In 1958, as rumors of rivalry between King Sa'ud and Crown Prince Faisal began to circulate privately, some of this was reflected in newspaper columns which made subtle comparisons between the two princes. The government decreed a merger of four papers into two, and in 1960 banned four prominent writers from writing in the press—moves which clearly signaled official determination not to let criticism go too far, and which helped mute the outspokenness. Then Faisal's accession to the throne in 1964 brought a considerable measure of stability and consensus to Saudi politics that was reflected in a more quiescent press.

By 2003, the Saudi press had become more willing to criticize the government, but still only within limits. The editorials and news play sometimes cast the health and education ministries in a bad light but they do not criticize Saudi foreign policy or the top leadership.[43]

Similarly, in Bahrain, the press became bolder, more outspoken, and independent of the government in periods of domestic ferment and relative weakening of governmental authority.

In Bahrain, the short-lived experiment with an elected parliament, 1973–1975, also saw a brief upsurge in press outspokenness, reflecting the political debate and ferment that parliamentary activity unleashed. The December 1973 election results revealed more radical and leftist strength than most conservatives had anticipated, and the liveliness of the debates in the assembly surprised and irritated the government. When the government suspended the assembly indefinitely in August 1975, and parliamentary discussion of controversial issues such as security legislation ceased, the press also became more bland in content.

Oman is a monarchy ruled by the al-Bu Said family since the eighteenth century. Qabus bin Said has been sultan since 1970. There are no political parties or elected representative institutions. Oman has no freely elected legislature but does have consultative councils appointed by the government, one created in 1991 and a second added in 1997. In 1996 the sultan promulgated a basic law, the first written constitution, which provides for freedom of speech for the first time in law, but as of 1999 this was not implemented.

In the UAE, the political leadership started making some steps toward liberalization in 1998, led by Information Minister Shaikh Abdullah bin Zayid. In November 1999 he said there was a need for independent and private media institutions since "the public will no longer accept media that are controlled by the government, that seek to provide them with a limited and partial view of events." He said the UAE had "a policy of promoting greater self-confidence in our media and of encouraging its freedom. We want our media to develop the confidence to discuss and to criticize, where criticism is needed. In government, we need to know what concerns our people, what suggestions they have for the improvement of the way in which government serves them."[44]

GUIDANCE MECHANISMS

In the loyalist press system, the regime does not have at its disposal the mechanisms for guiding and influencing that exist in the mobilization system and which derive from ownership of the press by a political agent of the regime. Since the loyalist press is in private hands, the regime must use indirect methods to influence newspaper personnel. These methods have already been alluded to in this chapter, but we shall summarize them here.

The most common mechanism ensuring newspaper loyalty to the basic policies of the regime and to its top leadership is anticipatory self-censorship based on sensitivity to the political environment. The editors and other journalists usually know, without any specific guidance, what the regime expects them to say in their newspapers and they usually comply for the reasons outlined in this chapter. Second, the regime makes known, through public acts such as statements of policy or appointments of personnel, what is important to it and what the official line is. These acts, publicized first through official press releases and by the government-owned radio and television, are recognized as important by journalists in the private press who treat them accordingly. Occasionally the government will specifically praise a newspaper for "balance" and "objectivity," a pat on the back designed to signal approval of the editorial line. Third, in all of these countries the government operates a national news agency which indirectly gives the private press guidance signals each day by the way it treats and comments on the news.[45] Fourth, government officials in these countries from time to time contact newspaper personnel informally and privately to make clear on specific issues such as what government policy is, what the regime would like to have emphasized, and what is sensitive, but usually the guidance is general and the government usually does not clear texts.[46]

And finally, the government has some powers under the law that it uses on those relatively rare occasions when it believes direct action must be taken against a disloyal newspaper.

For example, in Saudi Arabia, there is a Higher Council for Press, which includes key members of the royal family and is chaired by the Interior Minister. It ultimately decides basic policy for the media, even giving instructions to the Information Minister who is nominally responsible in that area, and the Minister in turn keeps the press informed on government policy with respect to sensitive issues.[47]

In summary, the press in Saudi Arabia, Bahrain, Qatar, the UAE, Oman, and Palestine is basically loyal to the regime and nondiverse, despite the fact that it is essentially not government owned. Although the regime does not control the newspapers directly through a political agent as in the mobilization system, it does evoke loyalty to its policies and top personnel because of the legal, financial, and especially the political conditions under which the press functions. The newspapers do not aggressively promote revolutionary change as they do in the mobilization system; instead they loyally support the nonrevolutionary regimes which hold power in these countries. The means of government influence over the press and the reasons for their effectiveness, as well as the style of the press itself, is unique to the loyalist system.

NOTES

1. Although Palestine is not at the time of this writing an independent sovereign state, we are using this term for convenience to refer to the West Bank and Gaza, parts of which during the 1990s achieved varying degrees of autonomy under the Palestinian Authority.

2. Afaf Hamod and Elise K. Parsigian, "Bahrain" chapter, and Hana S. Noor Al-Deen, "Oman" chapter, in Yahya R. Kamalipour and Hamid Mowlana, Eds., *Mass media in the Middle East: A Comprehensive Handbook,* Westport, CT: Greenwood Press, 1994, pp. 28–29, 187–88.

3. Mohamed M. Arafa, "Qatar," chapter 16 in Kamalipour and Mowlana, pp. 233–35.

4. Interview with informed observer in Doha, June 2001.

5. Khalid Muhammad Ahmad, lecture, conference in Abu Dhabi, January 19, 2003.

6. Orayb Aref Najjar, "Palestine" chapter 15 in Kamalipour and Mowlana, pp. 215–17; and interview with Hanna Siniora, Ramallah, February 8, 2000.

7. Najjar, pp. 214–17.

8. Najjar, p. 214.

9. Kuldip R. Rampal, "Saudi Arabia" chapter in Kamalipour and Mowlana, p. 255.

10. Hana S. Noor Al-Deen, "Oman" chapter in Kamalipour and Mowlana, pp. 194ff.

11. *1999 World Press Freedom Review.*

12. *Emirates Bulletin* No. 080, April 30, 2001.

13. Mohamed M. Arafa, "Qatar," chapter 16 in Kamalipour and Mowlana, p. 240.

14. Sources: Europa, *The Middle East and North Africa 2000,* 46th Edition, Europa Publications Ltd., UK, 1999; and Editor and Publisher, *International Yearbook 1999,* 79th edition, Part I, and various interviews in 2002 and 2003 with senior editors from these countries. Private sources usually differ from published figures which are usually higher.

15. U.S. Department of State, *1999 Country Reports on Human Rights Practices,* Saudi Arabia section, February 25, 2000; and interviews with Saudi journalists in Washington D.C., in 2002.

16. Interview with Saudi journalist, May 2002, Washington D.C.; and Abdal Rahman Rashed in *Arab News,* July 23, 2001.

17. MEMRI, Special Dispatch No. 535, July 9, 2003; no official reason was given for his firing but private sources are convinced it was his editorials.

18. Interview with informed observer, Jerusalem, February 10, 2000.

19. Interview with Hana Siniora, editor of *al-Fajr,* Ramallah, February 8, 2000.

20. Tarek al-Muayyid, the then Information Minister, created *al-Ayam* and gave it substantial assistance in starting up. Interview with Mansoor al-Jamri, Chief Editor, *al-Wasat,* January 19, 2003, Abu Dhabi.

21. Interview with Mansoor al-Jamri, chief editor, *al-Wasat,* January 19, 2003, Abu Dhabi.

22. Mohammed El-Nawawy and Adel Iskandar, *al Jazeera: How The Free Arab News Network Scooped the World and Changed the Middle East,* Cambridge: Westview, 1967, pp. 72–78, 87.

23. Dr. Ahmad Abdal Malik, former chief editor of *al-Sharq* newspaper, interview, January 19, 2003, Abu Dhabi.

24. Interview with Dr. Ahmad Abdul Malik, chief editor, *al-Sharq* and *The Peninsula,* in Doha, June 2001.

25. Kuldip R. Rampal, "Saudi Arabia" chapter in Kamalipour and Mowlana, op.cit., p. 255.

26. Kuldip R. Rampal, "Saudi Arabia" chapter in Kamalipour and Mowlana, p. 255; U.S. Department of State, *1999 Country Reports on Human Rights Practices,* Saudi Arabia section, February 25, 2000.

27. Donna Abu-Nasr, "Saudi Newspaper Said to be Censored," Associated Press, March 23, 2002.

28. Interview, informed observer, Doha, June 2001.

29. Mohamed M. Arafa, "Qatar," chapter 16 in Kamalipour and Mowlana, p. 231.

30. Afaf Hamod and Elise K. Parsigian, "Bahrain" chapter in Kamalipour and Mowlana, pp. 40–41.

31. Interview with al-Jamri, Abu Dhabi, January 19, 2003.

32. Anantha S. Babbili and Sarwat Hussain, "United Arab Emirates" in Kamalipour and Mowlana, op. cit., p. 307; and U.S. Department of State, *Country Report for Human Rights Practices for 1999,* February 25, 2000.

33. Statements by UAE Information Minister Shaikh Abdullah bin Zayid, January 9, 2001 and March 7, 1998, Abu Dhabi, *Emirates Bulletins* Nos. 007–2001 and 05398, January 10, 2001 and March 8, 1998.

34. Interview with Shaikh Sultan bin Zayid published by *al-Ittihad* in October 1999. U.S. Department of State, *Country Report for Human Rights Practices for 1999,* February 25, 2000.

35. U.S. Department of State, *Country Reports on Human Rights Practices,* 1998 and 1999, "The Occupied Territories," February 26, 1999 and February 25, 2000; *1997 World Press Freedom Review.*

36. Orayb A. Najjar, "The 1995 Palestinian Press Law: A Comparative Study," *Communication Law and Policy journal,* Vol. 2, No. 1, Winter 1997, pp. 41–43, 55–56, 78, 92, 98.

37. U.S. Department of State, *1998 and 1999 Country Reports on Human Rights Practices,* section on "The Occupied Territories," February 26, 1999 and February 25, 2000, respectively; and *1997 World Press Freedom Review.*

38. Interview with Saudi journalist, May 2002, Washington D.C.

39. Interview with informed observer, Bahrain, June 2001.

40. Interview with Saudi journalists, Washington D.C., May and September 2002. The Board in 2002 included Salih Kamel, Khalid Olayan, Abdullah Bahamdan, Muhammad Amoudi, and Muhammad Allaisi, and was chaired by Prince Ahmad bin Salman.

41. Najjar, in Kamalipour and Mowlana, p. 214.

42. Minister Muhammad Abdu Yamani, quoted in *al-Jazirah,* May 13, 1976, p. 12.

43. Interview with Talaat Wafa, chief editor, *Riyadh Daily,* January 19, 2003, Abu Dhabi.

44. *1999 World Press Freedom Review*, reporting a November 1999 statement in Gulf News.

45. Saudi News Agency was established in 1971, Qatar and Omani News Agencies in 1975 respectively, and news agencies in Bahrain and the UAE in 1976.

46. Interview with Ibrahim al-Abid, special advisor to the Information Minister, January 19, 2003.

47. Interview, Saudi journalist, May 2002.

5

The Diverse Print Media: Lebanon, Kuwait, Morocco, and Yemen

A third major type of print media system appeared in the Arab world in the second half of the twentieth century. It can be called the diverse press because its most significant distinguishing characteristic is that the newspapers are clearly different from each other in content and apparent political tendency as well as in style. They are all privately owned and reflect a variety of viewpoints. In mobilization or loyalist press systems, by contrast, similarities outweigh any differences among papers within one country, but the opposite is true with the diverse press. The degree and quality of differences among newspapers is difficult to quantify or describe precisely, but regular newspaper readers perceive them quite easily.

Substantial diversity in the press implies that at least some of the newspapers, if not all, print news and opinion that is not supportive of the regime in power. Newspaper readers in this system have access to a greater variety of information than do readers of the loyalist or mobilization press, where all newspapers uniformly support the regime's basic policies and leaders. The diverse press is therefore relatively free, even if individual newspapers may be strong promoters of the regime, because some newspapers are somewhat independent of the regime and because the reader has more information and opinion to choose from.

The clearest and most consistent example of this type of press system has been seen in contemporary Lebanon. Kuwait, Morocco, and Yemen have also developed press systems which in many respects follow patterns similar enough to put them in this general category, too, although with some qualifications because the Kuwaiti, Moroccan, and Yemeni newspapers also have some of the loyalist press characteristics. In addition, as we have seen above (in Chapter 3), the press in four other countries passed through a factional stage characterized by diversity and relatively greater freedom, before it developed further to become mobilized. The diverse press seems to be a type that can and does emerge in the Arab world in various places, at various times.

Iraq is a special case that will be discussed at the end of this chapter. Under Saddam Hussain, the Iraqi media had been under a strict mobilization system, but when his regime fell in 2003, it emerged as a diverse type, although still in transition as of 2004.

What are the conditions under which this system emerges? In the case of the factional stage of the mobilization press, we have seen that three major factors helped diversity develop: the end of colonial restrictions, the appearance of openly competing political factions, and a national government that exercised restraint in dealing with the press. When the competition among political groups ended in those countries and the government intervened more directly and forcefully in the publishing business, the factional phase and substantial diversity ended. Similarly in Lebanon, and to a degree in Kuwait, Morocco, and Yemen also, the key factors seem to be these: political pluralism, patronization of the newspapers, and a relatively restrained approach to the press by the regime.

By political pluralism we mean the existence of readily identifiable groups or factions with distinguishable philosophies or approaches to public policy. This pluralism may manifest itself in organized political parties or in other forms, but the public can discern some clear choices among alternatives within the basic national consensus. Some of these groups establish direct or indirect ties with specific newspapers, creating a symbiotic patronization or sponsorship arrangement which, as we saw in Chapter 1, is not uncommon in the Arab press. Since the basic political system has manifest elements of pluralism in it, this is reflected in the press, as competing groups sponsor different newspapers. The regime in power may participate in the patronization process, sponsoring its own newspapers, but for the system to work it must show restraint in the exercise of governmental authority and political power over the press. The government may from time to time take legal or other action to restrict the press, but it does not go so far as to silence criticism totally or create complete uniformity.

Looking more closely at the system of a diverse press, we see that conditions that gave rise to it do vary from country to country; there can be many reasons for pluralism and for governmental restraint. Likewise the degree to which the system is in effect varies also. So to understand its dynamics we must examine individual cases.

At first glance, the four countries have rather different political systems. However all four countries have elected legislatures, and a considerable degree of political pluralism.

Lebanon is a parliamentary republic, whose unwritten National Pact of 1943 allocates parliamentary seats and political posts to the leading religious sects: the President is a Maronite Christian, Prime Minister is a Sunni Muslim, and the Speaker of the Chamber of Deputies is a Shi'a Muslim.

In Morocco the constitution provides for a monarchy with a parliament and an independent judiciary. But the king appoints all ministers and may dissolve the parliament and rule by decree. Since the constitutional reform of 1996 there is a lower house elected by universal suffrage and an upper house chosen by organizations. The lower house may dissolve the government. In March 1998 King Hassan II named a coalition government headed by opposition leader Abderrahman Youssefi and composed mostly of opposition party ministers, the first such government in decades and the first coalition cabinet of socialists, leftists, and nationalists. King Hassan, who ruled for thirty-eight years, died in July 1999, and was succeeded by his son Muhammad. King Muhammad VI has expressed support for "political pluralism . . . human rights and the protection of individual and collective rights."[1] He has however not made major changes in the structure of the Moroccan media.

In Kuwait, citizens cannot change their head of state, the amir, who has executive power. He is a member of the al-Sabah family that has ruled Kuwait for two centuries. He also has the authority to suspend the parliament, and he did so in 1976–1981 and in 1986–1992. However, parliamentary elections were held in 1992 and again in 1996 that were considered free and fair. The Kuwaiti government prohibits political parties, so candidates for the Assembly must nominate themselves, but there are informal groups in the Assembly.

The Republic of Yemen was created in 1990 out of a merger of the northern Yemen Arab Republic (YAR) in the north and the People's Democratic Republic of Yemen in the south. YAR President Ali Abdullah Salih became president of the new state, and he was reconfirmed as president by the legislature in 1994 and then in subsequent direct presidential elections into the twenty-first century. His General People's Congress (GPC) party has dominated the legislature and the cabinet, but several other political parties exist, including the Yemeni Socialist Party (YSP) representing southern interests, and the Reform (Islah) party representing Islamic, tribal, and other interests. Sixteen parties participated in the 1993 elections, and twelve in the 1997 elections. The government provides financial support to the parties including a small stipend to publish their own papers.[2]

Looking at the print media, first we will take Lebanon, since the press has come the closest to the diversity model and has sustained these characteristics over the longest period of time. The Lebanese civil war, which began in the spring of 1975, continued sporadically for seventeen years until 1992, seriously threatening to destroy the political basis on which the press had functioned for more than thirty years. Afterwards however the basic structure of the press remained as it had been. After discussing that structure, we shall turn briefly to the Kuwaiti, Moroccan, and Yemeni types, and the Iraqi press since 2003.

THE LEBANESE PRESS

Lebanon has more newspapers than any other Arab country. Prior to the civil war, there were over four hundred outstanding valid licenses to publish periodicals, including approximately fifty for daily newspapers and forty-five for political weeklies. Not all of these publications appeared, however. In fact more than three quarters of them were at times unable to be published for financial reasons although the owners kept their licenses. During the civil war, about fifteen dailies were printed regularly, and this number fell lower in times of civil disturbances, and the largest circulation daily in 1988 only could print about 34,000 copies. Then after the civil war ended, the government sought to bring some order into the chaotic press scene and a new press code passed in 1994 limited political publications to twenty-five including fifteen Arabic dailies.[3]

The quality of the papers varies considerably; a few may be the best in the Arab world, while some are among the shoddiest, most irresponsible, scurrilous papers anywhere. Many Lebanese newspapers fail to present facts objectively, or to do careful research, and they tend to be subjective, provocative, and sensationalist, like Western tabloids.

Some newspapers have small circulation figures, but others are read widely at home and abroad. Lebanon has the highest literacy rate of any Arab country, and it has been estimated that daily newspapers are read by three-quarters of the adult population on a regular basis. Earlier, Lebanon exported many of its newspapers to other Arab countries, but the numbers diminished considerably because of the civil war, competition from emerging newspapers in the Gulf and elsewhere.

Lebanese newspapers are not only numerous but taken as a whole they present readers with the widest variety of opinion and the most complete collection of information on a given topic of any Arab press. Almost all significant currents of Arab thought can be found represented in the Lebanese press. Readers of the Lebanese press believe that most publications with political content have one political bias or another that they can detect in the news selection as well as in the editorials. They usually attribute this bias to a secret understanding of some kind between a newspaper's editors and a specific Lebanese political faction and/or foreign groups. They infer this secret understanding from the content of the paper since editors as a rule do not admit that they have any such connections. Indeed, even the editors themselves typically accuse each other of receiving hidden financial subsidies or other benefits from political patrons in return for support in the paper. The typical editor denies that he biases his paper in return for a subsidy. And when the education minister declared that "all our newspapers and all our journalists can be bought, sold, and hired," for example, the president of the Lebanese Press Syndicate felt compelled to respond with a strong attack on the minister and defense of the press without denying the charge.[4]

There is no doubt that patronization of the press for political purposes does take place in Lebanon although it is impossible to determine the extent or precise nature of these connections. In some cases, the editorial tendency of a paper may be determined in large part by the personal attitude and philosophy of the publisher and only secondarily or marginally by any outside connections or subsidies. A few newspapers have achieved sufficient variety and balance within their own pages so that observers often have difficulty identifying a clear bias and some even call them objective. Other papers change their political orientation frequently so that it is difficult to categorize them except as opportunistic.

For example, before the civil war, it was assumed by readers of the Lebanese press that *al-Nida, al-Sharq, al-Safir,* and *al-Kifah* had connections with, and probably received subsidies from, Russia, Syria, Libya, and Iraq, respectively, while *al-Hayat* was thought to have Saudi and conservative Lebanese backing. Readers believed that *al-Amal* and *al-Jarida* must have had Lebanese nationalist financing of some kind, while Palestinians and Pan-Arab nationalists supported either *al-Muharrir* and *al-Liwa'* or the more moderate *al-Anwar* and Sawt *al-'Urubah.* Some papers, however, were more difficult to categorize so neatly because they showed mixed tendencies. *Al-Nahar* has been essentially a family enterprise since Jubran Twaini established it in 1933; his son Ghassan and now his grandson Jubran have managed it successfully. Family pride in the paper help explain *al-Nahar*'s courage in expressing occasional criticism of Syria more than most Lebanese papers.

For purposes of illustration, Table 5.1 gives some indication in simplified form of the variety of political tendencies that were observed by readers in the leading Lebanese dailies. Observers generally believe they can detect political tendencies in the dailies on three levels: national politics and religious affiliation, regional politics including the Arab-Israeli question, and international relations. The table lists the estimated circulation of daily newspapers from among the Lebanese dailies that appear regularly and comparative figures for them from 1975, just before the civil war, and 1999 plus a simplified annotation indicating the orientation their readers generally perceive.[5]

The many weekly and other publications that appeared before the civil war, and the ones that survived or emerged after it, cover the same broad spectrum of political orientations as these dailies. Competition and rhetorical conflict among them has been vigorous and lively, as has the criticism and defense of the government's policies and leaders. This type of press has developed in Lebanon because of the particular political circumstances

TABLE 5.1   Leading Lebanese Daily Newspapers (1999)

Name	Estimated Circulation (in thousands)			Predominant orientation	
	1999	1975	First published	Religious	Political
Al-Liwa' (The Banner)	79	3	1939	Sunni	Arab nationalist pro-Syrian
Al-Nahar (The Day)	65	55	1933	Gr. Orth.	Indep., moderate
Al-Anwar (The Lights)	59	40	1959	Gr. Orth.	Moderate Arab nationalist
Al-Safir (The Messenger)	50	2.5	1974	Muslim	Arab nationalist
Al-Sharq (The East)	36	3	1926	Sunni	anti-West, anti-U.S. pro-Syria
Al-Amal (Hope)	35	7	1939	Maronite	Phalange Party
Lisan al-Hal (The Spokesman)	33	8	1877	Gr. Orth.	pro-West
Sada Lubnan (Echo of Lebanon)	25	?	1951	Sunni	pan-Arab
L'Orient le Jour†	23	18	1942		independent, pro-West, Leb. nationalist
Al-Jarida (The Newspaper)	23	4	1953		Independent
Al-Diyar			1990s	Christian	centrist, young professionals
Al-Mustaqbal (The Future)	20	0	1999	Sunni	pro-Hariri, pro-Syria
Le Soir† (The Evening)	17	1.5	1947	Arm. Orth.	Independent, pro-West
Al-Kifah al-Arabi (The Arab Struggle)	?	2	1974		socialist, pan-Arab
The Daily Star*	11	6	1952 (relaunched 1996)	Shi'ite	pro-West, pro-PLO
Al-Nida (The Appeal)	10	3	1949	Shi'ite	Communist Party

*Published in English.
†Published in French.

in that country and the way that journalism emerged over the years. What are those circumstances?

Development of Press Patronization and Diversity

Lebanese newspaper journalism began in the middle of the nineteenth century, when the territory was under Ottoman rule. Although newspapers had appeared earlier in Egypt, Beirut has the longest continuous press history, and because of its early emphasis on education it had a higher concentration of newspapers from the beginning. The first Arab daily was started in Beirut in 1873, and about forty other newspapers and periodicals appeared there between 1870 and 1900. The first newspapers were elitist, written by and for intellectuals, whose liberal ideas frequently got them into trouble with Ottoman authorities. They were influenced by Western, particularly French, ideas and journalism, and their publications—in French or Arabic—often resembled contemporary French journals.[6]

Periodic strict censorship, especially during the reign of Sultan Abdal Hamid (1876–1909), caused some journalists to flee to Egypt where they could establish newspapers with fewer restrictions. But after the more liberal press law of 1909, Lebanese newspapers were able to play a definite role in the Arab nationalist movement. Their activities were still watched by the government, however; in May 1916, for example, sixteen of the thirty-one Arab leaders hanged in Beirut and Damascus for demanding independence and stirring up public opinion were journalists.[7] Under the French Mandate (1920–1941), more newspapers appeared, and many became politically involved, although the French maintained and even tightened controls on the press. By 1929 there were many papers in Lebanon, and some editors risked suspension, fines, or jail because they called for independence in their editorials.

In 1943, Lebanon became essentially independent, but France in fact retained some powers, and authority to regulate the press was not turned over to the Lebanese until 1946, when French troops finally withdrew. The newly independent Lebanese political system was based on a careful balance of a variety of interest groups, which has been maintained to this day, and which underlies the system of the press. Lebanon has always been a refuge for minorities, particularly religious sects, who maintained their autonomy and frequently competed vigorously against each other. An unwritten agreement of 1943, now referred to as the National Covenant (al-mithaq al-watani), was made between the two outstanding Christian and Muslim leaders. All groups and factions accepted a *de facto* coexistence which entailed, among other things, the proportional allotment of high political offices on the basis of factional membership. The competitive balance underlying the Lebanese polity is not only among confessional groups, but among secular ideological, social, economic, geographic, personal, and family ones as well.

The Lebanese press reflects these multiple divisions. In addition, disagreements among political officials, which result from splits and the necessity of coalition government, made the state relatively weak against organized interest groups. In such an environment, newspapers proliferated, many became highly political, and most reflected interests of special groups or parties. The newspapers frequently came into conflict with the government, but in contrast to most other Arab states, the government was not able to reduce the level of dissent or diversity significantly.

The Lebanese press was relatively strong from the beginning of the modern era. It exposed the corruption of the first regime after independence, and accused the government of rigging the elections of 1947. The government reacted by imposing more restrictive press regulations in 1948.

The new government that came into office in September 1952 was grateful to the press and passed a more liberal publishing law that lifted most of the restrictions in October. But the editors did not stop their criticism. In fact, the power of the press increased during the 1950s, especially as politicians and groups recognized its value as an ally in their battles. As their importance grew, the number of newspapers increased rapidly, so that before long Beirut alone had more than fifty dailies.[8]

From time to time, in spite of some self-regulation, the government has stepped in to exercise direct control over the press. During the 1958 civil war, the government suspended several opposition papers—two defied the ban by publishing in the rebel-held Basta District of Beirut, and also used its power to censor specific items in the press. But even when censorship is imposed, the Lebanese papers usually show their independence by publishing with blank spaces as a signal to readers that they have been restricted, a practice generally not allowed elsewhere in the Arab world.

The severity of the 1958 crisis also led the government to ban the importation of some foreign publications, particularly Egyptian and Syrian, and on a few other occasions the authorities have stopped single issues, although as a rule there are no such restrictions and virtually any foreign publication can be found in Beirut.

The Lebanese press law of 1962 continues to be valid with some amendments. It does prohibit the publication of "news which endangers the national security, or unity or frontiers of the state, or which degrades a foreign head of state." The Lebanese press has over the years tended to interpret these rules somewhat liberally and to see to its own observance of them. The 1962 law supported the Press (owners') Syndicate and Writers' Syndicate, and provided for a self-regulating body. The government has ordinarily not found it necessary to intervene directly, since the press syndicates functioned well in practice. This law has helped reinforce in the press a "high degree of freedom," and Lebanese editors are proud of their practice of self-regulation, which has usually avoided government censorship.[9]

The Lebanese civil war, which began in early 1975 and lasted for seventeen years, created special pressures on the press as it did on all Lebanese institutions. Lebanon's "social mosaic" which had provided the pluralist base of an open democracy for thirty years, began to come apart over economic and social issues, over the allocation of shares of political power, over the proper role of the Palestinians in Lebanon, and other questions. Contending factions became frustrated with the dialogue in the press and parliament and sought to achieve their ends by violent means. Divisions cut across different lines, religious, rich/poor, Arab nationalist/Lebanese nationalist, pro- and anti-Palestinian, and national leaders lost enough of their control so that private militias took over the streets and revealed the inability of the state to keep order.

Most of the major daily newspapers continued to appear, but with fewer pages and virtually all of their space devoted to strictly Lebanese events. Distribution of each paper became restricted to the area or areas controlled by the paper's supporters, as Lebanon and particularly Beirut became divided along geographic lines into enclaves. The level of responsibility and veracity in the press diminished as the crisis worsened; those papers lacking ties to patrons with armed militias became circumspect or went out of business while the rest became more vociferous. Journalists, like national political leaders, at first remained immune to deliberate physical attack, but in January 1976 the top editors of two important dailies died as the result of raids on their newspaper offices that may have been politically inspired. The Minister of Information, himself a prominent editor, issued only a mild reproach after the raid but did nothing, showing the government's powerlessness to protect journalists or anyone else.[10]

In the fall of 1976, agreement was reached among major Arab countries to establish an Arab Deterrent Force to help the Lebanese government restore order. Syria, which had sent its own military units into Lebanon during the peak of the civil war, was dominant in the ADF as Lebanon began to return to normalcy. While some of the Lebanese press supported Syria and the ADF, a number of newspapers were critical of developments. In December 1976 Syrian troops of the ADF occupied the offices of several newspapers, including the independent daily *al-Nahar* and the pro-Libyan daily *al-Safir,* which suspended publication. A few weeks later, the ADF allowed the restricted papers to resume publication. But in the meantime, the Lebanese government had issued a decree imposing precensorship on the press, giving the Directorate General of Public Security the power to preview everything before publication. The Interior Minister declared that no one should publish "material stirring up sectarian strife, . . . instigating actions endangering public safety and security, [or] . . . causing arguments leading to a renewal of fighting." First violations were punishable by fines and imprisonment, second violations by rescinding the license to issue the publication.[11]

The Lebanese government thus had decided that self-regulation was not sufficient and direct censorship had become necessary, because the internal situation was still not fully settled. But the civil strife did not destroy the characteristic multiplicity and diversity of the Lebanese press. Of the twenty-one most widely read dailies that existed in 1975, nine were no longer being published at all in 1979, and eight others were still below their 1975 circulation levels. Nevertheless, several new dailies had emerged, of which three were going strong as of 1979, and one of these had even climbed to second place in circulation. Equally important was the fact that clear differences in orientation of the various newspapers, across a considerable spectrum, had also returned by 1977 and were still present in 1979. During that four years, the pro-West Greek Orthodox *Lisan al-Hal* had disappeared, but the new and successful *Reveil* had the same tendencies; and pro-Iraqi *al-Kifah* folded, but *al-Liwa'* was still defending Iraq, among other causes.

Although Lebanon's civil turmoil, exacerbated from outside, continued into the 1980s, affecting distribution and other aspects of publishing, many newspapers continued to appear, and by 1986, fourteen of the fifteen dailies were still being published (*Sawt al-Uruba* had disappeared but a new daily, *al-Haqiqa,* representing labor views, had started). The independent *al-Nahar* and the pro-Libyan *al-Safir* were reaching the most readers with 60,000 circulation each, and all dailies together had a combined circulation of about 175,000, that was the highest in Lebanon's history.

After the civil war, the Lebanese print media continued to face serious problems, stemming from the weak economy, increased competition regionally from well-funded newspapers that had emerged in the Gulf and abroad, and from satellite television (see below). Moreover, the legal situation changed somewhat. The constitution provides for freedom of the press but the government partially limits it, intimidating journalists into self-censorship. The law prohibits attacks on the dignity of the head of state or foreign leaders. The government may prosecute offending journalists in the special Publications Court. The Surete Generale has authority to approve all foreign publications. Lebanese editors say that Surete officials occasionally phone them to provide guidelines on specific stories, and that the sensitive issues usually involve Syria or one of the top Lebanese officials, including the president, the prime ministrer or the speaker of parliament.[12]

A new press law was passed in 1994 which brought some order into the chaotic press situation caused by the civil war. The law reduced government power by ending preventive arrest of journalists, and it allowed prior censorship only in extraordinary cases approved by the Council of Ministers, or for imported foreign newspapers. It did stipulate heavy fines for violating enumerated rules, and it reiterated government authority to issue and revoke licenses or suspend publications, all of which would be reviewed by a special tribunal. The listed prohibitions included offending recognized religions or advocating racial or religious hatred. Also, the Press Syndicate adopted an "honor code" that amounts to self-censorship.

Domestic issues are often more sensitive than foreign ones. Even Israel, the hottest foreign issue, can be treated within limits. Lebanese newspapers regularly print excerpts from the Israeli press and quote liberally from Israeli leaders and citizens, but interviews by Lebanese journalists are not allowed, nor are contacts with Israelis, because Lebanon is still officially at war.[13] In April 2002 the government called for legal action against the Daily Star because the International Herald Tribune, which the Star publishes in Beirut, carried an ad which the authorities said was Israeli propaganda which is prohibited by law.[14]

One key issue affecting the Lebanese press in recent years is the fact that Syria has considerable influence over Lebanese politics. Tens of thousands of Syrian troops remain in the country and the 1991 Lebanese-Syrian security agreement stipulates a prohibition on publication of any information deemed harmful to the security of either state. Because of the risk of prosecution, Lebanese journalists censor themselves on matters relating to Syria. Lebanese journalists say that they must be careful about what they say about Syria, especially its internal affairs. They say it is possible in an editorial to recommend that Syria "rethink" its Lebanon policy, but never to equate the Syrian presence with Israel's occupation of Palestine. *Al-Nahar* is notable for its occasional criticism of Syria which has enhanced its reputation among Lebanese readers (the paper is banned in Syria), but it too tries to avoid criticizing Syria's internal affairs.[15]

In 1999 President Lahoud announced that during his tenure no charges would be brought against any journalist because of his writings or opinions. But the government does take action against individual papers. For example, in 1993, the government shut down *Nida al-Watan* for thirty-eight days; it is owned by a vocal Maronite critic of Prime Minister Hariri and was accused of inciting sectarian discord, by alleging that Hariri was buying church property in order to Islamize Lebanon. In 1993 the government closed *al-Safir* daily for one week for publishing state secrets when it printed the text of an Israeli proposal submitted to the Lebanese delegation in peace talks. The government closed *al-Sharq* for one week for printing a cartoon insulting the president's family. In October 1993 the public prosecutor charged *al-Liwa'* and *al-Diyar* with slandering government officials. In 1998 the government filed charges against several newspapers. In February 1998 it indicted the newspaper *al-Diyar* three times for defaming the president, the Prime Minister, and the judiciary. In January 1998 the supreme court endorsed a 1997 verdict by the Publications Court sentencing the chief editor of the daily *al-Kifah al-Arabi* to pay a fine of $30,000 for insulting the king of Saudi Arabia. In 1999 a court case was brought against *al-Nahar* journalist Pierre Atallah, charged in absentia in 1998 for defaming the judiciary and entering Israel.

During 1996 the Lebanese government filed charges against several newspapers, for example in one ten-day period it charged three dailies (*al-Diyar, al-Liwa'* and *Nida al-Watan*) and two weeklies (*al-Kifah al-Arabi* and *al-Massira*) with defaming the president and prime minister, and publishing materials deemed provocative to one religious sect. *Al-Diyar* was indicted five times and both owner and chief editor faced sentences of two years in jail and large fines. Yet dozens of newspapers are published with different views, financed by domestic and foreign groups, and newspapers often reflect the views of their financial backers. Daily criticism of political leaders by many publications continues.

Lebanese weekly magazines, like the daily newspapers, have exhibited a variety of political and religious orientation that has not been erased by the civil strife. The number of weeklies was reduced by the unsettled conditions in the country, but as of 1986 there were still about thirty political weeklies, and they represented a fairly broad range of editorial opinion. The weekly *al-Massira* expressed the views of the Christian Phalange, *al-Amal* spoke for the moderate Shiite Amal Party, *al-Ahd* spoke for the radical Shiite Party of God, and *al-Anba'* for the Druze PSP party. In addition, several publishers had moved their headquarters from Beirut to Europe during the civil war, so that Lebanese-owned weeklies were being published in Paris and London and not only read by expatriate Arabs but also sent into the Arab countries, including Lebanon, from there (see Chapter 8). By the year 2000, there were more than fifty existing daily newspaper licenses but fewer than half were being utilized; another fifty or so publications were however appearing.[16]

Two factors have made the Lebanese press one of the freest in the Arab world. First, the state failed to silence press criticism to the extent that other Arab states have, and the press has developed a measure of self-regulation to protect itself as an institution. Second, and more importantly, the continuation of the pluralist society and confessional democracy was and is reflected in the genuine diversity of the Lebanese press. The Lebanese newspaper reader may not always find objectivity in one newspaper, but taken as a whole, the Lebanese press provided him with a broad spectrum of views and news unparalleled in the Arab world, and from which he could make his own choices. This press system was built on a political base of institutionalized pluralism that other Arab countries lacked. As that base crumbled in the civil war, the press became more limited to functioning as a narrow channel of communication among members of one group, and it became more irresponsible and tied to agents of violence, and pluralism turned to fragmentation. After the war, factionalism remained and was mirrored in the press. Diversity continues although it has been reduced somewhat because of Syria, the economy and media developments in the region.[17]

THE KUWAITI, MOROCCAN, AND YEMENI PRESS SYSTEMS

The print media systems in Kuwait, Morocco, and Yemen have some structural similarities with the press in Lebanon, and also a few differences.

Kuwait produces a large number of newspapers for its size, and the quality of its press reached a remarkable level as early as the 1970s. By 1979, seven daily newspapers (five in Arabic, two in English) with an estimated circulation of over 124,000 were being published in Kuwait, although the population was still under one million and adult literacy was only 60 percent. By 2002, the seven dailies were distributing a total of nearly half a million copies, although the population was still only 1.8 million and literacy was 78 percent. In addition, more than a dozen weeklies and an equal number of other publications were appearing in that country. All of the dailies were known outside of Kuwait, where they sold well. They were popular in the Gulf states, but some had gained readers elsewhere in the Arab world too.

Morocco, too, has a relatively large number of newspapers. In 2003 it had nineteen daily newspapers (twelve in Arabic, seven in French), with a total circulation of more than four hundred thousand copies, and it had dozens of other publications. It is true that the quality of the Moroccan press does not match that in Lebanon or Kuwait, although it is improving. Its journalism is relatively weak. It has neither a long tradition of journalism like Lebanon, nor the money to hire outside talent as Kuwait does. Nevertheless, the three countries do share other press characteristics.

In Yemen, the press system is rather new. The current structure of the Yemeni press dates only to 1990, when an entirely new political situation was created following the merger in that year of north and south Yemen. With the new state came elections and multiple political parties for the first time, and an extraordinary degree of press freedom that had not been seen in Yemen before. Newspapers have limited circulations and most are nondailies, but there are dozens of different ones, providing a broad spectrum of opinion.

Diversity among Newspapers

The press in Kuwait, Morocco, and Yemen, as in Lebanon, is basically in private hands, and it shows a significant degree of diversity.

Kuwaiti Print Media

Kuwaiti print media have developed a degree of diversity, competition, and outspokenness, that make the Kuwaiti press somewhat similar to the Lebanese, although in Lebanon they are more pronounced and newspaper traditions are more firmly established because the press began seventy-five

TABLE 5.2   Kuwaiti Daily Newspapers[18]

Name	Estimated circulations (in thousands)		First published
	2003	1986	
Al-Watan (The Homeland)	65	60	1972
Al-Ray' al-'Aam (Public Opinion)	65	87	1961
Al-Qabas (The Beacon)	60	80	1972
Al-Anba' (The News)	50	107	1976
Al-Siyasa (Politics)	17	70	1965
The Kuwait Times*	25	28	1961
The Arab Times*	20	42	1977

*Published in English.

years earlier. It seems that the relatively young Kuwaiti press (the first publication of any kind appeared there in 1928) is tending in the direction of the Lebanese press, although its political environment is somewhat different.

All Kuwaiti newspapers are owned by Kuwaiti families. Al-Qabas (The Beacon) is a consortium of five families, and the others are single family enterprises—and are run as family businesses. All dailies are showing a profit because of good advertising revenues plus subsidies from the government, and the fact that radio and television do not carry ads.

Since the liberation of Kuwait from Iraqi occupation in 1991, the Kuwaiti press has become much more focused on internal affairs and much less on regional and international matters. Prior to Desert Storm (1991), Kuwaiti papers focused heavily on regional pan-Arab issues, and this was partly due to the large number of non-Kuwaiti Arabs who had links to the region. After Desert Storm the press focused much more on local news. Also, editorial orientations of individual newspapers are more difficult to categorize as they change over time and with the issue, for example all of them have criticized the government and the parliament and all have defended both. Nor is ownership necessarily a predictor of editorial policy, for example the speaker of parliament is a part owner of al-Qabas but that has no discernible impact on al-Qabas editorials or news play. All newspapers respect certain basic taboos, namely not to criticize directly the Emir, the Crown Prince, or Islam.[19]

Kuwait's oldest successful dailies are al-Ray al-'Aam (Public Opinion) and al-Siyasa (Politics), both having been established in the 1960s. Al-Ray al-'Aam (Public Opinion) maintains a uniform and consistent editorial policy, strongly supporting the royal family while criticizing individual government officials and public figures. Lately it has tended to be the most sensationalist of the dailies. Al-Siyasa tends to be somewhat more outspoken, liberal, and diverse in its interpretation of events. It tackles a variety of problems with vigor, and a considerable variety of viewpoints is expressed in its editorials, subjecting public figures of any persuasion to its close scrutiny. It often presents interviews with Arab leaders, and some of its editorials show strong support for Saudi Arabia. However *al-Siyasa* does tend to support the ruling family, and it tends to advocate moderate courses of action, treating issues in a less emotional fashion than other papers do. *Al-Qabas* is a paper with a different editorial approach, which is quite successful. Established in 1972, in four years it had achieved the highest circulation of any daily, although it later dropped to third place. *Al-Qabas* does not advocate any one political line but seeks to satisfy all Kuwaiti factions. It is rather liberal and fairly objective in its presentation of news and commentary. Financed by a group of local businessmen, it gives especially good coverage to economic matters, giving emphasis to Kuwaiti business interests, and it specializes in educational and environmental matters.

A fourth daily, *al-Watan* (The Nation), has in the past shown special concern for foreign affairs, especially the Gulf area. Since liberation it has given more space to Islamic writers which has attracted readers especially interested in religion. It has often been outspokenly critical of the Kuwaiti government. Finally, the fifth and newest Arabic daily, *al-Anba'* (The News), which has strong ties with the Kuwaiti business community, is a staunch advocate of capitalism and Arab family traditions. Since liberation, it has been an outspoken critic of Yasir Arafat and the Palestine Liberation Organization. Its board chair is the only Arab female in that position in the Arab world.

The English-language daily, *The Kuwait Times,* has existed since independence, and it presents a moderate, liberal point of view. Its long-time competition, the more conservative *Daily News,* ceased publication in 1976, when Abdul Aziz Masa'id sold it to the al-Ghanim family, that was unable to keep the publication going. A new competitor emerged in 1977 when al-Siyassah Publishing House sold *The Kuwait Times* and began a new liberal English daily, the *Arab Times,* that has a lively style, and because it uses material from *al-Siyasa* it has better circulation than *The Kuwait Times.*

Several weekly newspapers are published in Kuwait, including *al-Talia, al-Ula,* the Islamic paper *al-Furqan,* and *al-Hadaf,* which specializes in women's issues. Like the dailies, Kuwait's weekly publications also present a spectrum of viewpoints and orientations.

Moroccan Print Media

The Moroccan press, too, is spread quite widely across a political spectrum in that country. After King Hassan appointed opposition leader Abdelrahman Yousifi as Prime Minister in 1998, government restrictions on the press eased somewhat, and some further liberalization took place after Muhammad VI became king in 1999. The press is now freer to criticize national institutions such as the judiciary, which it could not do in the past. The press however still avoids direct criticism of the king, Islam, or the government's policy on the Sahara.[20]

Two of the highest circulation dailies, for example (see Table 5.3) represent views other than the government's. *Al-Alam* and *l'Opinion,* are Arabic and French sister papers published by the Istiqlal party, which for many years was in the opposition but has also been in the government. They are the two oldest dailies in existence—*al-Alam* was started in 1944—and like the Istiqlal party itself, they have been part of the political scene in independent Morocco for so long that they are virtually part of the establishment. They are regularly critical of the status quo, however.

One traditionally independent newsaper is the daily *al-Ittihad al-Ishtiraki* (The Socialist Union). Since May 1983 it has been the successor to *al-Muharrir* (The Editor), which was suspended after the June 1981 Casablanca riots, and has been published by the Socialist Union of Popular Forces (the USFP). The USFP party that was formed by a group of politicians who broke with the

TABLE 5.3   Selected Moroccan Daily Newspapers (2003)[21]

	Date established	Circulation estimates	Editorial tendencies
Al-Ahdath al-Maghribiya	1999	80,000	independent
l'Opinion*	1965	70,000	Istiqlal Party organ
Al-Ittihad al-Ishtiraki	1983	65,000	USFP organ
Le Matin*	1971	50,000	semi-official
Assahra al-Maghribiya	1990s	30,000	semi-official
Al-Sabah	1990s	20,000	independent
Attajdid	1990s	25,000	Unity & Reform Party
L'Economiste*	1998	22,000	independent
Al-Alam	1944	18,000	Istiqlal Party organ
Maroc Ouest	1990s	20,000	independent
Aujourd'hui Le Maroc*	2001	20,000	independent
Bayane al-Youm	1972	15,000	PPS Party
Al-Bayan*	1972	5,000	PPS Party
Liberation*	1990s	5,000	USFP
L'Independent*	1998	5,000	independent
Al-Munaatif	1990s	1,000	MP Party, conservative
Al-Amal al-Dimukrati	1990s	750	OADP Party
Risaalat al-Umma	1983	500	Constit. Union Party

*Published in French.

Istiqlal party has over the years been critical of the government's economic and educational policies and its European and American ties. However, after 1998 when King Hassan made Abdul Rahman Youssefi, the head of the USFP, Prime Minister, the paper has muted some of its criticisms of the government. Youssefi retained his post as chief editor of *al-Ittihad al-Ishtiraki*, and after Muhammad became king, he kept the Prime Ministerial post also. The paper has continued to appeal especially to university students, younger professionals, and government employees.

Official policy since Youssefi became prime minister and Muhammad VI became king has been more liberal, although the government has occasionally suspended papers that became strongly critical of the administration.[22]

Private newspapers published by the Maroc Soir Group, now owned by prominent businessman Othman Benjalloun, have for years tended to support the government's policies and are generally considered to be "semi-official." This publishing house puts out two of the country's highest-circulation dailies, the thirty-year-old French paper *Le Matin* and the newer Arabic paper *Assahra al-Maghribiya* (The Moroccan Sahara). In news selection and commentary, their tendency is to support the monarchy, the Establishment, business and private enterprise, and they are relatively more friendly to Western countries.

Two other dailies, *al-Maghrib* in French and Arabic and *al-Mithaq al-Watani* (The National Pact) also support government policies. The daily *al-Anba'* (The News), published by the Ministry of Information, is consistently progovernment, and has the advantage of being able to scoop the competition with government news, and they present a supremely optimistic tone which contrasts with that of the other papers.

Morocco has a number of newspapers which represent the varied views of different political parties. Nine of the papers are dailies. *Bayane al-Youm* (Today's Dispatch) in Arabic and *al-Bayane* in French are the official organs of the Party of Progress and Socialism (PPS), which is the former Moroccan Communist Party. *Attajdid* (The Renewal) in Arabic is owned by the Unity and Reform Islamist movement. It was formerly known as *al-Raya* (The Banner), and changed its name in 1999. *Al-Amal al-Dimukrati* (The Democratic Worker) is owned by the Organization of Popular Democratic Action (OADP), a far-left party. *Risaalat al-Umma* (The National Message) is owned by the Constitutional Union Party, the main opposition party in parliament. And *al-Munaatif* (The Path) is owned by the Forces of Democratic Front, a party that split off from the PPS. *Al-Haraka* (The Movement) is an Arabic daily owned by the Voice of the Popular Movement (MP) Party, a conservative rural Berber party. Three other party papers are weeklies: *al-Assr* (the Evening) is owned by the moderate Islamist Party of Justice and Development (PJD); *al-Ittihad* (the Union) is owned by the USFP party; and *al-Sahwa* (The Awakening) is owned by the Islamist Unity and Reform movement.[23]

The opposition press is often critical of the government. The tone of these editorials became especially sharp during the 1993 election campaign.

In addition, there are six daily newspapers and sixteen weeklies which are independent of the government or any party, and most of them regularly express criticism of the government (see Table 5.4). Among the dailies, *al-Ahdath al-Magribiya* (Moroccan Events) has the largest circulation of the independents. It is controlled by former USFP politicians and journalists, and its tendency is secularist, often critical of the Youssefi government. Two other large circulation independent dailies, *al-Sabah* (The Morning) and *L'Economiste* are business-oriented. *Maroc Ouest*, *Aujourd'hui le Maroc* and *L'Independent* are independent dailies with smaller circulations.

TABLE 5.4   Moroccan Weekly Newspapers[24]

	Estimated circulations	Editorial tendencies
Al-Usbu' (ex-Usbu' Siyasi)	75,000	independent, sensationalist
Al-Sahifa	45,000	independent, political, and economic
Al-Ittihad	44,000	USFP socialist party
Al-Ayam	40,000	independent, oppositionist
*Le Journal Hebdomaire**	30,000	independent, political, and economic
Al-Hadath al-Sharqi	30,000	independent
Al-Assr	25,000	Party of Justice and Development
Demain Magazine	10,000	independent, political, and economic
La Gazette du Maroc	10,000	independent, political, and economic
*La Verite**	15,000	independent
Asdae	15,000	independent, sensationalist
*La Vie Economique**	15,000	independent, business
Al-Bidawi	15,000	independent, oppositionist
*Maroc Hebdo**	17,000	independent, political
*La Nouvelle Tribune**	9,000	independent, political
Al-Sahwa	5,500	Unity and Reform movement
Business News†	4,000	independent, business
Al-Maydane	5,000	independent
Al-Khadra al-Jadida	3,000	independent

* Published in French
† Published in English

Yemeni Print Media

In Yemen, prior to unification, the press was weak and very much under government control in both the north and the south. In the south, in 1946 the Free Yemeni movement bought printing equipment and started the newspaper *Sawt al-Yemen* (Voice of Yemen) to spread its antigovernment ideas, but once in power the Yemeni leaders in the south banned private and party papers and issued their own. The government of the People's Republic of Southern Yemen published a daily paper, *14 October,* named for the date in 1963 when the National Liberation Front in the south declared its intention to lead an armed struggle against Britain. Its circulation was about 20,000 copies. The southern regime also published several nondailies, including the weekly magazine *al-Thawra* (The Revolution), that was the organ of the Yemeni Socialist Party Central Committee. In North Yemen, the government-owned Saba General Organization for Press published two daily newspapers, *al-Thawra* (The Revolution) in Sanaa and *al-Jumhuria* (The Republic) in Taiz, and it also published a weekly for the armed forces named *26 September,* named for the date in 1962 of the military coup in the north against the ruler, Imam Badr. Some of these pre-1990 publications continued after unification, alongside the new ones.

Immediately after Yemeni unification in 1990, the government declared that political parties would be allowed and that for the first time, parties and private individuals could issue newspapers. Literally hundreds of publications appeared. During the next four years, 1990–1994, there was a high degree of press freedom, as the government did little to try to dictate what news the newspapers carried or what the editorials said. In the spring of 1994, a civil war broke out between elements in the south which opposed the northern-led national government. After the war ended in the summer with a northern victory, the government became somewhat less tolerant of press freedom. Nevertheless, a large number of newspapers— more than one hundred—continued to appear and they had considerable latitude in what they could print. Most of them appeared weekly or less frequently, but they had political influence nevertheless.

Since Yemen is one of the world's poorest countries, with a per capita GNP of under $300, the economy cannot sustain expensive newspapers and most of them were unable to publish every day. In fact, Yemen has only two daily newspapers, *al-Thawra* and *al-Jumhuria.* They had been published by the North Yemeni government prior to unification and continued since. Most papers publish only a few thousand copies, and only a few of them have circulations over ten thousand. There is genuine variety and diversity in the Yemeni press, however, when seen as a whole, including the weekly and other nondaily publications, as Table 5.5 shows.

After Yemeni unification, several government publications, carried over from both northern and southern regimes, continued to appear. The northern

TABLE 5.5   Yemeni Print Media (1999)[25]

	First published	Location	Editorial orientation
Government newspapers			
Al-Thawra	1962	Sanaa	progovernment
Al-Jumhuria	1960s	Taiz	progovernment
14 October	1968	Aden	Yemeni Socialist Party
26 September	1982	Sanaa	Yemeni Army
Al-Mithaq		Sanaa	General People's Congress (GPC)
Opposition party newspapers			
Al-Sahwa	1985	Aden	Islah Party
Al-Shura		Sanaa	Union of Popular Forces, Islamist
Al-Thawri			Yemen Socialist Party (YSP)
Al-Wahdawi	1992	Sanaa	Nasserist People's Un.
Al Umma	1990		Party of Truth
Al-Tajammu'	1998	Sanaa	Yemeni Union Gathering
Al-Jamahir			Ba'th Party
Al-Ihya'	1997	Aden	Ba'th Party, pro-Iraq
Al-Haq	1997	Aden	Connection Party
Al-Ra'y	1951	Sanaa	Sons of Yemen League
Private newspapers			
Al-Ayam	1950	Aden	independent
Al-Sharmu'			independent
al-Usbu'			independent
al-Masar			progovernment
Sawt al-Ummal			progovernment unionist
Yemen Times*	1990	Sanaa	independent
Al-Wahda	1991	Sanaa	progovernment
al-Ra'y al-'Aam	1985	Sanaa	independent, conservative
Al-Tariq	1996	Aden	independent
Al-Balagh	1993	Sanaa	independent
Yemen Observer*	1996	Sanaa	independent

*Published in English.

government's two dailies, *al-Thawra* and *al-Jumhuria,* its army weekly *26 September,* continued, and President Salih's party, General People's Congress, put out a new newspaper, *al-Mithaq* (The Pact). The southerners continued to put out *14 October,* their old official newspaper, as the primary organ of the Yemeni Socialist Party (YSP), the leading party of the south that had become part of the unified political spectrum.

The Yemeni opposition parties maintain their own newspapers to propagate their policies. The Reform (Islah) Party, that has been part of a coalition government and also outside it in opposition, maintains the weekly newspaper *al-Sahwa* (The Awakening), that carries its official views including some Islamist editorials, and it sells perhaps 20,000 copies because party members buy it. The Yemeni Socialist Party (YSP) was established in 1979 in Aden as a merger of several southern parties, and claims to represent southern interests broadly in unified Yemen. It publishes *al-Thawri* (The Revolutionary) as a YSP organ. The Union of Popular Forces (al-Ittihad al-Quwa al-Sha'bia) headed by Ibrahim al-Wazir since its establishment in 1959, calls itself a nationalist, democratic, and Islamic party. It publishes the newspaper *al-Shura* (The Consultation), and it is one of the largest-circulation papers with up to 20,000 copies sold. The Nasserite Popular Unionist Organization (Tanzim al-Wahdawi al-Sha'bi al-Nassiri) was established in Taiz in 1965, and it publishes the weekly newspaper *al-Wahdawi* (The Unionist). The former Endowments Minister Ahmad al-Shami, who established the Party of Truth (Hizb al-Haq) as a rival to the Islah Party, established the newspaper *al-Umma* (The Nation) to disseminate his views, and it also tends to feature religious writers.

The Yemeni Unionist Gathering Party (al-Tajammu' al-Yamani al-Wahdawi), founded by Omar al-Jawi, publishes *al-Tajammu'* (The Gathering) newspaper. There are two Ba'athi newspapers. The Ba'th Party, which originated in Damascus in the 1940s, emerged in both Yemens in the 1950s, and in the south it published the newspaper *al-Ba'th*, but that disappeared and Ba'athi views are represented in unified Yemen by *al-Jamahir* (the Masses) and *al-Ihya'* (The Revival) newspapers. The former is published by a party headed by Abdal Wahab Mahmud and is supportive of the government, while the latter is the organ of an opposition party led by Qasim Salam.[26] The Connection (Rabita) Party publishes the newspaper *al-Haq* (The Truth). The Sanaa weekly *al-Ra'y* (Opinion) is published by the League of Sons of Yemen party (Rabita Ibna al-Yemen), an opposition party that emerged in 1990 as successor party established in Aden in 1951 under the name League of the Sons of the South, which had existed in Aden since 1951.

There are also several privately owned Yemeni newspapers. One of them is the independent paper *al-Ayam* (The Days), that was established in Aden before unification and is now owned by the son of the founder, Hisham Bashraeel of the Liberation Party (Hizb al-Tahrir). *Al-Ayam* is a popular nongovernment newspaper which enjoys the largest circulation of any paper, and which the government closes periodically but it is widely read. *The Yemen Times* was established by Dr. Abdalaziz Saqqaf, a Western-educated university economics professor. He periodically wrote editorials critical even of the army and the president, and his readership included most of the foreign embassies and the Western community. After he died in an accident in June 1999, his son Walid continued the newspaper but it lost some of its editorial edge. Other private, independent newspapers include *al-Sharmu'* (The Candles), *al-Usbu'* (The Week), *al-Tariq* (The

Path), *al-Balagh* (The Message), the conservative *al-Ra'y al-Aam* (Public Opinion), the progovernment but independent papers *al-Masar* (The Road) and *al-Wahda* (Unity), and the progovernment trade unionist paper *Sawt al-Ummal* (Voice of the Workers).

Criticism and Government Restrictions

In Kuwait, the press tends not to go as far as the press in Lebanon in its attacks on the government. The Kuwaiti press is forbidden by law from criticizing the ruler (amir) or quoting him without authorization, and it may not publish information which would "affect the value of the national currency or create misgivings about the Kuwaiti economy," advocate the overthrow of the government by force, publish official secrets, harm public morality, slander, belittle religion, or defame individuals.[27] In practice, newspapers publish criticisms on most social, economic, and political issues. They frequently criticize government policies and officials, including the Crown Prince who is also the prime minister. The only subjects they always avoid are the amir and attacks on Islam.

The 1962 Kuwaiti constitution provides for freedom of the press, printing and publishing "in accordance with the conditions and manner specified by law." Citizens criticize their government in private, but journalists practice some self-censorship. Several laws empower the government to impose restrictions on freedom of the press. The Press Law prohibits the publication of any direct criticism of the amir, government official communications with other states, and material that serves to "attack religions" or "incites people to commit crimes, creates hatred, or spreads the dissension among the populace." The Information Ministry practices informal censorship by pressuring individuals who they believed crossed the line. Also, the General Organization of Printing and Publishing controls all Kuwaiti printing, publishing, and distribution of print materials.[28]

The Kuwaiti press has considerable freedom to criticize. Between the press law amendments of 1972 and 1976, the government could not take direct action to suspend a newspaper that broke the rules but could only take it to court; in practice this is a long drawn-out process that reduced the number of governmental actions and gave the press additional freedom. For example, in June 1999 a number of party and independent weeklies strongly criticized the government for corruption, inflation, and election fraud.[29]

The August 1976 Kuwaiti press law amendment gave the government the power to suspend or cancel a newspaper (a) which served "the interest of a foreign state or organization," (b) which "obtained any sort of assistance from a foreign state," or (c) if "its policy contradicts the national interest." The Prime Minister explained that "with unlimited freedom the press became irresponsible. . . . Giving it freedom without controls have made some papers obedient instruments in the service of objectives alien to our country, which work to corrupt society, propagate self-interested rumors, and sow trivialities and sedition among our ranks."[30] The government issued a press law in 1985 and a statement on the press in July 1986, which broadened media restrictions and censorship somewhat—for example, establishing a vague prohibition on "incitement of hatred among the people."

The Kuwaiti government used this new authority to take action against newspapers for certain controversial editorials and so news items that have political significance. But as a rule the actions are relatively mild, involving brief suspensions by the Information Minister for less than three months rather than longer suspensions or cancellations which the Council of Ministers was empowered to order. Precensorship is not used except in a national emergency such as the 1967 war, and censorship of imported print materials is as rare as it is in Lebanon. The Kuwaiti press continues to challenge the regime and the government's primary means of influence is persuasion.

A 1988 Amiri decree, issued when the national assembly was dissolved, gave ministers discretion to treat as state secrets practically all documents that were not officially declassified, and journalists who revealed their contents could be criminally prosecuted. Article 111 of the Kuwaiti Penal Code provides for one year in jail for disseminating opinions that include sarcasm, contempt, or the belittling of religion. Article 204 provides for three years in jail or a 3,000 dinar fine for printing anything immoral.

In order to begin publishing a newspaper in Kuwait, publishers must obtain licenses from the Information Ministry. They may lose the license if the publication does not appear for six months. In 1992 the Kuwaiti government rescinded the 1986 decrees that provided for prepublication censorship. With that, the Kuwaiti press became its own censor, subject to government legal action. In 1993 for example, the government sometimes used the law to punish the press. But the press exercised some independence, for example, in 1993 the Attorney general ordered the press not to report on financial scandals, but the press wrote editorials denouncing the ban and violators of the ban were not punished. But in 1993 the Kuwaiti press criticized senior officials, including the Prime Minister, and the ministers of defense and interior, all of whom are members of the ruling family, without being punished.

The Kuwaiti courts often play a role. The constitution says "judges shall not be subject to any authority" and although they are appointed by the amir, they sometimes strike down punitive sentences, for example, several times in 1999.[31]

In Morocco, too, the press enjoys some freedom to criticize the government and the politically powerful. The Moroccan constitution provides for freedom of expression, and in fact newspapers representing a spectrum of views from socialist to nationalist to Islamist do publish rather freely.

Since 1956, when Morocco gained its independence and colonial controls on the press by France and Spain were lifted, the Moroccan newspapers have as a whole shown a consistent willingness to criticize and debate the issues. The government has not always tolerated this criticism and from time to time has used various legal and political means against individual newspapers. Each time, these measures evoke protests from the editors and publishers in question, so there has been a kind of ongoing tug-of-war over how far the press can and should go. Moroccan press laws provide for fines and prison terms for offenses against the royal family, the public peace, the morale and unity of the armed forces and police, and external security.

A 1958 decree, which is still valid, gives the Moroccan government the authority to license the press. Article 55 of the Press Code empowers the government to order newspapers not to report on specific items. The Moroccan Press Code allows the government to censor newspapers directly by ordering them not to report on specific items or events. The government in the past influenced the press through guidance issued by the Interior Minister but the government tolerates strong editorial criticism in the party dailies. Law and tradition prohibit criticism of three topics: the monarchy, sanctity of Islam, and Morocco's claim to the Western Sahara, although in October and November 1999 several leading journals published articles critical of the government's past handling of the Western Sahara.[32]

The competition between the Moroccan government and opposition newspapers increased during the political crises of the 1960s. Some papers were vehemently critical of government policies and officials, but the government made regular use of its authority to seize and censor individual papers. The suspension of the Istiqlal daily *la Nation Africaine* in February 1965 for publishing an antimonarchical quotation from a nineteenth-century Egyptian philosopher led to a parliamentary crisis and an amendment to the press code canceling the government's power to suspend or ban a newspaper, but this in turn sparked the king's decision to take personal control of the government in June. The "state of exception" was lifted in July 1970, but the government continued to act against the opposition press with suspensions and arrests of editors. Most Moroccan journalists however welcomed the government's suppression in 1971 of the French-owned Mas Group newspapers. The Mas dailies *La Virgie Marocaine* and *Le Petit Marocain* had survived the transition to independence, and their circulations were three to four times that of next leading daily, *al-Alam*, because of the quality of journalism and objectivity of news coverage. The Mas Group papers had consistently opposed independence before 1955, and had even called for the deposition of Sultan Muhammad V, applauding his exile in 1953. But just before his return in 1955 they suddenly switched sides and supported him. After independence, they avoided all political involvement and fulfilled a strict information function; because of this and the relatively smooth transition to independence, they were able to continue publishing.

Their continuation was, however, an irritant to many Moroccans, especially to the opposition Istiqlal and other political groups that resented this "foreign press" succeeding in their country. The press code of 1958 required, at the request of the Istiqlal, that all papers had to be controlled by Moroccan nationals, but the government did not enforce this rule against the Mas papers. In 1963, the National Press Union filed suit against the Mas papers, and the court agreed that they were being published illegally, but levied only a small fine against them. An Istiqlal attempt to pass a law against them in June 1965 was diverted by the government's "state of exception."[33] Finally, on October 7, 1971, the government revoked the licenses of the two Mas Group dailies, and by November 1, *le Matin* and *Maroc Soir* appeared to take their places. The new papers were published by the staffs of their predecessors, but new Moroccan chief editors were installed to take full responsibility for editorial decisions.[34]

Government actions suspending newspapers briefly for specific violations of the press law continued, and at times became a frequent occurrence for such opposition dailies as *l'Opinion* and *al-Ittihad al-Ishtiraki* and its predecessor, *al-Muharrir*. But the papers do not tire of continually testing how far they can go, and in the process considerable open debate on issues takes place.

The Moroccan government owns the daily *al-Anba,* and the official press agency MAP. The government supports two semiofficial dailies, *Le Matin* in French and *al-Sahra* in Arabic. Also the government provides subsidies through price supports for newsprint. A 1958 decree gives the government the licensing authority for print media. The Press Code allows the Interior Minister to confiscate publications the government deems offensive, and the Prime Minister may order indefinite suspension of a publication. A publication deemed a threat to state security can be seized and the publisher's license suspended. The Interior Minister can seize foreign publications but he did not do so in 1998 or 1999. In 1999 the government did not use its licensing authority but the press censored itself.

The Moroccan government has from time to time taken action against individual publications for what they have printed. For example, in 1996 the OADP daily *Anoual* was seized twice, the weekly magazine *Maroc Hebdo* was sued for defamation because of its reports implicating high level Moroccans in drug trafficking. In November 1996 the government banned the weekly *al-Usbu' al-Sahafi wa al-Siyaasi* indefinitely, apparently for a series of articles on the sons of the Prime Minister. In 1997 *al-Usbu' al-Siyaasi* was banned for libel but resumed publication in March 1998 as *al-Usbu'.* In May, 2000 the government banned two weekly magazines, *Le Journal* and its sister *al-Sahafa.* Since 1998 these two papers had become the most daring of Morocco's independent newspapers and they became very popular, running articles criticizing the Interior Minister ("Bahri Must Go") and publishing interviews with Polisario opposition leaders.

Muhammad Masiri, Minister of Communications, said there was no place for publicity for the Polisario because Morocco was at war.[35]

Yemen

In Yemen, the opposition party newspapers that emerged in 1990 and afterwards, and many of the independent ones, tend to publish reports and editorials consistently critical of the government, directly and indirectly. The new liberal press policy quickly became clear when newspapers even raised questions about presidential bribes and the writers went unpunished.[36] Criticism of government bureaucrats became commonplace. Only the most sensitive issues were treated with caution.

The Yemeni Law on Press and Publications of December 1990 guarantees to every citizen, party, organization, and ministry the right to publish newspapers, but it prohibits the denigrating of Islam or other faiths, publishing state secrets, causing tribal or sectarian discrimination, spreading ideas against the Yemeni revolution, libel, "spreading chaos or confusion," incitement to violence, and criticism of the head of state unless the criticism is "constructive," without further defining all the terms. It allows seizure or closure of newspapers but only with due process before the courts.[37] The government issued additional press regulations in 1998 that require newspapers to be licensed and to have a working capital of at least YR 700,000 (then equal to $4,375), in order to put some limits on the establishment of newspapers. The government in practice has retained and used its authority to influence the press, through legal means involving the courts, and sometimes has used extra-legal means including harassment and intimidation by security officials. A Special Media Court was created to hear cases brought against journalists. In addition, journalists sometimes censor themselves, for example in writing about subjects they know are sensitive, such as official corruption, or relations with Saudi Arabia and other foreign countries.[38]

For example, articles critical of Saudi Arabia led to the closure from December 1998 until May 1999 of the independent weekly paper *al-Ra'y al-Aam,* and then to the detention for six days in August 1999 of the editor of *al-Wahdawi* newspaper. An article on corruption and President Salih led to the suspension in February 1999 of the newspaper *al-Shura,* organ of the Islamist opposition party Union of Popular Forces, a case went through the court system for months. A report that Yemen had given the U.S. a military base on Socotra led to the incarceration in March 1999 for four days of the chief editor of *al-Haq,* the organ of the opposition Rabita party. Articles saying that northerners unfairly controlled the south led to a court case and fines and suspended jail time in May 1999, for the chief editor and a journalist at the Aden weekly *al-Ayam.* The system however has also protected journalists, for example although the government brought a case against the opposition newspaper *al-Shura* in 1995 for

slander against a leader of the Islah party, and the court ordered the newspaper closed and journalists flogged, the Justice Ministry suspended the
sentence and the case was settled amicably with an apology. When *al-
Ayam* in August 1999 published an interview with Abu Hamza al-Masri, a
Yemeni in London convicted in absentia for terrorism, its chief editor was
charged with a crime of publishing false information instigating terrorism.
An article in *al-Ayam* in February 2000 about government demolishing a
nineteenth-century synagogue in Aden led to the arrest of the editor for
instigating "sectarian feuds."[39]

WHAT CAUSES DIVERSITY AND RELATIVE FREEDOM?

What are the reasons behind the diversity and relative degree of freedom
in the Kuwaiti, Moroccan, and Yemeni print media? The newspapers tend
to be owned by active, ambitious men, who see the press as a means to
make their voices heard and to increase their political and economic power.

In Kuwait, *al-Ray al-Aam* is a family run paper, published and edited by
a prominent Kuwaiti who headed the foreign affairs committee of parliament until its abolition in 1976. *Al-Anba'* and *al-Qabas* were founded by
leading groups of Kuwaiti businessmen who had ties with different families and sectors of society. *Al-Watan* is owned by a group of wealthy land-
lords and contractors, while *al-Siyasa* is run by a young journalist with
excellent connections in Kuwaiti and some foreign government circles. All
of these people have a personal stake in their newspapers so the orientation and style of a paper is influenced by their personalities.

In Morocco, too, individuals with political interests feel they gain by the
promotion of their ideas through their newspapers. The clearest examples of
this are *al-Alam* and *l'Opinion*, the two Istiqlal Party newspapers. The chief
editor of *al-Alam* is a central committee member of the Istiqlal, Abdel Karim
Ghallab, who has quite distinct political views and ambitions. He is one of
Morocco's best journalists and at the same time a leading opposition politician. The chief editor of *l'Opinion* is also an Istiqlal politician. Both of them
use the papers to reach Istiqlal Party members with political opinions and
analyses. Similarly, the daily *le Matin* is run by Moulay (prince) Ahmed
Alawi, a cousin of the King; it clearly reflects his monarchist, loyalist views,
representing an obvious political counterbalance to the political attitudes
conveyed in the Istiqlal papers. Finally, the newspapers *al-Ittihad al-Ishtiraki*
and *al-Bayan,* too, are in effect used by their chief editors as political outlets
for their own partisan views. The two parties which back them, the USFP
and the PPS, respectively, have been restricted in their activities by the government, so the chief editors are even more anxious to exploit their newspapers as channels for political expression.

In Yemen, since 1990 when the country was unified and parliamentary
elections and political parties were permitted for the first time, newspapers

affiliated with parties or owned by individuals were allowed to appear. When they emerged, they represented a wide variety of viewpoints. Some did not survive, and many were nondailies, but a diverse spectrum of views remained.

Secondly, the political system in the country is such that this open competition and rivalry is possible. In Kuwait, for example, the National Assembly is elected, but it is not a fully representative democratic institution, although it has held vigorous debates on sensitive issues and publicly expressed considerable criticism of government policy. Not only were the major merchant families well represented but the leftists, trade unionists, and the Arab nationalists had articulate spokesmen there whose views were amplified in the press. The Kuwaiti government still retains considerable authority, but it diminished over the years as the parliament became stronger and more outspoken, enhancing press freedom. This trend was set back in 1976 with the abolition of parliament and promulgation of a stricter press law, but it resumed when the Kuwaiti elected parliament was restored in 1991 and became a major locus of vigorous policy debates and criticism of the government.

In Morocco, too, the political system helps make press diversity and competition possible. This system allows a degree of political competition to prevail in the open. The Moroccan print media system is not a completely open system like the Lebanese, but there has been a clearly defined political spectrum in Morocco since independence in 1956. At that time, Sultan Muhamed V recovered full sovereign powers in treaties with the French and Spanish, but he set up a government containing representatives of a number of different parties including the Istiqlal and the Democratic Independent Party. Since the parties were legitimate and open, it was natural that newspapers emerged reflecting their diverse views. Journalism in Morocco had begun in the nineteenth century but it had taken on a strong nationalistic political tone in the 1930s when nationalist leaders tried to use the press against the colonial French. After independence the papers were regarded as political tools. One observer puts it this way: "As newspapers were considered the very heart of politics, representatives of every political tendency attempted to publish at least one, and sometimes two or three papers in Arabic to advance the views of their leaders."

The Istiqlal in Morocco maintained its position as the loyal opposition, but it was unable to dominate the nationalist movement. The Communist Party and some other small ones such as the Popular Movement were also active, as were several trade union organizations and most of these groups sponsored newspapers. The Communist Party was outlawed in 1959, but much of its leadership and membership was later allowed to join together in the so-called Party of Progress and Socialism that came out with a new Marxist-oriented newspaper. The government and its supporters also promote newspapers.

Thus several political groups compete for power under the watchful eye of the king, who has periodically allowed general elections and the formation of parliaments. Although the political process in Morocco sometimes is paralyzed by the variety of interest groups and parties, observers agree that the diversity is based on the underlying political competition that takes place in the system.

In Yemen, the fact that print media emerged along with elections and political parties, and at the same time North-South unity combined two very different political systems, led to a very diverse press. Newspapers supported by southerners tended to have a pro-socialist and south-oriented approach while Northern papers tended to be more conservative and focus on Northern issues.

The third factor behind the Kuwaiti and Moroccan systems is governmental sensitivity to its international position, that seems to make it more tolerant of a lively and diverse press.

In Kuwait the government is quite conscious of the fact that the country is a very small state surrounded by larger and more powerful neighbors, and even the resident population of the country is more than half non-Kuwaiti. As a consequence, the government has adopted a circumspect policy of cooperation with everyone and toleration of virtually all important political movements in the area. The fact that every newspaper has non-Kuwaitis in influential positions (usually Kuwaiti journalists are in the minority) reinforces the toleration of diverse viewpoints. Also, both the government and members of parliament like to point with pride at the country's free and vigorous press.

The Moroccan government, too, is sensitive to foreign opinion. Many Moroccan leaders including the king support the continuation of press freedom partly because the press is free in Europe, and the European countries, particularly France, are still looked upon as models to be emulated in many ways. Despite the nationalist anticolonial hostility directed against France in the 1950s, the influence of French culture is still strong in Morocco and this is one manifestation of that phenomenon. It must be added, however, that the Moroccan press has not lived up to the expectations of the Francophile elite that support press freedom, so many educated Moroccans still prefer to read *le Monde* or other French newspapers.

The Yemeni government found itself isolated regionally and internationally in 1990, just at the time of unification, when it supported Iraq in the crisis over Kuwait while most Arab states and the West were in confrontation with Iraq. At the same time, the Soviet Union, which had been South Yemen's main patron, collapsed and that support ended. Since 1990, Yemen has sought to gain assistance for its economy, which has considerable needs, by arguing that its development of democracy and freedom deserve to be supported.

Thus the press systems in Lebanon, Kuwait, and Morocco have a degree of diversity and freedom that set them apart from the other press systems in the Arab world. There are significant differences among these three systems; the Lebanese press (in normal times) exercises considerable self-regulation and is relatively free from government control, while the Kuwaiti and Moroccan newspapers operate within stricter boundaries. Nevertheless they all reflect a political diversity and a degree of open debate in the political system itself which make press diversity and freedom possible.

THE IRAQI PRESS

Iraq after the fall of Saddam Hussain's regime in the Spring of 2003 is a special case. Although as of 2004 it is still subject to change because of the unusual circumstances of its political development, it does show many of the characteristics of the diverse type of print media (for radio and television, see Chapter 10).

Post-Saddam Iraq

The American-led military attack on Iraq that began on March 20, 2003, led in April to the collapse of Saddam Hussein's regime and his control over the Iraqi media. The American-British occupation authorities, who then took control of the country, permitted Iraqis to publish newspapers. The occupiers, calling themselves the "Coalition Provisional Authority" (CPA) led by Ambassador L. Paul Bremer, abolished Saddam's Information Ministry, sacking more than five thousand employees who had worked there, and they created the "Iraqi Media Network" that was an interim body to replace it, controlled by the occupiers. Generally speaking the media environment was quite free and totally different from what had prevailed under Saddam, although the CPA did set some rules. They prohibited incitement to violence against U.S.-British forces and incitement to ethnic or religious hatred. It required all media to obtain CPA licenses, that could be cancelled for "promoting civil disorder, rioting, or damage to property," advocating support of the Ba'th Party, or putting out news that is "patently false and calculated to promote opposition to the CPA."[40] In July 2003 for example, Iraqi police closed *al-Mustaqilla* newspaper and arrested its managing editor for publishing an article headed "Death to all Spies and those who cooperate with them; killing them is a religious duty."[41]

The print media suddenly were transformed from a mobilization into a transitional system. New newspapers appeared everywhere. By mid-July observers counted more than one hundred different papers in Arabic, plus a dozen in Kurdish, although only a few of them appeared on a daily basis and most were weeklies. Ownership and sponsorship of the newspapers was diverse. Nearly half identified themselves as official organs of political or religious groups. For example, the Supreme Council for the Islamic Revolution in Iraq, a leading Shia group that had opposed Saddam from a safe haven in Iran published *al-Adala* (Justice) and *Nahrayn* (Two Rivers); the Iraqi National Congress headed by returned exile Ahmad Chalaby published *al-Jamahir* (The Masses) and *al-Mazwsil* (Mosul); the pro-Shia Islamic Da'wah Party published *al-Bayan* (The Dispatch) and *al-Da'wa* (The Call); the Sunni-led Iraqi Unified National Movement published *al-Sa'a* (The Hour); and there were several simply religious-oriented papers. The two main Kurdish parties that had operated freely in the North during the 1990s, the Kurdish Democratic Party and the Patriotic Union of Kurdistan, began distributing their Arabic and Kurdish newspapers all over the country. But the vast majority of the new papers claimed to be independent. There were no Iraqi government publications early in the occupation because there were no independent Iraqi authorities, but the U.S.-British authorities, exercising governmental powers, sponsored their own Arabic newspaper, *al-Sabah* (The Morning), to disseminate their views.[42]

The occupation authorities from the beginning made clear that they were determined to establish a democratic political system and a free press, and Iraqi leaders echoed those desires. Iraq's pluralistic society with multiple ethnic and religious divisions made a diverse press natural as long as the central government allowed it. The occupation authorities insisted their control of the country was temporary. As of 2004 therefore, the print media, reflecting the underlying political system, fit quite well into the diverse category.

NOTES

1. *1999 World Press Freedom Review,* quoting the king's speech of July 30, 1999.

2. U.S. Department of State, *1999 Country Reports on Human Rights Practices,* Yemen section, Febuary 25, 2000.

3. Mahmoud M. Hammoud and Walid A. Afifi, "Lebanon" in Yahya R. Kamalipour and Hamid Mowlana, Eds., *Mass Media in the Middle East: A Comprehensive Handbook,* Westport, CT: Greenwood Press, 1994, pp. 163, 170.

4. *Al-Nahar,* December 1, 1974, p. 3, quoting Minister Majid Hamadah and Syndicate President Riad Taha.

5. These figures and the political and religious orientations of the tables were given to the author by independent, qualified observers in 1974, 1975, and 2001.

6. Nabil H. Dajani, "The Press in Lebanon," Gazette 17 (3), 1971 pp. 163–67; Ghassan Tueni, *Freedom of the Press in a Developing Society* (Beirut: al Nahar, 1971), pp. 5–8.

7. Dajani, "The Press in Lebanon," op. cit., pp. 157–58.

8. Dajani, "The Press in Lebanon," pp. 59, 159.

9. *Journalism Quarterly* 43 (3) (Autumn 1966): 513; and Dajani, "The Press in Lebanon," p. 161.

10. On January 31, 1976, the offices of *al-Muharrir* and *Bayrut* were attacked by a large force, apparently of the Syrian-backed Palestinian group, Saiqa.

Al-Muharrir Chief Editor Shublaq and *Bayrut* Deputy Chief Editor 'Amir died as a result of the attack.

11. *Arab Report and Record,* January 1–15, 1977, p. 9; Prime Minister's announcement of January 2, 1977. Prime Minister's statement of January 3, 1977. Prime Ministers statement, Beirut Radio, 1200 GMT, January 2, 1977, FBIS, January 3, 1977, p. C-2.

12. Interview with Lebanese editor, Beirut, June 16, 2001.

13. For example in May 2001, the Lebanese government issued a warrant for the arrest of journalist Raghida Dergham, based in New York, for participating in a panel discussion with an Israeli official. *Mid-East Realities Bulletin,* June 11, 2001.

14. The ad was placed in the tribune by the pro-Israeli American Anti-Defamation League (ADL). Jim Quilty, "The Wrong Kind of Message," *Middle East International,* April 19, 2002.

15. Interviews with journalists and editors in Lebanon, June 2001.

16. Magda Abu Fadl, "Setting Trends," IPI Report, first quarter of 1999, p. 22.

17. Interview, Prof. Mahmoud Tarabay, Lebanese American University, June 15, 2001.

18. Circulation figures are from informed observers, and are the best obtainable, but they should be considered estimates. Other data is from interviews and from Mruwa, *Al-Sahafa,* pp. 403–405, and USIA "Media Directories" for Kuwait, and private communications.

19. Interview with Wafa'i Diab, Deputy Chief Editor, *al-Anba,* May 29, 2002.

20. Interview with informed observers in Rabat, January 18, 2001.

21. Moroccan Press Distribution Agency (SAPRESS), January 2003, reported by MAP January 2, 2003, for most figures, and U.S. Embassy Rabat, Morocco Media Directory, January 2003.

22. For example Youssefi suspended two opposition papers on December 3, 2000, but after a public outcry reinstated them January 19, 2001; *Middle East International,* January 26, 2001, p. 14.

23. U.S. Embassy Rabat, Morocco Media Directory, January 2003.

24. Moroccan Press Distribution Agency (SAPRESS), January 2003, reported by MAP January 2, 2003, for most figures, and U.S. Embassy Rabat, Morocco Media Directory, January 2003.

25. Information from interviews in Yemen, June 1999, and U.S. Department of State, *1999 Country Reports on Human Rights Practices,* Yemen section, Febuary 25, 2000. In 1999 a second *al-Shura* newspaper appeared because of an ideological split in the UPF party, but the courts decided that only one could use that name.

26. Interview with Dr. Muhammad Mutawakkil, Sanaa, June 29, 1999.

27. Law No. 3 of 1961 on printing and publishing (Qanun al-Matbuat wa al-Nashr) amending Kuwait's first publishing law of 1957.

28. U.S. Department of State, *1999 Country Reports on Human Rights Practices,* Kuwait section, Febuary 25, 2000.

29. *Al-Shura, al-Sahwa, al-Ra'y al-Aam,* and *al-Wahdawi,* June, 17, 20, 22 and 22, respectively.

30. Radio and TV address to the nation, August 31, 1976, by Prime Minister Jabir al-Ahmad al-Sabah, FBIS, September 1, 1976, p. C-1.

31. U.S. Department of State, *1998 and 1999 Country Reports on Human Rights Practices,* Kuwait sections, Febuary 26, 1999 and Febuary 25, 2000, respectively.

32. U.S. Department of State, *1999 Country Reports on Human Rights Practices*, Morocco section, Febuary 25, 2000.

33. *Le Monde Diplomatique*, Paris, January 1972.

34. Al Alam, October 8, November 2, 1971. A Spanish daily was also taken cover and a new Moroccan daily in Spanish, *Actualidad*, appeared in its place.

35. U.S. Department of State, *1996 and 1998 Country Reports on Human Rights Practices*, Morocco section, January 30, 1997 and Febuary 26, 1999; *Middle East International*, May 5, 2000, pp. 6–7; and Marvine Howe, "Fresh Start for Morocco," *Middle East Policy*, vol. VIII, no. 2, June 2001, p. 61.

36. Abdalaziz Saqqaf editorial, *Yemen Times*, 1991.

37. Law No. 25 of December 22, 1990.

38. U.S. Department of State, *1999 Country Reports on Human Rights Practices*, Yemen section, February 25, 2000.

39. U.S. Department of State, *1999 Country Reports on Human Rights Practices*, Yemen section, February 25, 2000; Committee to Protect Journalists, New York, statements August 1999 and May 15, 2000.

40. Bremer's Orders No. 6 and 7 of June 2003, cited in Reporters Without Borders, "The Iraqi Media Three Months After the War: A New But Fragile Freedom," Report, July 22, 2003 (http://www.rsf.fr). By the end of July the restrictions had been used only twice, to close a radio station and a newspaper.

41. *Hartford Courant*, August 4, 2003.

42. BBC Monitoring Media Services, "Iraq: The Media in Post-war Iraq," July 15, 2003 (http://www.ifj.org). This report contains lists of newspapers being published as of July 15, 2003.

6

The "Transitional" System of Print Media: Egypt, Jordan, Tunisia, and Algeria

By the beginning of the twenty-first century, four Arab countries—Egypt, Jordan, Tunisia and Algeria—had developed what could be called a "transitional" system for their print media. It is transitional because it has undergone steady change for more than a decade, and because the system itself still remains under debate, and appears to be unsettled. It is a rather complex system that contains strong elements favoring governmental controls over the press, alongside elements that provide some measure of freedom of expression and diversity. Some of the newspapers are owned by the government, others by the private sector and by political parties. The former, "national newspapers," tend to have larger circulations and more influence on the public debate than the latter, however. Also, although the constitution speaks about free speech and press, there are many laws on the books which give the government the power to take action against newspapers and journalists for what they publish. It is in fact characteristic of these systems that cases involving journalists are frequently brought to court. The government also has leverage over the print media through economic means. The government does not hesitate to use these powers, but the powers are generally based on laws passed by elected parliaments, or legal decrees.

OWNERSHIP

Ownership of the print media in these four countries is in several hands. The government has ownership in some of the key newspapers and magazines, either full ownership or controlling interests. Other newspapers are privately owned, either by individuals or by groups of private individuals.

Still others are owned by political parties, which are legal in all of these countries. The party papers openly express the official views of the sponsoring party, including views opposed to the government, through their editorials and the news play. In all of these four countries, there are distinct differences among the political parties and these views to a large extent can be expressed in the print media. Differences find their way into print even though the means of expression vary among the four countries.

In Egypt, for example, ownership of the so-called "national press" including the largest circulation dailies, is in the hands of the Supreme Press Council (SPC) and the Shura (consultative) Council (upper house of parliament). The Shura Council, established in 1980, legally owns the national press, and the SPC, established in 1975, has the authority to issue licenses to publish and to practice journalism. Both councils are in effect controlled by the regime's political party, and the president ultimately has the ability to appoint their chief editors. The national publishing houses also put out weekly and monthly publications, many of which are quite influential, such as *al-Musawwar, Akhir Sa'a, Rose al-Yusif,* and *Sabah al-Khair,* as well as *al-Ahram Iqtisadi* and *al-Ahram Duwali.* The Egyptian constitution allows ownership by public or private legal entities, political parties or corporate bodies, although no individual may own more than ten percent of the shares of a publication. A 1998 law requires that papers managed by joint stock companies have the prime minister's approval. However, Egyptian law also allows political parties to publish newspapers, and as of 2003 five of the sixteen legal parties had their own papers. The daily *al-Wafd* speaks for the Wafd Party, while the weeklies *al-Ahali, al-Ahrar, al-Arabi,* and *Mayo* speak for the leftist Tagammu', Liberal, Nasserite, and ruling National Democratic Parties, respectively. Although avowedly Islamist political parties like the Muslim Brotherhood are illegal, Islamist political views have been expressed regularly through *al-Shaab,* the newspaper of the opposition Labor Party, which however as of 2003 was suspended. Thus the main opposition political parties have vehicles from with which they propagate their views and criticize the government.

In Algeria, since the 1990 Information Law, ownership of newspapers by political parties and private individuals has been permitted, and only slightly restricted. Islamist parties are allowed to exist in Algeria, although they are not permitted to own newspapers directly, and they must express their views through the independent papers. In 2003, the government owned four daily newspapers, two in Arabic and two in French. Two independent dailies in French were close to the government. Three independent dailies, two in Arabic and one in French, were pro-Islamist, and one independent French daily was antiIslamist. The rest were independent, some with various connections.

In Jordan, the law allows private and party ownership but requires that owners be Jordanian nationals. The Jordanian government holds controlling

TABLE 6.1   The Transitional Press: Major Daily Newspapers[2]

	Estimated circulations		First published
	In 2003	In 1985	
Jordan			
Al-Dustur (The Constitution)	90,000	40,000	1967
Al-Ra'i (Opinion)	90,000	45,000	1971
The Jordan Times*	10,000	7,000	1975
Al-Arab al-Yawm (Arab Today)	30,000	0	1996
Tunisia			
Al-Shuruq (The East)	80,000	50,000	1985
Al-Sabah (Morning)	65,000	46,000	1951
Al-Hurriyya (Freedom) (formerly Al-Amal)	50,000	15,000	1934
Le Renouveau† (formerly L'Action)	33,000	13,500	1932
La Presse†	42,000	15,000	1934
Le Temps†	25,000	19,000	1975
Al-Sahafa (The Press)	18,000	0	1989
Le Quotidien†	15,000	0	2001
Egypt			
Al-Akhbar (The News)	700,000	650,000	1952
Al-Ahram (The Pyramids)	700,000	550,000	1875
Al-Gumhuriya (The Republic)	400,000	400,000	1953
Al-Masa' (The Evening)	350,000	50,000	1956
Al-Wafd (The Delegation)	60,000	0	1988
Ahram al-Masa'I (Evening Pyramids)	50,000	0	1990
The Egyptian Gazette*	20,000	10,000	1880
Le Journal d'Egypte†	10,000	10,000	1936
Le Progress Egyptien†	10,000	8,000	1893
Al-Alam al-Yawm (The World Today)	15,000	0	1991
Al-Ahrar (The Liberal)	5,000	NA	1977
Algeria			
Al Khabar (The News)	400,000	0	1990
Le Quotidien d'Oran†	200,000		1990s
Le Matin†	170,000		1990s
Liberte†	160,000	0	1990s
Horizons†	130,000	0	1990s
El Watan (The Nation)†	120,000	0	1990
Le Soir d'Algerie†	50,000	0	1990s
La Tribune†	40,000	0	1990s
El Moudjahid† (The Fighter)	30,000	350,000	1956
Al Bilad (The Nation)	30,000	0	1990s
Al Yawm (The Day)	30,000	0	1999
L'Authentique†	30,000	0	1990s
Le Jeune Independent†	25,000	0	1997
Sawt al Ahrar (Liberal Voice)	25,000	0	1990s
Al Sha'b (The People)	20,000	75,000	1962
La Nouvelle Republique†	15,000	0	1990s
Al Massa (The Evening)	5,000	0	1990s
Echourouk El Youmi (Eastern Daily)	NA	0	1990s

* Published in English.

† Published in French.

ownership shares in two key daily newspapers, but there are many weeklies that are owned by the political parties and private individuals. Throughout the 1990s there has been discussion in Jordan of privatization of the print media owned by the government, and this effort gathered momentum at the beginning of the twenty-first century, but as of 2003 had not succeeded (see next chapter).

In Tunisia, newspapers are owned by political parties, individuals, and the government. Since many Tunisians are bilingual, in Arabic and French, several publishers put out papers in both languages. Thus four of the eight daily papers are in Arabic and four are in French, and there are several bilingual weekly news magazines. Two sister dailies, *al-Hurriyya* and *Le Renouveau,* are organs of the ruling Democratic Constitutional Rally party (RCD) which finances them in part, and RCD members occupy key positions on their editorial staffs as well as their boards of directors. (When these two papers were founded before independence they were named *al-Amal* and *l'Action,* respectively, and in 1988 they changed their names.) Two other sister newspapers, *La Presse* and *al-Sahafa* are also controlled by the regime. In addition, there are four independent dailies: the sister papers *al-Sabah* and *Le Temps,* and the sister papers *al-Shuruq* and the relatively new *Le Quotidien.*[1] There are two RCD weeklies, but the rest of the newspapers are nongovernmental, including five weeklies.

GOVERNMENTAL CONTROLS

Ownership does not tell the whole story. The governments in these countries have several means to exercise influence over the print media. They license newspapers and can suspend them or shut them down for what they publish. They can impose fines on newspapers and journalists. They can have journalists arrested or in some cases dismissed for what they write. They may ban them from travelling abroad. Often several different agencies of government, including the Information Ministry, the Interior Ministry, and the Defense Ministry, have authority to take action against newspapers and journalists. The governments often influence the content of the print media indirectly, or by persuasion, and journalists practice some self-censorship.

The governments have several legal means of control and influence over print media, including enforcement of taboos spelled out in the law; litigation of other legally designated offenses; economic pressure; and control over the importation of foreign print media.

In Tunisia, the government controls the movement of journalists, for example in 1996 it prevented journalists from attending a UN-sponsored conference in Yemen on freedom of the press, and in the spring of 2000 a journalist went on a hunger strike to protest his travel ban.

In Egypt, the regime influences the press in a variety of ways, through its domination of the Supreme Press Council (which licenses newspapers), the Shura Council, control over formation of new political parties, and through various laws including emergency and antiterrorism legislation. The emergency laws passed in 1967 at the time of a crisis with Israel, and antiterrorism laws passed under President Mubarak, are still on the books and they allow government censorship of the media.

Explicit Taboos

The laws in these countries include various prohibitions on freedom of expression, which give the government the authority to act against any infractions. Typically, newspapers are not permitted to incite to violence; to publish libelous attacks on individuals, especially on government officials; to insult the head of state or the head of state of a foreign country; to criticize the armed forces; or to publish security-related information without permission. Criticism in any of these taboo areas usually invites a strong government reaction in the form of a legal suit against the offending journalists and possibly also their newspaper as well.

In Egypt, under the Penal Code, journalists can be fined or imprisoned for insulting the Egyptian president, the president of a foreign country, government officials, the armed forces, or the parliament. In addition, there are provisions in emergency and antiterrorism laws which the government can use to restrict publication of news and commentary that may be considered to "disrupt social peace" and other vaguely defined acts. For example, in 2001 the authorities closed the Coptic weekly newspaper *al-Naba* for publishing a story about a priest which "undermined public order."[3]

In Jordan, private citizens can be prosecuted for slandering the royal family, the government, or foreign leaders, or for sowing sedition. The Jordanian penal code also authorizes the state to take action against anyone who incites violence, defames a head of state, disseminates "false or exaggerated information outside the country that attacks state dignity" or defames a public official.[4] Jordan's Press and Publication Law, first passed in 1953 and modified in 1955 and 1973, gives the government the authority to license all newspapers and magazines, and to withdraw the license if a publication "threatens the national existence" or security, infringes on "the constitutional principles of the kingdom," harms the "national feeling" (al-shu'ur al-qawmi), or offends "public decency" (al-adab al-amma). The law specifically forbids publication of news about the royal family unless approved by it, or articles defaming religion or contrary to public morality or unauthorized military and secret information."[5] The 1998 law gave the government powers to issue fines, withdraw licenses, and shut down newspapers. Persons accused of violating this law are tried in a special court for press and copyright cases. Religious sensitivities are also protected, for example in January 2003, the Jordanian State Security Prosecutor closed the weekly newspaper *al-Hilal* and jailed two of its editors and a reporter for allegedly defaming of the Prophet Muhammad.[6]

In Tunisia, the Press Code contains provisions prohibiting defamation and subversion but they are broadly written and not clearly defined. The Tunisian Press Code affirms freedom of the press but limits it where necessary "to protect society from anything injurious to tranquillity, security, and public order," and "to protect the state and the constituted agencies of government against anything liable to cause foreign or domestic disorders."[7]

In Algeria, a 1990 law stipulates that freedom of speech must respect "individual dignity, imperatives of foreign policy and the national defense," and a 1999 decree requires that independent newspapers print security information only from official sources. During the 1990s, the Algerian government suspended many newspapers because of ongoing security problems and some of them never reappeared.

Litigation

Periodically, often several times each year, the authorities arrest journalists and bring them to trial for what they write. These countries all have elected parliaments which have passed a variety of laws affecting the media, and the government freely uses these means to punish journalists who are responsible for publishing news or opinion that the government objects to seeing in print. The authorities arrest and interrogate journalists, bring some of them to trial, and impose often heavy prison sentences. Generally, the government resorts to the judicial system rather than to extra-legal means to block the expression of opinion or the publication of a story. The government does not win all of its cases against newspapers and journalists, but the act of taking them to court tends to make them somewhat more cautious next time.

Jordanian law gives the government powers to issue fines, withdraw licenses, and shut down newspapers. Persons accused of violating this law are tried in a special court for press and copyright cases. In Jordan in 1995, for example, there were twenty cases and in 1997 there were thirteen cases in the press and copyright court. However, most cases never come to trial and in 1995 only two resulted in guilty verdicts.[8] In 1998 the authorities arrested several editors and held them in prison for between four days and six months. In 1999 they made three arrests of journalists.

In Egypt, between 1996 and mid-1999, the Public Prosecutor referred 175 journalism cases to court (117 misdemeanors, 55 criminal, 3 military); 4 cases resulted in prison. The law gives the Public Prosecutor power to ban publication of news related to a case involving national security. In Egypt, the emergency law that has been on the books since 1981, authorizes prepublication censorship, confiscation of newspapers, and closing down of publications. The Egyptian Penal Code has a chapter with thirty-one articles on "crimes of the press." The Egyptian government has the power to license print media and uses it occasionally to punish publications for what they print.

Economic Pressure

The government also has the ability to exercise economic pressure on newspapers and journalists, and this has an impact. The use of advertising revenue by government agencies is one common form of inducement. Monopolistic government control of printing facilities and the import of newsprint is another. Government subsidies are sometimes granted, even to opposition newspapers that have limited financial means, making them at least somewhat dependent. Also laws requiring minimum capitalization for the establishment of a newspaper can be used to inhibit the proliferation of small publications that may be politically opposed to the government.

In Egypt, the government-controlled publishing houses have a monopoly over the printing and domestic distribution of newspapers, including those of the opposition. The Supreme Press Council, which the regime also controls, has influence over newsprint and advertising distribution. The authorities occasionally use these powers to restrict free expression. To cite one example, in 1998 the government withdrew printing access for the Arabic weekly newspaper *al-Dustur,* which was operating under a license from Cyprus but being printed in an Egyptian government printing facility, and the paper ceased to exist, because of articles about religious strife. *Al-Dustur* had started publishing on December 13, 1996 and was confiscated twice 1996–1998, and was frequently censored, and it had a circulation almost as large as *al-Akhbar.*

In Tunisia the print media have periodically faced financial difficulties which make them vulnerable to government pressures. For example, in 1993, when a Tunisian news magazine published an article showing the country in a negative light, the government withdrew its advertising as a punishment.

In Algeria, the government exercises financial influence in one way through its monopoly on newsprint imports, and ownership of the five main printing companies, plus a ban on private presses, all of which constitutes leverage over newspapers which it occasionally uses. Newsprint imports are controlled by the state-owned company l'Algerienne de Papier (ALPAP), and when private groups have tried to set up presses they have been shut down. Much of the advertising in the Algerian press comes from the public sector, and for many newspapers this is a decisive factor for their existence. For example, in 1998 *El Watan* and *Le Matin* ceased publication because of pressure by the government-owned Algerian Printing Society (Societe d'impression d'Alger, SIA) to pay their printing debts totally and immediately, despite an agreement by SIA to receive staggered payments. Journalists suspected the ultimatum resulted from publication of articles in these papers critical of the Justice Minister. In 1999 such pressure was used against the daily paper, *Demain Algerie.*[9] Also, the state-owned advertising agency ANEP was created in 1996 and it decides the allocation to media of all government advertising, which is considerable. The government uses

ANEP to place ads more in newspapers which follow government policies such as an anti-Islamist line, regardless of the price the newspaper charges for the ad.[10]

In Jordan, the government uses official advertising as leverage. For example in July 1999, when the daily *al-Arab al-Yawm* published a series critical of Prime Minister Abdal Raouf Rawabdeh and the government, the government stopped its advertisements and had the news agency Petra stop providing news to the paper.[11]

Import Restrictions

These four countries also control the import of print media published outside the country. Journalists sometimes seek to evade local restrictions by having their publications licensed and printed abroad, but they still must clear local censors when they have the newspapers or magazines sent in.

For example, Tunisia has frequently stopped the French newspaper *Le Monde* from entering the country, and at the time of the October 1999 elections, the government blocked entry for many foreign publications that were discussing the electoral process.

In Egypt, the Interior Ministry can ban foreign publications on the grounds of protecting public order. The Defense Ministry may ban reports on sensitive security issues. Also the Censorship Department of the Egyptian Information Ministry must approve the distribution in Egypt of print media published outside the country, and it uses this authority to block the import of publications it objects to.

Egyptian censors have periodically banned the London-based pan-Arab newspaper *al-Hayat*. For example it seized the paper in 1992 when it reported government failures to deal with an earthquake, in 1993 when it printed an interview with Islamist Shaikh Omar Abdalrahman, and in December 1998 for printing an interview with a leading Islamist of the Gamaa Islamia organization.

Also the Egyptian owners, of the weekly newspapers *al-Tadamun, Cairo Times,* and *Middle Eastern Times,* who failed to gain permission to publish in Egypt, decided to publish them in Cyprus and take their chances by sending them into Egypt through the censors. Most of the issues get through, although occasionally the editors are asked to delete stories or editorials which contain criticism of President Mubarak, the Egyptian military, the status of Coptic Christians, or unacceptable material on Islam.[12]

The Scope for Free Expression

Therefore there are significant governmental restrictions on the print media, and journalists practice self-censorship. The newspapers in these countries, however, still manage to display some freedom of expression and some diversity, within limits.

The Tunisian print media are lively, despite the authoritarian nature of the regime, and its close monitoring of what is published. In Algeria, for example, even during the very serious security situation that prevailed throughout most of the 1990s, and which led to restrictions on the print media, most of the opposition political parties and many private individuals continued to publish newspapers expressing a variety of views including some criticism of the government. Then toward the end of the century, as Algeria's security problems diminished, the scope for expression of opinion and printing of news increased in the print media.

Guidance

In all of these countries, the government from time to time passes guidance on content to the print media, directly or indirectly. Journalists know the government position on most key issues from official statements carried by various channels including the national news agency, which is controlled by the government. Official government news agencies have existed in all four of these countries for many years: Egypt's Middle East News Agency (MENA) started in 1956, Tunis Afrique Presse (TAP), Algerie Presse Service (APS) started in 1961, and Jordan News Agency (JNA) in 1965.

Also, government officials from time to time convey guidance informally to print media journalists. The chief editors of the government-owned newspapers typically hear from senior officials about how they would like a major issue to be portrayed in the media, an instruction they always take seriously although sometimes they fail to follow it. Officials also seek to pass guidance in various ways to nongovernment media, which are less likely to follow it but sometimes do.

Occasionally there are strong personal ties between officials and editors. The most famous example of the symbiotic relationship between an Arab leader and a journalist is that of Gamal Abdul Nasser and Muhammad Hassanain Haykal in Egypt during the 1950s and 1960s. Haykal, Chief Editor of al-Ahram, was President Nasser's confidante and by far the most influential journalist during the Nasser period. He stayed on as head of al-Ahram for three years after Nasser's death in 1970 and more than a million people inside and outside of Egypt continued to read his weekly column "Speaking Frankly" (Bisuraha). His column however increasingly reflected his disagreement with post-Nasser government policy and in February 1974, after he expressed fundamental opposition to the way Sadat had conducted the October 1973 war and to Sadat's direct appeal to the United States to solve the Arab-Israeli problem. Sadat, in his capacity as chairman of the Arab Socialist Union, removed him from al-Ahram. After that Haykal concentrated on writing books and articles for publication outside Egypt. As Sadat implemented his policy of rapprochement with the West and criticism of the Soviet Union, the influence of Nasserites, Marxists, and other leftists in the press diminished, especially in the daily newspapers. Prominent journalists who had been exiled or jailed during the Nasser period were rehabilitated and given responsible press positions. For example, Mustafa Amin, one of Egypt's leading writers, was jailed by Nasser in 1965 on charges of spying for the United States, and he and his twin brother Ali, who went into exile, were rehabilitated in January 1974. In February the government eased press restrictions.

NEWSPAPER CONTENT

What is the impact of this complex system of laws and political influences on the content of the print media, both in news play and in commentary? Does the system permit the press to express diversity of opinion, and criticism of the government, and if so to what extent? In fact there is some criticism of the government in the print media, primarily in the opposition party press, but also in the national newspapers. Unlike the loyalist or mobilization systems, there is some diversity among newspapers, reflecting their political orientation. Even government press controls are criticized. It is characteristic of the print media systems in these countries that the systems themselves have been in a constant state of adjustment in recent years and are subject to regular discussion in the political arena including the press. Unlike the countries where a truly diverse system exists, however, the print media that are progovernment tend to have larger circulations and a greater ability to influence the overall tenor of public debate.

For example, the Jordanian press has for years criticized government officials for not resolving such problems as water shortages or the failure to control inflation. Most of the negative press treatment concerns domestic issues, although occasionally it deals with foreign policy issues of a secondary nature. The Jordanian daily newspaper with the closest ties to the regime, *al-Ra'y,* tends to be more optimistic about internal issues or on the Arab-Israeli problem, and responds more quickly to the defense of Jordan in the face of foreign criticisms than other dailies, which tend to be somewhat more pessimistic, printing more news with negative overtones without becoming stridently critical. *Al-Dustur* tends to be in the latter category, although it can also print strongly progovernment views.

In Tunisia, the press does not discuss the pros and cons of very sensitive issues such as the Arab-Israeli conflict or Tunisian-American relations, but it does sometimes deal with the less vital Asian or Latin American questions. In the Bourguiba era, there was little essential difference on major stories between the PSD-owned papers and the private ones. All of them received the bulk of their news and information from the government-owned news agency, although PSD-owned papers tended to add details and vary their interpretations somewhat. Yet even then the private papers, especially the sister papers *al-Sabah* and *Le Temps,* owned by wealthy businessman Habib Cheikh-Rouhou, tended to have a slightly more aggressive style.

In Algeria, in 2003 the independent newspapers enjoyed much larger circulations than the government-owned papers. The French language daily *El Moudjahid,* founded in 1956, that had the highest circulation of any newspaper in the 1980s with well over 300,000, by 2003 had fallen to only 30,000. Three other government-owned dailies, the Arabic language *al-Sha'b* and *al-Massa,* and the French language *Horizons,* had even lower circulations. On the other hand, the six most popular newspapers, all with circulations estimated at over 100,000 each, were independent. Some independent dailies tended to have connections with special interests. For example, two of them, *al-Bilad* and *al-Yawm* tended to be sympathetic to Islamic concerns, while *Le Matin* and *Liberte,* tended to support Berber interests, and *Le Matin* was generally leftist and anti-Islamic. The daily *L'Authentique* was a nonpartisan daily owned by General Betchine. The four government-owned papers, and two small-circulation progovernment dailies, tended to defend the government consistently, but many of the other newspapers did not hesitate to criticize the government and even the president in editorials, cartoons and headlines.[13]

In Egypt, the mass-circulation "national" daily newspapers are similar in content in that they deal with almost the same news stories and treat them with similar priorities. There are, however, clear differences in journalistic style and in the types of readership addressed. *Al-Ahram,* which has a hundred-year history, tends to be more conservative in style, more careful to be accurate, and it appeals more to government officials, businessmen, and university professors. It has specialized in publishing important commentaries and essays from prominent writers and journalists. *Al-Akhbar,* on the other hand has been known for its excellent news reporting and for professional journalism. It has a slightly higher circulation, is somewhat more sensational and popular, quicker to publish stories, and appeals more to bureaucrats, students, and others who prefer its livelier approach. It has specialized in publishing important commentaries and essays by well known Egyptian writers. As one journalist put it, *al-Akhbar* tries to be "like the pretty girl who wears a new dress every day, and who turns heads when she enters a room." *Al-Ahram,* on the other hand, is like an old man in a top hat and morning coat with a walking stick."[14] Both of them enjoy a fifty percent increase in circulation on weekends.

Al-Gumhuriya, the third leading daily, in the early years stressed Arab socialist ideological issues, but then in the Sadat era became more like *al-Ahram* and *al-Akhbar* in tone and content. Although it was founded by the leaders of the Egyptian revolution, it later fell behind *al-Ahram* and *al-Akhbar* in reputation, and some observers consider it too close to official policy to be credible. These differences in the national press are essentially stylistic. The Egyptian press as a whole, however, shows some diversity and independence, primarily because of the daily and weekly newspapers that are owned by the opposition political parties.

There are several important Egyptian weeklies. *Rose al-Yusif* has gone through several policy changes in its long history, from critical to compliant, and in 2003 it tended to support the government. *Akhir Sa'a, 14 October,* and *al-Musawwar* tend to be progovernment, although *al-Musawwar* does publish critical articles. *Al-Arabi, al-Usbu',* and *Sawt al-Umma* tend to be more critical of the government. The political party papers, which are all weeklies except *al-Wafd,* closely follow their respective party lines (see next chapter).

In these countries, the style of print media and their content derives from several basic factors related to the legal structure of the media themselves plus the character of the underlying political system. Following is a discussion of the most important factors at work.

POLITICAL CONDITIONS

Several aspects of the political system tend to bring about this transitional system of print media organization. The four countries that fall into this category share some of basic political characteristics. The first is political pluralism. Political parties and other such organizations are allowed to be formed outside of the direct control of the government in power, and they espouse views and opinions that are at least sometimes at variance with those of the government. Second, elections take place on a regular basis, at least for a parliament if not for the chief executive, and these elections allow political parties and individuals an opportunity to compete for access to political office. Third, the government deals with opposition elements primarily with legal means through the political process and the courts, using existing law rather than extra-judicial measures. Fourth, the law and prevailing practice permit opposition organizations and individuals to have at least some access to mass media by which they can communicate with the public. Fifth—and this distinguishes these countries from those where the press is diverse—the government's influence over the political discourse and means of expression including the print media is significantly and disproportionately greater than that of opposition elements. Sixth, the government and its supporters have significantly more economic power than its opponents which helps them to communicate their views. And finally, the underlying political system itself has been undergoing change and adjustment as leaders inside and outside government debate what the appropriate political philosophy for the country should be.

Political Pluralism and Elections

The single most important factor in determining the nature and extent of free expression in the print media is the degree and character of pluralism in the political environment.

In Tunisia, which was a one-party state for the first fourteen years after independence, political pluralism gradually increased after 1970, and since 1990 selected opposition political parties have been allowed to function in the political process. Since 1999, the opposition has been permitted to run candidates for president. President Zaine El-Abdine Ben Ali and his Constitutional Democratic Rally (RCD) have controlled both the executive and the legislature since 1987. In 2002 a referendum that reportedly passed by 99.52% amending the constitution gave him twelve more years in office.

In Algeria, the 1989 constitution provided for conversion from a single-party socialist state and although the process was set back for much of the 1990s, it has expanded. Since 1997, Algeria has had a multiparty parliament, and many parties of different political philosophies including Islamist, although the Islamic Salvation Front (FIS), which had ruled Algeria alone for a quarter century after 1962, continues to be banned. In the 2002 Algerian election, the FLN, which had ruled Algeria alone for a quarter century after 1962, returned to power.

Jordan too has undergone a process since 1989 of some democratization and dismantling of the martial laws that were on the books. Since 1992, political parties have been legal and have participated in the elections, although the monarchy remained.

In Egypt, political pluralization began in the 1970s and evolved into a multiparty system. The law prohibits parties based primarily on religion and thus the previously prominent Muslim Brotherhood is not a legal party, although some known MB adherents have served in parliament ostensibly as independents or as members of other parties. New parties must have the approval of a semi-official Parties Committee, which is controlled by the ruling party, but whose decisions can be appealed in the civil courts. By the beginning of the twenty-first century, there were thirteen recognized political opposition parties. At the same time, however, the emergency laws, which were passed in October 1981 after the assassination of President Sadat, continue to exist, having been renewed in the year 2000. The government has continued to justify repressive measures on the need to combat an Islamist insurgency, and the Presidency has since 1981 been in the hands of Husni Mubarak, who was re-elected for a fourth six-year term in a September 1999 referendum. Mubarak's National Democratic Party (NDP) also holds a large majority in the People's Assembly and in the Consultative (Shura) Council, which have substantial influence over the press.

In summary, the print media system in these four countries is complex. Ownership is in various hands, including those in power in the government. The authorities also have other means to influence the content of the press, but the most common ones are enshrined in the law, and litigation is common. There are explicit taboos in the law, but government officials also use informal means to affect newspaper content. Economic factors are also important. The most decisive factor in press freedom, however, is the existence of political pluralism and opposition political parties. At the same time, these systems are in flux.

SYSTEMS IN FLUX

It is characteristic of these four countries that the system governing print media has been undergoing fairly constant change over the past two or three decades, and that change is continuing. This is not surprising in view of the changes in the underlying political system that have been taking place, since media systems here (and throughout the region) are so heavily influenced by their political environments. The question of media structure is therefore debated regularly as to what is the appropriate system for the press, and appropriate legislation governing the media. Journalists of various political persuasions, even ones generally supportive of the government or with close connections to high officials, speak out from time to time calling for more press freedom. Legislation is debated and passed by parliament, and then amended again within months or a few years. The same government officials speak sometimes of wanting to have more press freedom and at other times of the need for responsibility and restraint. These changes in law and official policy depend partly on changing circumstances inside the country or in the region, but they are also symptomatic of the fact that there is no firm and fixed consensus on the role of the press in society. We call these systems "transitional" but it is not clear which way they are headed or indeed that they are in fact in transition to a different type of system that will stabilize and remain for a long time.

In the following chapter, we will briefly review the changes that have occurred in the print media systems in each of these four countries over the recent past, to illustrate the fact that the rules are continually being modified, albeit within certain parameters mentioned above.

NOTES

1. U.S. Embassy Tunis Public Affairs Office, "Media Directory 2000," and information from the U.S. embassy in Tunis in January 2003.

2. Sources: *The Middle East and North Africa 2000*, 46th Edition (Europa Publications Limited: U.K., 1999); and Editor and Publisher, *International Year Book, The Encyclopedia of the Newspaper Industry* 79th Edition, Part 1, Editor and Publisher, 1999; Egyptian journalist interview January 2003 for Egyptian figures; and U.S. Embassy Algiers, "Media Directory Algiers," November 2002 for Algerian papers.

3. *Middle East Journal*, vol. 55, no. 4, Autumn 2001, p. 671.

4. U.S. Dept. of State, *1999 Country Reports on Human Rights Practices*, Jordan chapter, January 25, 2000.

5. Press and Publication Law No. 33, articles 10, 38, and 213, which replaced Law No. 16 of 1955; see also 'Adib Mruwa, *Al-Sahafa al 'Arabiyah*, Beirut: Dar al Hayat, 1961, p. 347.

6. *Jordan Times,* January 26, 2003, p. 5.

7. Press Code of February 9, 1956, as amended in April 1975, in JPRS 65003 U.S. Commerce Department, June 13, 1975.

8. U.S. Dept. of State, *1996 Country Reports on Human Rights Practices,* Jordan chapter, January 30, 1997.

9. *World Press Freedom Review,* editions of 1998 and 1999.

10. In the 1990s, for these reasons the newspapers *Le Matin* and *l'Authentique* received more government ads than did *L'Opinion;* U.S. Department of State, *Country Reports on Human Rights Practices,* 1996 and 1999, Algeria Chapter, Washington D.C., January 30, 1997 and February 25, 2000.

11. *1999 World Press Freedom Review.*

12. *1999 World Press Freedom Review,* and cairotimes.com (2002).

13. U.S. Embassy Algiers, "Media Directory Algiers," November 2002; interview with well informed Algerian observer, March 2003.

14. Interview no. 13, Egyptian journalist, Cairo, May 8, 1973. On the history of *al-Ahram,* see Dr. Ibrahim 'Abdu, *Al Ahram, Tarikh wa Fann 1875–1964,* Cairo: Mu'assasat al 'Arab, 1964.

7

Development of the Transitional System of Print Media

The transitional system of organization of print media that exists in four Arab states—Jordan, Algeria, Tunisia, and Egypt—developed over the last half of the twentieth century. Each country had its own unique characteristics, but there were some common elements that helped the system to emerge. Trends in media structure were not linear but reflected periodic and ongoing debates in all four countries over what the proper course should be. In this chapter we will summarize the experiences of each of the four, which help illuminate the common causative factors, primarily the underlying political environment, and the fact that these print media systems have undergone transitions.

JORDAN

Prior to 1948, the only newspapers being published in Jordan were two low-circulation Amman weeklies, *al-Nasr* and *al-Urdun,* and the latter had been controlled since its establishment in the 1920s by a Lebanese family. In 1948 when Israel was founded, some leading publishers and editors who had worked in Palestine after World War II, fled from Israeli occupation to Jordan's East Jerusalem where they established Jordan's first daily papers.[1] The print media developed in quality and in independence during the 1950s and early 1960s. For example, *al-Urdun,* which in 1949 became a daily and under Dr. Hanna Nasr, the son of the founder, did not hesitate to criticize the government. In 1959 and 1960, the dailies *al-Jihad* and *al-Manar,* respectively, were established. In that period also the weeklies *Amman al-Masa'*, *Akhbar al-Usbu'*, *al-Sabah*, and *al-Hawadith* began to appear.

In the early years after World War II, the Jordanian government periodically used its authority to control press content. For example, in March 1967, after the press expressed dismay at the inability of the army to respond adequately to Israeli military raids across the border, Prime Minister Wasfi Tell declared that the newspapers had "failed to meet the level of responsibility expected of them" in the crisis, and he had all publishing licenses revoked. The government was especially sensitive on this issue at the time because some Arab countries, notably Egypt and Saudi Arabia, were criticizing Jordan for its "weakness" toward Israel. Then the June 1967 Arab-Israeli war, which resulted in Israel's occupation of East Jerusalem, also impacted on the press as most of the Arab journalists fled further eastward. The government then issued new licenses on condition that the four old Jerusalem dailies would merge into two Amman dailies: *Filastin* and *al-Manar* merged into *al-Dustur* while personnel of *al-Difa'a* and *al-Jihad* joined to publish a new daily, *al-Quds*. This merger was ostensibly to improve the quality of the press but the move was widely regarded as an attempt to evoke more support for the government through this warning. In 1968 a new daily paper *al-Difa'a* emerged as the third reincarnation of the old Jaffa paper.

In the summer of 1970, when the Palestinian commando (fida'iyeen) movement seriously challenged the Jordanian government and took over parts of the country, the government used its powers to control the press. It closed the two dailies *al-Dustur* and *al-Difa'a* on June 14 when they carried on their front pages a fida'iyeen communiqué blaming the "reactionary regime" for the conflict. The government allowed them to reopen two weeks later because it was not strong enough to control the new fida'iyeen daily *al-Fatah*, which took their place and became an even more outspoken pro-Palestinian critic of the Jordanian government. Other Jordanian newspapers also became more critical as the government seemed to weaken, and the Palestinian militants grew stronger. But after the final showdown in September 1970, in which the government regained control of the country, *al-Fatah* disappeared, and the authorities again withdrew the license of *al-Difa'a* as punishment. At the time, the government established a new paper, *al-Ra'y*, to help promote the official viewpoint.

Because the Israeli-Arab issue remained a sensitive one for the government, its treatment was often an issue in government-press relations. For example, in December 1975, the government closed *al-Akhbar* after its editorials said that the new Jordanian currency carried "the Star of David, Israel's flag," while the other papers carried the government's denial. During the 1980s, primarily for the same reasons, Jordanian print media were under strict government censorship and control, and journalists were frequently detained. The Palestinian uprising which began in December 1987 was so important to Jordan politically that it was an added incentive to the government to maintain controls over the press. In 1988 the government issued executive orders dissolving the boards of directors of the three existing daily newspapers and forcing private newspaper owners to sell their shares to the government, which then appointed many of the top managers of the country's newspapers.[2]

By the end of the 1980s, the situation started to change. Jordan's democratization process gained momentum in November 1989, when an election for a new parliament took place, that was the first Jordanian election in twenty-two years. After the election, the atmosphere for freedom of expression in the print media improved. The government that took office in December 1989, headed by Prime Minister Badran, promptly removed several categories of offenses from the martial law legislation on the books. It allowed the deposed boards of directors to return to the three newspapers, in effect lifting the direct government controls imposed in the previous year. Then in 1991, Prime Minister Taher al-Masri's government repealed most of the martial law categories that had been in effect since 1967. In August 1992 martial law was finally abolished, and in September 1992 parliament passed a law legalizing political parties. Thereafter political party newspapers began to appear, and some of them clearly took positions in opposition to the government. They participated in the elections that took place in the summer of 1993.

In 1992, even after the emergence of the party press, the political system remained a monarchy although a parliamentary system was also functioning. The government still retained the right to issue licenses to publish, and it had significant ownership in key dailies. It owned 61 percent of the Jordan Press Foundation which had published the daily *al-Ra'y* newspaper since 1971, and 40 percent of the Jordan Press Company which had published the dailies *al-Dustur* and the *Jordan Times* since 1967 and 1975, respectively. Government agencies also owned 67 percent of the fourth daily, *Sawt al-Sha'b*, established in 1983. Ownership implied some loyalty to the government, but all of the dailies showed some independence, especially *al-Dustur* and *Sawt al-Sha'b*.[3] The private and party press in 1992 was concentrated in the weeklies, including *Akhbar al-Usbu'*, *al-Sahafi*, the Islamist paper *al-Liwa*, and *The Star*, plus a political magazine *al-Ufuq*.

In 1993, a new Press and Publications Law replaced the law of 1953 as amended in 1973. It removed many of the repressive provisions of the 1973 press law, making the press freer than at any time in its history. However, it retained the provision that the government had the sole authority to license print media and could withdraw licenses if the publication "threatened national existence" or security, infringed on Jordan's constitutional principles, harmed "national feelings," or offended "public decency." It forbade news about the Royal Family unless approved by it, articles defaming religion or contrary to public morality, or unauthorized military information.

Although the 1993 law liberalized the print media somewhat, a number of journalists held a demonstration outside parliament demanding still more liberalization of press rules.[4]

Following passage of the 1993 law, the Jordanian government granted licenses to six party affiliated weekly newspapers:[5]

- *al-Mustqbal* (The Future) of the Future Party
- *al-Ahd* (the Pledge) of the Pledge Party
- *al-Hurriya* (Liberty) of the Liberty Party
- *Nida al-Watan* (Call of the Homeland) of the Popular Unity Party
- *al-Masira* (The March) of the Jordan Progressive Democratic Party
- *al-Jamahir* (the Masses) of the Communist Party

The multiparty elections of 1993 provided an opportunity for these new newspapers and others to participate actively in the political debate.

In January 1995, King Hussain asked Prime Minister Abdal Karim Kabariti to design a communication policy to "deepen people's practice of democracy, instigate a dialogue between them and foster the creation of constructive criticism" between officials and citizens. The Prime Minister appointed Marwan Muasher as Information Minister, which the press welcomed, and Kabariti's government expanded press freedoms during its tenure, which lasted until March 1997. For example, the government issued forty press licenses in 1993–1997 including some to political parties.[6]

The 1993 law had promised some privatization of the press, in Article 19(d), which called for the government, which owned the main newspapers, to reduce its ownership of the press to thirty percent by 1997. On May 17, 1997, however, the deadline for government reduction in ownership of the press, the government promulgated a temporary press law that was in fact more restrictive and dropped Article 19(d), the provision that the government reduce its ownership to thirty percent. The government still owned two-thirds of the Jordan Press Foundation and one-third of the Jordan Press and Publications Company and the change in the law permitted that to continue. At the time, the King said, "Freedom has its limits. The limits are: not encroaching on other people's freedom, not harming the nation, and not mocking national interests and unity."[7]

In September 1997 the Jordanian government shut down thirteen weekly newspapers for not meeting the capitalization standard of $420,000 required in the May 1997 Press and Publication Law amendments. Protests against the law broke out including demonstrations in late May. The International Press Institute (IPI) and Human Rights Watch condemned the law. Some nongovernmental Jordanian newspapers published editorials criticizing this change. The Supreme Court later cancelled the May 1997 law as unconstitutional however, because parliament had not ratified it. The weekly papers that had been closed, therefore resumed publication in February 1998.[8]

In 1998 King Hussain instructed the government to prepare a new press law to prevent what he considered to be slanderous reporting on the Palestinian-Israeli talks. In a letter to the Prime Minister he said the law should "deter anyone from harming Jordan's ties with Arab states or adversely affecting national unity." The government's press bill was ratified by parliament on August 9, 1998 and promulgated in September. It contained several articles reversing the democratization and freedom of the press and giving the government more control. It eliminated appeals to the denial of licenses, it banned any news relating to the armed forces or security forces or defamed heads of Arab friendly and foreign states, and allowed the courts to close publications for reasons of "public interest" or "national security." The 1998 law gave the government powers to issue fines, withdraw licenses, and shut down newspapers. Persons accused of violating this law are tried in a special court for press and copyright cases. The penal code also authorized the state to take action against anyone who incited violence, defamed a head of state, disseminated "false or exaggerated information outside the country that attacks state dignity," or defamed a public official. When combined with the Press Association Law of 1998, it placed some new restrictions on the print media. It drew strong Jordanian and international criticism for increasing the capitalization requirement for newspapers, provided very high fees for violations.[9]

When Abdullah II became king in February 1999, following the death of his father, he began to take some small steps toward greater liberalization of the print media. In March 1999 he said press freedom "should be as high as the national flag."[10] He intervened directly on several occasions to secure the release of jailed journalists. In February 1999, for the first time since 1967, the government allowed Palestinian newspapers to be sold in Jordan, where sixty percent of the population is of Palestinian origin. In May 1999, he ordered abolition of censorship of foreign publications entering Jordanian territory. In September, in a special session summoned by the king, parliament amended the highly controversial press law in force since September 1998, revoking certain particularly restrictive articles concerning press freedom, such as the prohibition of any information considered to be an attack on the royal family, the army, the currency, the legal system, national unity or Arab heads of state (provisions already contained in the penal code) and the suspension of any publication during legal proceedings. Critics however said the reforms did not go far enough, and asked for cancellation of the heavy fines allowed against journalists who contravene the press laws, and changes in the penal code provision for imprisonment for crimes of opinion.[11]

In November 1999, King Abdullah called for a Media Free Zone near Amman where publications would not be subject to censorship. The purpose would be to attract foreign investment.[12] In February 2000, Jordan passed a law implementing this idea. Prime Minister Rawabdeh said investors would have total freedom of expression and could hire anyone they wished. The Zone was to be run by a commission appointed by the government. The project was similar to one in Egypt and the UAE.[13]

Complete privatization of the press, which has been a frequent subject of discussion in Jordan for a decade, surfaced again after Abdullah became king, and became subject of government statements, public discussion, and parliamentary debate. In 1999 and 2000, King Abdullah said several times that privatization of the press would be a good thing, and in his letter of designation to the new Prime Ali Abdul Ragheb in July 2000, he urged that the issue be addressed seriously.[14] At the time, the Jordan Investment Corporation, the investment arm of the government, still held fifteen percent of the capital of the Jordanian Press Foundation (JPF) that published the mass circulation daily *al-Ra'i,* the English language daily *Jordan Times,* and the children's magazine *Hatem.* The Social Security Foundation (SSC), a government institution chaired by the Labor Minister, held 47 percent of the foundation's shares, and the SSC also owned 30 percent of the newspaper *al-Dustur* and 22 percent of al-*Arab al-Yawm.*

In July 2000, Information Minister Taleb Rifai said that he expected privatization to be complete in three months. However, privatization was then postponed indefinitely. In August 2001, because of the unstable regional situation, the Jordanian government began to restrict press freedoms, closing newspapers and arresting editors, reversing some of the liberalization started a decade earlier. By 2003, four dailies—*al-Aswaq, Sawt al-Shaab, al-Akhbar,* and *Arab Daily*—had been shut down, leaving only one English and three Arabic dailies appearing.[15]

ALGERIA

Algerian print media have gone through several different stages of organization. When the French administered Algeria as a department of France, French settlers living there in the second half of the nineteenth century had such firm control over Algerian economic, political and cultural life that the Arab press was not able to develop. The political parties that became active after World War I did appeal to Arabs for support but they were controlled by Europeans. All newspapers and most periodicals were owned by Europeans, printed in French and ignored Arab news. Even after World War II and up to independence in 1962, the seven dailies and most of the other publications in Algeria were published in French by Frenchmen. Arab nationalists were able to publish a few modest weeklies for a while, but France suppressed them in 1955 as the war for independence began. In addition, the French administration prevented the importation of foreign publications which supported the nationalists. As a result, an underground

Algerian nationalist party press developed. For example in 1956 the National Liberation Front started its newspaper *El Moudjahid*, first in French, and then after 1957 also partially in Arabic. It was printed in Tunis and smuggled into Algeria prior to independence. Only in 1960, after Paris had decided on self-determination for Algeria, did the French administration there allow for publication of some of Arab nationalist views.[16]

When Algeria became independent in 1962 under President Ahmad Ben Bella and his National Liberation Front (FLN), initially the print media showed some independence and diversity, to a large extent as supported by the different political parties that suddenly became active in the country. The Communist-backed newspaper *Alger Republicain,* which the French had banned in 1955, reappeared, and the newly formed Algerian Peoples Party (PPA) began publishing its official newspaper. The FLN, which had led the fight for independence, moved its official weekly *El Moudjahid* from Tunis to Algiers in 1962. There was, briefly, criticism of the government in the parliament and in the press.

The multiparty system was however so weak it did not survive more than a few months, and press diversity disappeared with it. The regime banned the Communist Party and the PPA in November 1962, forcing their newspapers to close. The new parliament that was formed in August 1963 included only delegates who were loyal to the government or who eschewed public criticism.[17] Consequently when the new constitution of August 1963 proclaimed Algeria a one-party state, the press had lost most of its diversity. From 1963 until 1989 the press was dominated by the regime, and Algeria had a mobilization type of system. The press reflected uniformity in the public arena, that the government reinforced by using its censorship authority to deal with any nongovernmental private newspapers which stepped out of line. The regime promoted its weekly *El Moudjahid,* and during 1962 and 1963 established three new daily newspapers and ten other publications, to spread the regime's point of view.[18] Then in September 1973, the government banned private newspapers, leaving only those controlled by the regime and its party. When it did so, government-controlled Algiers Radio broadcast a commentary which said that this decision would end "attacks on our country," and praising the nationalization of the press as "a great victory over hired pens, absurd, tendentious propaganda," and "filthy psychological campaigns."[19] In September 1963, Algeria's president Ben Bella himself was personally involved in the dramatic seizure of the European-controlled *La Depeche d'Algerie,* whose facilities were turned over to the FLN daily *Le Peuple.*[20]

By the end of 1963, the one remaining private newspaper *Alger Republicain,* which had been pro-Communist, had become a supporter of the regime. In June 1965 it was merged into the FLN daily *Le Peuple,* and since then this paper has appeared under the name *El Moudjahid.*[21] Algeria's ruling party declared that there was a "need to heighten political sensitivities and to improve methods of action to achieve more effective mobilization behind the goals of the Revolution" including eliminating "the after-effects of colonialism."[22]

After Houari Boumedienne replaced Ben Bella in a coup d'etat in 1965, he continued to impose strict controls on the Algerian press. When Boumedienne died in 1978 and Chadli Benjedid became president, he too continued strict controls for another decade. In 1989 however, a new constitution provided for conversion from a single-party socialist state to a multiparty parliamentary system, opening the way for significant changes in the press. In period from 1989 through 1991, under Benjedid, the Algerian political system was becoming somewhat more democratic, and the print media were expanding Algerian freedom of expression. The 1989 constitution provided for freedom of speech, which corresponded with the expressed desire of the political leadership to open up the political system itself. The 1990 Information Law permitted nongovernmental ownership of newspapers including by political parties, and in 1990 the government set up a fund to help promote print media, giving $10.4 million to government publications but also giving $7.9 million to nongovernment publications.[23] Between 1989 and 1991, the number of newspapers and magazines in Algeria proliferated from 31 to more than 160, including 18 daily newspapers and 69 weeklies. Moreover, newspaper ownership was diverse. In December 1991, the state owned 37, private individuals owned 96, political parties owned 8 and various associations owned 28. The total circulation of the 18 dailies was over 800,000, of which fifty-nine percent was of nongovernmental papers.[24]

The democratic trend was cut short, however. When the Islamic Salvation Front (FIS) in December 1991 won the first round of the multiparty elections, the army intervened in January 1992, cancelled the second round and aborted the election process. The growth of political pluralism was severely restricted but not entirely stifled by the regime's emergency security measures, the violent reaction by Islamist political elements, and several years of serious security clashes. A five-man High State Committee replaced the presidency, and promulgated laws that included new restrictions on the press. Armed Islamic groups began terrorist attacks on the government and its supporters that escalated and continued, lasting throughout the decade. This affected the press in several ways. Journalists were physically at risk because they were targeted or caught in the violence. The government, seeking to suppress the Islamic activists, took security measures that affected the media.

The December 10, 1992 state of emergency decree and the antiterrorism laws affected the press directly and indirectly, allowing the government to suspend a publication for up to six months without going to court. The law spoke about threats to public order but in effect left it to the government to determine what constituted such a threat. The ensuing security situation and the government's reaction to it led to direct government press controls. In 1992, for example, the government suspended seven newspapers, and in 1993 it suspended three more dailies, including not only independent ones but also government-owned ones. In 1993, the government announced that security related stories would require prior government approval.[25]

Under President Liamine Zeroual (1994–1999), the government conducted an ongoing battle with terrorists. A June 7, 1994 government decree required that all security related information had to come from the Algerian Press Service, and the government established review committees at the printing plants to review publications for what it considered security material.[26]

For several years, the level of terrorism continued high, despite strong measures by the government to try to end it. Independent and party newspapers however continued to express a range of viewpoints and some succeeded in criticizing the government's broad economic and social policies. When they accused specific ministers of crimes or even policy failures, however, the Interior Minister and the courts usually took action against them. The government also during the 1990s used its control over advertising by official agencies to assist newspapers which were clearly anti-Islamist or which did not investigate government corruption.[27]

Journalists also suffered from the terrorism itself. Between 1993 and 1996 alone, when many thousands of Algerians were killed or injured, sixty journalists died. Then the government made housing available to journalists where their safety could be assured, and in the 1987–1988 period none lost their lives.[28] All of these circumstances served to inhibit free expression in the Algerian print media. In addition to the direct government restrictions, journalists often practiced self-censorship in anticipation of official punishments on the one hand, or of terrorist attacks on the other.

After 1996, the Algerian security situation improved somewhat, and the Zeroual regime began to ease its tight restrictions on political life. In June 1997 Algeria held its first legislative election since the one that had been aborted in January 1992, and Algerians elected the first multiparty parliament in their history. Candidates representing 39 political parties plus several independents participated, although the FIS continued to be banned. The government party, the National Democratic Rally, won 154 seats; two Islamist parties won 103 seats between them and two Berber parties together won 39 seats, while four small parties won 9 other seats; and independents won 11.[29]

During the June 1997 parliamentary election campaign, a variety of party and independent newspapers carried a range of viewpoints in supporting different candidates. Just as the election produced a range of views in the new parliament, a fairly broad spectrum of opinion was also found in the print media at the time. The government handled the Islamist issue

by allowing most Islamist parties to function legally, although not to publish newspapers; nevertheless it permitted several nongovernment newspapers regularly carried the views of these parties.[30]

At the same time, however, the government continued to use the judicial
system and existing laws to try to restrict what the newspapers were saying. According to the Justice Ministry, between the years 1996 and 2000,
the government brought charges against 141 journalists in 156 cases
involving libel, insult, and abuse, and some journalists claim the figures are
actually higher.[31]

By the end of the 1990s, the security situation had shown some
improvement, and the press was allowed more latitude in its reporting.
Although the emergency and security regulations were still in effect, by
1999, the independent press was reporting regularly on security matters to
a much greater extent than before without being punished. Newspapers
even used nonofficial sources for security stories despite the fact that they
were still ostensibly required to use only the official news agency.[32]

For example, the Algerian dailies *al-Watan* and *al-Khabar,* which had
been established in 1990 during the liberalization period by groups of
journalists, managed to survive despite suspensions during the 1990s. By
2002 they were thriving, with claimed circulations of 100,000 and
400,000 respectively.[33]

By the beginning of the twenty-first century the Algerian political system
and the press showed some genuine diversity. Many independent newspapers were able to criticize the government, although the government itself
still controlled several important papers directly. By the year 2003, the
Algerian print media were quite fragmented, with about thirty daily newspapers appearing, representing different views. Only four of the dailies
were owned by the government, and two others were close to the government, but the rest conveyed a variety of views. Many of the newspapers
were highly critical of the government including the president. The
national election in April 1999, that resulted in Abdalaziz Bouteflika
replacing President Zeroual, was disputed by several political parties and
their newspapers were outspoken, criticizing Bouteflika openly, and they
continued to do so afterwards.[34] As President, Bouteflika warned the press
to be careful not to tarnish Algeria's image, but he allowed criticism to
continue.[35]

TUNISIA

An indigenous press developed in Tunisia while the French exercised a
Protectorate over the country, 1881–1956, primarily by a group of middle
class writers and intellectuals who maintained contact with the Arab world
and Arab culture. The French however controlled the content of the
Tunisian Arab press during this period. They imposed strict censorship

during World War II, which they lifted in 1947, but they continued controls until independence in 1956.

Habib Bourguiba, who dominated the Tunisian political scene for three decades from independence until 1987, had a personal interest in and association with party newspapers dating from the early years of his political career in the 1930s. In 1930, at the age of 27, he was writing for the Destour Party newspaper *La Voix Tunisienne,* and in 1932 he established his own political newspaper *l'Action Tunisienne,* which the French closed in 1933. In 1934 when the Neo-Destour split from the Destour, it began publishing *l'Action* and Bourguiba wrote for it.

When Tunisia became independent in 1956 and Bourguiba became its president, he continued to have a special interest in the press, and he had his political party continue to publish newspapers because he saw them as an important part of his political success. From independence until 1970, the print media in Tunisia were uniform and closely managed as part of a one-party political system.

The Tunisian government under Bourguiba periodically used its powers to close or suspend newspapers. For example in 1962, the government closed the Communist monthly *al-Tali'a* and the pro-Communist monthly *Tribune de Paris,* following an attempt on Bourguiba's life. In January 1957 it suspended the weekly *l'Action* for a week for criticizing the government and its trials of former Protectorate collaborators; the paper was then closed in September 1957 after the PSD Political Bureau denounced it for "using the prestigious name of the paper founded by the party leader" for waging an "insidious campaign of confusion."[36]

Starting in 1970, political pluralism in Tunisia has very gradually replaced what was a one-party state for the first fourteen years after independence. In 1970, Tunisia began to develop multiple political parties, and the structure of the press also began to become somewhat freer and more diverse. In the beginning, however, the development of an independent press was slow. As one Tunisian journalist put it in 1973, "There is no opposition [mu'arada] in the nation, so there is no opposition press."[37] Another said in 1976, "A national Tunisian policy has been chosen [by the ruling elite] and all newspapers are supposed to support it. They are only free within that framework."[38]

It was only after the departure of Bourguiba, who was replaced as president by Zaine El-Abdine Ben Ali in 1987, that a trend began which led to the emergence of the party press and a modest increase in freedom of expression. The Ben Ali government from the beginning called for greater political pluralism, and supported a new Press Code which was promulgated in 1988 and eased some of the restrictions on the press. Then in 1990 the regime allowed opposition political parties to function openly. By 1993, opposition newspapers were again allowed to appear, and they played a role in politics.

In the parliamentary elections of the 1990s, progovernment parties won overwhelming majorities, but a few seats were reserved for opposition parties and this number gradually increased. Several opposition parties entered candidates in the 1994 parliamentary election, and 12% of the seats (19 of 163) were reserved specifically for them. These parties were able to convey their views to at least some of the electorate through their newspapers. The proportion of seats in parliament reserved for opposition parties was increased to twenty percent in the 1999 election. In July 1999 the constitution was changed to permit the opposition, for the first time in Tunisia's history, to run candidates for president; and two of them did so in the presidential election that fall. Opposition party newspapers spoke out during that presidential election. President Ben Ali was however reelected by 99.44% and in the October 1999 elections, Ben Ali's Constitutional Democratic Rally (RCD) won another overwhelming majority in the legislature. He and his RCD in fact continued to control both the executive and the legislature as they have since 1987, dominating Tunisian politics.[39]

In the late 1990s, however, government actions against opposition newspapers (arrests of journalists, seizures of newspapers, withholding ads) persuaded the Commission for the Protection of Journalists (CPJ) to declare Ben Ali an "enemy of the press" in 1998 and 1999.[40] Outside observers believe that although the party and private newspapers exist, their ability to criticize the government is diminished by government restrictions and self-censorship. And in May 2002, Ben Ali used a national referendum to increase his power still more.[41]

EGYPT

Egyptian newspaper publishing goes back to the nineteenth century. Although the first Egyptian newspapers were organs of the regime, nongovernmental private papers appeared during the cultural and intellectual renaissance of the 1860s and 1870s. A "virile party press appeared" after 1882, which was "lively, political and rebellious," although these early papers were not owned by the parties as such but merely patronized by them.[42]

In several cases, a writer would establish a paper, and slowly, as other like-minded people were attracted to it, they formed a party that became active on the political scene. For example, Shaikh Ali Yusif's Hisb al-Islah party grew up around *al-Muayyid* newspaper; the Hisb al-Watani party developed after Mustafa Kamel established *al-Liwa'* newspaper; and the Umma party emerged after *al-Jarida* newspaper was founded.[43] Since the British were more tolerant of partisan papers than of organized parties, the papers grew faster than the parties. Some papers, like the successful private dailies *al-Ahram* and *al-Muqattam*, both with long histories having been established in 1876 and 1889 respectively, continued and retained some of their independence. The reports and commentary discussion in these elite newspapers was, however, still kept within strict limits by governmental restrictions, despite the proliferation of journals and the increasing political nature of them.[44]

In the period before 1945, the Wafd Party used its newspapers as a chief weapon of political agitation because there was no opportunity for the nationalists to challenge the British militarily, so they took advantage of the press freedom to make their views known. Egypt's largest circulation paper, *al-Misri,* was close to the Wafd. None of the papers was revolutionary, however, nor did they threaten the basic political system. The 1923 constitution allowed the government to confiscate a newspaper to protect the "interests of the social system" but there was considerable diversity and competition. Except for the interlude of wartime censorship, the press was able to criticize policies, expose corruption in government, and reflect diverse philosophies and interests. One observer in the late 1940s found that Egypt had a vigorous and diverse party press, as well as a few nonpartisan dailies such as *al-Ahram.*[45]

The military officers who seized power in Egypt on July 23, 1952, and abolished the monarchy, quickly established their own "publishing house of the revolution," Dar al-Tahrir (Liberation House), in order to make known the ideas and personalities of the new leadership. By September 1952, Dar al-Tahrir had begun publishing a bimonthly magazine, *al-Tahrir,* which was anti-imperialist, leftist revolutionary in tone, and supportive of the ruling Revolutionary Command Council. Several of the RCC members wrote for it, including Anwar Sadat and Gamal Abdul Nasser, who were then still relatively unknown figures behind the presidency of General Muhammad Naguib. In December, the publishing house started its own daily newspaper, *al-Gumhuria,* on a license issued in Nasser's name. In the early years, *al-Gumhuria,* appealed especially to leftist intellectuals, workers, and others who liked its tendency to stress Arab socialist ideological issues and leftist causes. This newspaper's editors were very proud for many years that they still operated under a license issued in 1952 (the year of the Revolution) to Gamal Abdul Nasser, and for years were "influenced by the principles of the Revolution (mabadi' al-thawrah) more than the other papers, which focus on news."[46]

The Revolutionary Command Council also took direct action against the remaining influential privately owned newspapers. General Naguib increased press censorship when he became President of Egypt in September 1952. In January 1953 President Naguib announced the formation of a single new political organization, the National Liberation Rally, and banned all other parties and their journals as "prejudicial to the national interest."[47] Colonel Nasser tried to lift censorship when he emerged as Prime Minister in February 1954, but the subsequent outburst of criticism from the unshackled newspapers caused him to re-impose it a month later, and censorship has been used periodically ever since. Small-circulation papers that had no impact on Egyptian political life, such as *Journal d'Egypte,* were allowed to stay in private hands.

During the seventeen years when Gamal Abdal Nasser was in power, the regime used its licensing authority and other legal weapons against uncooperative papers and individual journalists. The creation of a monopoly political party had diminished the public debate over government policy, but still not enough to satisfy the ruling Revolutionary Command Council (RCC). Three private daily newspapers, *al-Ahram, Akhbar al-Yawm,* and *al-Misri* were popular and way ahead of the RCC's *al-Gumhuria* in circulation. The biggest, *al-Misri,* had a circulation of more than 120,000.[48] It tended to reflect views of the recently abolished Wafd Party and was critical of the regime, calling for real parliamentary rule. In 1954 it openly criticized Nasser after other newspapers had muted their opposition.

Al-Misri editors called Nasser a usurper of people's rights, and its editorials, under the heading "Back to your Barracks" directly attacked the RCC.[49] In April 1954 the RCC revoked the publishing license of *al-Misri,* and the Arab world's largest-circulation paper suddenly ceased to exist.[50] By 1954, three other independent daily newspapers, *al-Balagh, al-Zaman,* and *al-Muqattam,* were also gone.

Thus the measures that the RCC took during its first two years in power—abolishing political parties and groups, censoring, closing newspapers and newspaper guilds, and jailing prominent newspapermen, and at the same time creating its own publishing house—had the combined effect of severely limiting any criticism of the regime and its policies. The RCC did not take over direct control of all private newspapers, but these other measures made it very clear to Egyptian journalists that they had to stay within certain lines in order to continue writing and publishing.

Egypt's Law No. 156 of May 24, 1960, stipulated that no newspapers could be published without the permission of the country's only political organization, the National Union (later renamed Arab Socialist Union). The law also transferred ownership of the four large private publishing houses (Dar al-Ahram, Dar Akhbar al-Yawm, Dar al-Hilal, and Dar Rose al-Yusif) to the National Union, which already owned Dar al-Tahrir publishing house. The law also required that the National Union appoint the boards of directors for the newspapers it owned. This political organization, therefore, was given wide licensing, financial, and personnel powers over the press. Because the organization was controlled by the regime, the regime in effect controlled the press by these means.[51] The system was modified only slightly in March 1975, when a Higher Press Council was created which was given forty-nine percent ownership of the press and the power to issue publishing licenses. Because the key members of the Higher Council were the Minister of Information, ASU officials, and media officials, and since the latter were still appointed by the regime, the government did not lose its de facto control.[52]

It was significant that the Nasser regime's reorganization of the press took place in 1960, just a year before the Egyptian government's nationalization of important sectors of the economy. The regime apparently became convinced it could not nationalize the economy if the press was "still in the hands of the capitalists."[53] President Nasser and his associates saw the owners of most of the newspapers as big capitalists who would resist and possibly openly oppose the coming socialist measures, and an explanation attached to the Egyptian press law said public ownership of the means of social and political guidance was a way in the new society of prohibiting capitalist domination over the means of guidance, establishing democracy and the public ownership of the means of guidance, which is the press.[54]

The regime argued that what happened in 1960 was not technically nationalization of the press, because it was not the state or the government that took over ownership of the newspapers, but the Arab Socialist Union, which was the political agent of the regime. The 1960 law deliberately uses the phrase "organization of the press" (tanzim al-sahafah) rather than "nationalization" (ta'mim), and Egyptian law does not regard the National Union or ASU as an organ of the state. One legal expert adds that the publishing houses have "no connection with the authority of the state" (sultah al-dawlah). There is no regular government financial connection with the press.[55]

Egyptian newspaper editors during the Nasser era, 1953–1970, stayed within limits, but they were also able to criticize the status quo in subtle and indirect ways. They published short stories and even poetry by talented writers in order to convey criticism to readers through symbolic fiction. Some published economic analyses which described existing economic difficulties in restrained and matter-of-fact ways that did not politicize the issues or blame the leadership but made it clear that there are problems. Even in political commentaries, some writers were able to take gentle jabs at the system and the regime. In 1965 when Ali Amin was forced to leave the editorship of the paper he founded, he wrote: "I do not choose the songs I sing and I do not select the tunes [but] . . . I am infinitely optimistic. Many people are surprised at my optimism."[56] In short, the Egyptian press, even under Nasser's strong authoritarian rule, was not completely docile or subservient in the face of political realities, but there was evidence of vitality and professionalism in Egyptian journalism, though it was often restrained by the political system for the sake of current efforts by the leadership at unity in order to deal with overriding problems such as the Arab-Israeli conflict or economic development. Diversity has been seen primarily in the nondaily periodicals. During some of the Nasser era (1953–1970), leftist journalists were active in most of the media, but the monthly journal *al-Taliah* became a special organ of the dedicated Marxists, and the weekly *Rose al-Yusif* became an outlet for

irresponsible yellow journalism that carried the government's anti-imperialism
and other policies to excess.

Also, Muhammad Hassanein Haikal, the Chief Editor of *al-Ahram,*
had an extraordinary amount of influence over government policy and
public opinion as a confidante and defender of Nasser, and because of
his Friday columns in his newspaper, which attracted tens of thousands
of readers.

Under Anwar Sadat, who became president upon Nasser's death in
1970, the press system changed several times, both toward and away from
more diversity and freedom of expression. Sadat's attitude toward the
press, and toward freedom of speech generally was in fact rather ambivalent. He sought to increase democracy, but at the same time he retained a
strong concern that elements he considered unpatriotic would exploit the
freedom. The Sadat government at the beginning gradually showed a
greater degree of tolerance for political discussion and criticism, certainly
on the private level and to some extent in the press. Journalists who supported the government's policies were favored, however, and appointed by
Sadat to key press positions. He chastised press critics publicly. The Egyptian daily press under Sadat did not, however as a rule publish editorials
attacking the basic tenets of the government's foreign policy or its basic
principles—socialism, national unity, and social peace—and all political
discussion took place within the framework of the policy of the state. Criticism of government bureaucrats for their failure to execute policy did
appear in the press, but alternatives to the top leadership were not proposed by the daily newspapers.[57]

Early in his presidency, Sadat took some steps to liberalize the print
media. In 1973 he lifted the censorship that had been imposed earlier,
withdrawing the government monitors who had been sitting in the newspapers clearing content for many years. Also in 1973 the regime, however,
caused its political organization, the Arab Socialist Union, to withdraw the
professional licenses of more than one hundred journalists so that they had
to leave the newspapers. After six months, their licenses were restored and
they returned to their jobs, reminded effectively of their dependence on the
regime for their livelihood. For the most part they were paid salaries anyway during this period, as a humanitarian gesture; but the threat of being
prevented from exercising their profession on a long-term basis hung over
their heads as an incentive.

As Sadat said when he reinstated the journalists, "I meant and still mean
to give a warning. It has not been my aim nor is it my nature to harm any
person in his work, profession or livelihood. . . . I want freedom of the
press. At the same time I want it to be a dedicated press."[58] Two years
later, still involved in a discussion of press freedoms, Sadat recalled the
event in a similar vein: "I did not dismiss anybody. It was disciplinary punishment. I said: shame, behave yourselves. Why? Because I am in a battle

and a situation in which everyone is required to stand by their country—not by me personally—because it is their country. And on September 28, 1973, I came and said that all the journalists should go back to their newspapers."[59]

Unlike Nasser, Sadat during most of his presidency did not treat opposition journalists harshly by imprisoning them or depriving them of their means of livelihood. Muhammad Hassanain Haykal, the most powerful journalist under Nasser, is one example of that. Haykal continued to write during the Sadat era, but when he spoke out too obviously in opposition to government policy he simply lost his platform. Other columnists denounced Sadat for creating a "center of power" (markaz quwwa), a phrase Sadat himself had used to attack Ali Sabri and other opponents of the regime after 1970.[60] No one journalist emerged to assume the dominant position Haykal had held, but all of the chief editors fundamentally supported the government's policies. President Sadat publicly endorsed press freedom, but he also called on the media to be responsible. As he put it in one speech in 1975, "If freedom of expression is sacred, Egypt is more sacred and I am not prepared to relinquish any of her rights."[61] In early 1974, the government announced the easing of press restrictions, formally abolishing censorship. During 1974–1975 columnists in various papers engaged in debates in print over the need for a revival of political parties, over Nasserism, over student discontents, and over freedom of the press itself. There was even some investigative reporting of official corruption.[62]

In 1975, Sadat issued a decree establishing the Supreme Press Council which was empowered to issue licenses to publish, and to draw up a code of ethics for the print media.

The most outspoken criticism of the government during the early Sadat period tended to come from the nondailies. The monthly *al-Taliah* remained a Marxist organ, and the weekly *Rose al-Yusif*, which became very popular with some intellectuals, was also to the left of the mainstream. At the other side of the political spectrum, the two monthly magazines *al-Da'wah* and *al-Itisam,* which had been suspended during the Nasser era, represented the views of the religious conservatives. When *al-Tali'a* and *Rose al-Yusif* commented on the January 1977 rioting over consumer price increases by calling them a spontaneous expression of mass disaffection, this clearly was out of line with the government's view that the rioting was inspired by radical elements. Shortly thereafter, the chairman of al-Ahram Publishing House replaced *al-Taliah*, which this house published, with a science magazine, and the editor of *Rose al-Yusif* was replaced by a man more supportive of government policies, so both publications ceased carrying dissenting views.[63]

In 1976 President Sadat began to lay the groundwork for possible changes in the press structure, by allowing political parties to emerge and by permitting parties to publish newspapers.[64] Until 1976, the ruling group's political organization had been the only legal party in the country and at the same time the owner of all politically significant newspapers.

At the time of the parliamentary elections of 1976, Sadat declared the formation of three so-called platforms (manabir) of the Arab Socialist Union which could compete separately in the election campaign, representing leftist, centrist, and rightist tendencies, respectively. Then these three platforms became separate political parties. Law No. 4 of 1977 endorsed this change and made it possible for new parties to be formed by members of parliament. The ASU was thus made obsolete, and in June 1977 Sadat abolished all strata of the ASU except for the Central Committee, which remained pending a political decision on what to do with such matters as ownership of the existing newspapers, still legally in the hands of the ASU. The 1977 parties law also allowed the emergence of political party newspapers. After extended discussions among politicians and journalists, in 1980 Law No. 148, on Powers of the Press, was passed, giving to the Shura Council (upper house of parliament) legal ownership of the five major publishing houses, which publish the three "national dailies" and numerous magazines. The Shura Council appoints the chairman and eight of the fifteen board members of each house, and in practice the Egyptian president also approves the chairman and chief editor.

Some of the Egyptian political parties that emerged in the 1970s adopted a clear stance of opposition to the government. New parties (and their newspapers) needed, and still require, the approval of a semi-official Parties Committee, which is in effect controlled by the regime, but whose decisions can be appealed in the civil courts. Several opposition parties managed to survive. The law prohibits parties based on religion so the Muslim Brotherhood is illegal as a party, but some members have served in parliament as independents or members of other parties.[65] There is consequently no official Muslim Brotherhood newspaper but some other opposition papers reflect MB views.

The parties that emerged in Egypt in 1976 were permitted to publish their own papers, but they did not overnight create clear press diversity because policy differences among the parties remained small, and those journalists who were critical of the government had difficulty in publicizing their views.

In 1977, as the People's Assembly was discussing a new press law, President Sadat made clear that his concept of democracy required "public" control over the press: "Today, thank God, 25 years after our revolution, our country has regained its constitutional legality. . . . We now have a state of institutions [dawlit al-mu'assasaat] . . . the cabinet . . . the People's Assembly and . . . the judiciary. The fourth authority which we have created is the press. This is because the press has a great influence on public opinion. . . . We cannot allow our press, which shapes public opinion, to be controlled by an individual or by an opinionated and temperamental newspaper publisher, nor for that matter by a group of people who want to impose their will on the people. No, the press is the property of the people and will remain so."[66]

The new political parties did begin to publish their own weekly newspapers. *Garidit Masr* of Sadat's center party which started on June 28, 1977, was totally supportive of the regime, but criticism of policies came regularly from *al-Ahrar* of the rightist Liberal Party as soon as it began to appear on November 14, 1977, and even more so from the leftist Progressive Unionist (tagammu') Party's weekly *al-Ahali*, which first appeared on February 1, 1978. During the spring of 1978, a rather lively discussion on several domestic and foreign policy issues took place in *al-Ahali* and *al-Ahrar*, as well as in the People's Assembly, in the universities and elsewhere. But the party papers encountered serious financial difficulties in competing with the large publishing houses. In addition, *al-Ahali*, that regularly criticized what it saw as growing income inequalities and other negative effects of the government's economic policy, the American connection, and corruption by prominent personalities ran afoul of the Socialist Prosecutor who began on May 17, 1978 to seize issues for antidemocratic content, a charge that the court upheld.

Meanwhile, in a referendum on May 21, 1978 President Sadat secured approval for a new law banning political activity by Marxists, pre-revolutionary politicians, and others. He stressed in many public statements that he was committed to democracy, to freedom of the press, and to party newspapers, as long as these were tempered by responsibility.[67] Editors of the party weeklies continued their publication efforts through the summer of 1978, but by September most were gone, to a large extent reflecting the weaknesses of the new parties themselves. After this false start, the party press would emerge stronger later (see below); but meanwhile the religious magazines *al-Da'wah* and *al-Itisam* continued their rather independent course, even criticizing the government's peace initiative.[68]

In his last two years as president, 1979–1981, Sadat's ambivalence toward the press and his critics became even clearer: he sought to allow party activity and simultaneously sought to keep the public discussion within certain bounds, as party journalists attempted to speak out more. The initial focus of attention was the preparation for the June 1979 Peoples Assembly election. In anticipation of that, President Sadat in late 1978 created a new National Democratic Party, which the members of his government joined. This new regime-sponsored party began to issue a weekly newspaper, *Mayo* ("May," named after Sadat's so-called Corrective Revolution of May 1972), which was well financed and had the benefit of special news features and information provided by government departments, as well as exclusive interviews with the president.

In anticipation of the upcoming 1979 election, another new political party, the Socialist Labor Party, was formed by opposition elements, and it too began to issue its own newspaper, *al-Sha'b* (The People). In addition, the party weekly *al-Ahali,* published by the National Progressive Unionist Grouping, reappeared just prior to the election and joined *al-Sha'b* in leftist criticism of the regime. Neither of these papers was able to gain a large circulation (print runs remained well below 100,000 copies), and both encountered difficulties with the authorities over the contents of individual issues. For example, *al-Ahali* objected in print to Sadat's 1979 peace treaty with Israel and to the 1979 parties law amendment which required all parties to support certain principles including the treaty. Several issues of *al-Ahali* were confiscated because of these attacks, yet the two leftist opposition papers continued.

Then, in 1981, President Sadat lost patience with continuing criticism and attacks from a variety of sources, deciding that they represented a deeper hostility to the state that he could not tolerate. In September 1981, he reversed course on press freedom and reverted to direct state control over the press. He closed a number of newspapers and put many journalists in jail. He did so in the context of a general crackdown on various opposition elements, which included arrests of university professors and others as well. He took strong restrictive action against a wide spectrum of his political opponents, putting many leading critics of all kinds in jail and ordering the suspension of several party publications, including the leftist party papers *al-Sha'b* and *al-Ahali* and the Muslim Brotherhood monthly *al-Da'wa.* Their basic right to publish was never legally revoked, but the government found ways to stop them from appearing during this period. The ruling party's paper, *Mayo,* as well as the very mildly oppositionist paper, *al-Ahrar,* of the rightist Liberal Party, were, however, permitted to continue publication.

On October 6, 1981, in the midst of this confrontation with a wide spectrum of opposition elements, President Sadat was assassinated by Muslim extremists. Husni Mubarak, Sadat's vice president, succeeded him as president. The presidency has since 1981 been in the hands of Husni Mubarak, who was re-elected in successive six-year terms, the latest one being a September 1999 referendum. Mubarak's National Democratic Party (NDP) also holds a large majority in the People's Assembly and in the Consultative (Shura) Council, an important channel of influence over the press.

President Mubarak, like Sadat, has however been ambivalent about the press. Under Mubarak, arrests and abuse of journalists—police assaults and raids, detentions, even torture—continued, although not as severely as under Nasser and Sadat. Also in late 80s and early 90s violence by Islamic groups existed and liberal journalists were threatened, and government explanation puts government abuses of journalists within context of a security situation.[69]

Close observers of the press in Egypt believe that President Mubarak's treatment of the print media is inconstant and "shows confusion."[70] At first he continued Sadat's tough restrictions on the press, and he immediately had emergency laws passed which affected press freedom. After a few months in office, however, Mubarak lifted many of the direct press restrictions. He let the opposition leaders and journalists out of jail and allowed the opposition party newspapers to resume publication. He gradually liberalized the press during the following years, so that Egyptian journalists began to enjoy more freedom than they had had at any time in their modern history. When he released from prison most of the opposition writers whom Sadat had incarcerated, they soon found it possible to begin writing and criticizing again, within limits.

By the spring of 1982, the opposition party newspapers *al-Sha'b* and *al-Ahali* had resumed publication. In the fall of 1983, a fourth opposition party, the New Wafd, which had been founded in the late 1970s but was suspended after a brief debut, won a court case, and reemerged stronger than ever. By the spring of 1984 this new party was publishing its own weekly, *al-Wafd,* which quickly demonstrated the party's appeal by selling more than half a million copies each week. This was six to ten times the circulation of the other party weeklies, making the paper comparable to the leading dailies in readership. Finally, in 1984, the government lifted the ban on Coptic Christian and Muslim publications that Sadat had imposed in 1981, and the last of these particular press restrictions was gone.

During the period after 1982, there were five party weeklies—one government-controlled and four opposition—and they gradually became more outspoken in the freer climate that Mubarak allowed. President Mubarak continuously emphasized the importance of democracy and free speech. The opposition weeklies attacked the regime on various issues, such as the handling of the case of the Egyptian soldier who died in prison in 1985 after killing seven Israeli tourists, or the handling of the 1985 hijacking of an Egyptian airplane to Malta. Mubarak occasionally lectured the opposition, but he took no direct measures to silence media critics, and he seemed to be sincere in his desire to broaden the base of political legitimacy by allowing more freedom of discussion. In addition, the so-called "national press," including the three major dailies (*al-Ahram, al-Akhbar,* and *al-Gumhuria*), and several other older publications, occasionally carried news reports and commentaries that tended to put the regime in a negative light, even though they basically remained fully supportive of the regime and the Establishment. Because of the new atmosphere of greater liberalization, and because of the competition with the revived opposition party weeklies, even the national press showed increased willingness to report on all newsworthy events, and tackle controversial subjects, regardless of the political effect. In 1983 the International Press Institute stated that the Egyptian press under Mubarak had achieved the highest level of freedom since the fall of the monarchy in 1953.[71]

By 1993 there were five party newspapers with circulations of over 100,000 each: the Wafd Party's daily newspaper *al-Wafd;* the al-Tagammu' party's weekly *al-Ahali;* the Liberal Party's weekly *al-Ahrar;* the National (Watani) party weekly *Mayo;* and the Labor Party's weekly *al-Sha'b.* Other small papers appeared irregularly. *Misr* newspaper, owned by the political party of the same name, declined in circulation as the party faded from prominence, and in 1997 the party suspended it for lack of funds. But the three "national" daily papers reached large numbers of people, with circulations between 400,000 and one million. By 1993 there were 263 licensed newspapers of all kinds: 38 issued by national publishing houses, 38 by government organs, 11 by political parties, 24 by unions and companies, 79 by individuals and professional societies, 12 by universities, 18 by social clubs and youth centers, and 30 by provincial governments.[72]

At the same time, the state has retained many instruments of control and influence over the press, and has used them on occasion. The Mubarak government has justified some repressive measures against the press by reference to on the need to combat the Islamist insurgency that began in 1992. Antiterrorist Law 97, passed in July 1992, strengthened penal code provisions allowing the state to take action against a publication which it believes threatens the public order by "disrupting social peace" or "spreading panic," which are terms subject to varying definition. After the 1997 Luxor massacre, the insurgency diminished considerably, but President Mubarak never lifted the emergency laws, which have continued to exist now for decades; they were renewed again in the year 2000 so they can be used by the regime against the press.

In 1995, the government tried to tighten controls over the press by having parliament pass a restrictive Press Law Number 93. This proved to be a tactical error because it caused a very strong negative reaction from a wide spectrum of journalists including prominent ones generally loyal to the regime. Even senior editors of major newspapers who had been appointed by the government, such as Ibrahim Nafie, who was chief editor of *al-Ahram* and head of the Press Syndicate, protested against the new law, objecting to many of its provisions. Nafie and others engaged in lengthy negotiations with the government that resulted in their winning concessions in a new Press and Publications Law Number 96, passed in 1996.[73]

In May 1995, the Egyptian parliament passed Law No. 93 which increased criminal penalties for "publishing false information or forged documents liable to harm to the public interest" or to the national economy. It laid the burden of proof in libel cases on the press. Prominent journalists strongly criticized the law for its severity, one saying it would "turn Egyptian newspapers into press releases."[74] The Press Syndicate spoke out against the law and led a campaign for its cancellation that lasted more than a year. It held many meetings, staged protest strikes, and met with parliamentary officials. Dr. Mustafa Kamal Hilmy, chairman of the Shura Council and the Supreme Press Council agreed to have a committee review the law, and after Syndicate Chairman Ibrahim Nafie met with President

Mubarak on the matter in June of 1996, a new and more liberal Press Law 96 was passed.

The most widely publicized cases in the 1990s reflecting antagonism between the government and the press have involved the opposition Labor Party's newspaper *al-Sha'b*. The party had emerged in the mid-70s as the Socialist Labor Party during Sadat's party revival. The SLP was mildly leftist under ex-Nasserist Ibrahim Shukri. The Labor Party then became the sole legal outlet for Islamist views, and its fortnightly newspaper *al-Sha'b* in the 1980s and 1990s expressed those views. The paper took issue with government during the Iraq-Kuwait crisis of 1990, and then became increasingly antagonistic to the regime, leveling strong attacks on specific ministers.[75] As the newspaper stepped up its attacks on the government and its senior officials, the authorities occasionally arrested and questioned *al-Sha'b* journalists about their articles.[76] The disputes were taken up by the courts, as senior government officials and *al-Sha'b* editors filed charges and counter-charges before the judge.

In 1996, a Cairo court, citing Law 93 of 1995, sentenced the *al-Sha'b* editor Magdi Ahmad Hussein to jail and to pay a fine because of the paper's libelous articles against Alaa Hassan al-Alfi, son of Interior Minister Hassan al-Alfi. By this time at least twenty journalists from various papers had been tried in court under Law 93.[77] Then in 1998, Hassan al-Alfi, who left the government in November 1997, was tried in Cairo's criminal court on charges of corruption and abuse of power brought by lawyers for *al-Sha'b* newspaper. In court, al-Alfi said that *al-Sha'b* had brought the suit because it was "the mouthpiece of the outlawed Muslim Brotherhood" whose members he had brought to trial as minister.[78] In 1999, *al-Sha'b* published a series of articles over several months accusing Agriculture Minister Yusif Wali of treason for promoting trade with Israel, and in August 1999 the court sentenced the editor and others at the paper to two years in jail and fines of 20,000 pounds. The court of cassation overturned the verdict in December 1996, but the lower court in April 2000 sentenced them again to jail. During the long trial, a number of journalists staged a sit-in at the Egyptian Press Syndicate headquarters calling for the release of Hussain and cancellation of Law No. 96.[79]

In the year 2000, a novel by Syrian author Haydar Haydar, "Banquet for Seaweed," became an issue between *al-Sha'b* and the government. The newspaper led a campaign against the book saying it was offensive to Islam, and against the Minister of Culture for having it printed and distributed. The government-owned literary weekly *Akhbar al-Adib* defended the novel, but thousands of al-Azhar students rioted against it, and the authorities had to use force against them. In May, the authorities suspended the newspaper, and the Political Parties Committee, which is controlled by the regime, ordered the freezing of the Labor Party's activities on the grounds that the newspaper incited riots. Editors of *al-Sha'b* sought to hold a press conference about the novel at the headquarters of the Press Syndicate, but the Syndicate refused, reflecting sentiment among many journalists that the newspaper had gone too far.[80] Some commentators in national papers however came to its defense, for example, the chief editor of *al-Siyaasa al-Dawlia* journal published by al Ahram Publishing House, who was a member of the Press Syndicate Council, wrote an editorial in June 2000 which said the government's suspension of *al-Sha'b* by administrative decree was a "violation of press freedom." He said the government should have taken the case to court and its action "undermined democratic principles through arbitrary measures."[81]

The court case against *al-Sha'b* continued, and in January 2003 one judge ruled in favor of the newspaper, but the government blocked its reemergence anyway, and observers believe it will not reappear.[82]

At the beginning of the twenty-first century, many Egyptian journalists, including prominent columnists and editors writing in the national dailies, want to see more liberalization of the press from government influence and control. They argue, for example, that the penalties for libel, namely one year in jail and a fine of $300–$1500 for libel against a private individual and two years or a $1500–$6000 fine for libeling a public official are much too harsh.[83]

One of Egypt's most respected editors, Salama Ahmad Salama of the national daily *al-Ahram*, has written that the most important challenge facing the Egyptian press "is related to freedom; it will either be granted eventually or, if it continues to be denied, this will be a catastrophe. It is a matter of getting through the bottleneck." He argued, "There should be all sorts of freedoms: establishing newspapers, canceling provisions in the law that provide the imprisonment penalty for publication offenses, etc. If this does not happen we will not be able to have a leading position or compete with the international press."[84] Even the chief editor of *al-Ahram,* has said publicly: "We [journalists] must continue our struggle to regain more freedoms and have a press without restrictions or legislation that are fragile or far from the spirit of our age. . . . On issues such as the imprisonment of journalists, the penalty should be reduced to a financial fine paid by the journalist or his organization. . . . At the same time, we must remember our duties and follow the code of ethics. After all, a story could ruin a family or somebody's future. To gain our rights we must fulfill our duties."[85]

The Press Syndicate Council, representing all Egyptian journalists, in September 1999 issued an urgent appeal to President Mubarak, asking him "to give priority . . . to the revision of laws and legislation that restrict freedoms, guaranteed by the constitution, such as the freedom to publish and own newspapers and have access to information." It said, "The council believes that the time is due for revising the restrictive penalties for publication offenses in view of their grave consequences and negative reflection on the freedom of the press and their failure to establish a balance between freedom and responsibility. . . . The council's demand to replace jail sentences by monetary fines was not a response to the imprisonment of specific journalists but has been a basic demand of journalists in all their conferences and general assemblies." Since Law 93 was passed in 1995, journalists have tried to reduce its jail penalties; even after changes were made in 1996 the law still provided for jail sentences although shorter ones.[86]

The Syndicate also called for settling press cases amicably out of court. In 1998, Syndicate Chairman Makram Muhammad Ahmad negotiated with Prosecutor General Regaa al-Arabi and reached agreement that the syndicate should be given an opportunity to settle libel complaints without sending them to court. At the time, three journalists had just been sent to jail within less than a month and about sixty others were awaiting trial. The Council at the time also met with President Mubarak, who promised that no restrictions would be imposed on the press "other than those enshrined in the law and in the journalist's conscience." Yet in early 1998 the government banned *al-Dustur,* and transferred *Rose al-Yusif* deputy chief editor Adel Hammouda to *al-Ahram,* after both publications had printed a warning to Coptic businessmen allegedly from the Gama'a al-Islamia.[87]

The Egyptian press, therefore, plays a complex and constantly changing role in the Egyptian political process, although the fundamental system has retained most of its features under several regimes and in varying circumstances. The three "national" daily newspapers, which reach well over one million readers each, still fundamentally support the policies of the government, and the ruling party's own newspaper, *Mayo,* vigorously promotes the interests of the leadership. The existence of independent political parties is an essential element in the system. At the start of the twenty-first century, there were thirteen recognized opposition parties in Egypt, and several of them published newspapers regularly.[88] Key opposition newspapers including the Tagammu' party's *al-Ahali,* and the papers of the Nasserite and Wafd parties continue to appear as they have for many years and continued to criticize the government on a regular basis. The weekly *Rose al-Yusif,* considered by many to be a vehicle of irresponsible yellow journalism, also kept up its attacks. Yet except for *al-Wafd,* these nondailies which routinely criticize the regime generally have much smaller circulations and influence smaller segments of society. President Sadat allowed the beginning of a diversified, partisan press and then quashed it; President Mubarak gradually has allowed these elements to re-emerge, but they have not yet fundamentally altered the system. The potential is there for systemic change, but that will not happen unless and until the underlying political system becomes a more liberal and democratic one.

In short, print media in these four countries have gone through considerable change over the years, and their role in the political system is mixed and still being debated, so the issue was unsettled as of 2003.

NOTES

1. *Filastin* was established in 1911 in Jaffa by the Christian Arab family of Isa al-Isa, and *al-Difa'a* was established in Jaffa in 1933, and both moved to East Jerusalem in 1948.

2. Orayb Aref Najjar, "The Ebb and Flow of the Liberalization of the Jordanian Press: 1985–1997," *Journalism and Mass Communication Quarterly,* Vol. 75 No. 1, spring 1998, pp. 127–42.

3. Muhammad I. Ayish, Mohamed Najib El-Sarayah, and Ziyad D. Rifai, "Jordan" in Yahya R. Kamalipour and Hamid Mowlana, Eds., *Mass Media in the Middle East,* Westport, CT: Greenwood Press, 1994, p. 129–30.

4. Ayish et. al., p. 137; Najjar, pp. 127–42.

5. Ayish, pp. 129–37.

6. Najjar, pp. 127–42.

7. U.S. Dept. of State, *1996 Country Reports on Human Rights Practices,* Jordan chapter, January 30, 1997. These annual reports have also been used elsewhere in this chapter.

8. 1997 World Press Freedom Review; Najjar, op. cit., pp. 132–33; and U.S. Dept. of State, *1998 Country Reports on Human Rights Practices,* Jordan chapter, February 26, 1999; for details of this period, see Najjar, pp. 127–42.

9. U.S. Dept. of State, *1999 Country Reports on Human Rights Practices,* Jordan chapter, February 25, 2000; and *1999 World Press Freedom Review.*

10. *1999 World Press Freedom Review,* Jordan section.

11. Laid Zaghlami, "Algeria" chapter, in Kamalipour and Mowlana, op. cit., pp. 17–19; see also Simeon Kerr, ABC News, August 21, 2000; and *Reporters Sans Frontiers, 1999 Report.*

12. *1999 World Press Freedom Review.*

13. *1999 World Press Freedom Review,* and Lola Keilani, in *Al Ahram International,* Feb. 3–9, 2000, p. 5.

14. Ibtisam Awadat, *The Star,* Jordan, July 13, 2000.

15. Alia Shukri Hamzeh, "Government gives go-ahead on privatization of press," *Jordan Times,* August 31, 2000; Jillian Schwedler, MERIP Press Information Note #98, July 3, 2002; and informed observer, Amman, January 2003.

16. *New York Times,* April 29, 1960.

17. William Quandt, *Revolution and Political Leadership: Algeria 1954–1968,* Cambridge: MIT Press, 1969, pp. 193–95, 200.

18. The NLF began a French daily named *El Chaab* in Algiers, then in December 1962 renamed it *Le Peuple* and began a separate Arabic edition called *Al Sha'b.*

19. Algiers Radio, September 18, 1973, 1303 GMT.

20. *New York Times,* September 18, 1993.

21. *New York Times,* June 6, 1965; the Communist editor of *Alger Republicain* Henri Alleg, resigned in August 1964; *New York Times,* August 4, 1964.

22. Communique of a seminar on Information and Indoctrination held by the FLN, published in *Revolution Africaine,* Algiers, January 31–February 6, 1975, p. 20.

23. Reporteurs Sans Frontiers, 1999 report.

24. Laid Zaghlami, "Algeria" chapter in Kamalipour and Mowlana, op. cit., pp. 17–19.

25. In 1993 the government suspended the government daily *al-Massa'* and two independent dailies, *El-Watan* (in French) and *al Jaza'ir al Yawm;* U.S. Department

of State, *1993 Country Reports on Human Rights Practices,* Algeria Chapter, Washington D.C., 1994.

26. Reporters Sans Frontiers, "Five Journalists Still Missing," Paris, July 10, 2000.

27. U.S. Department of State, *1996 Country Reports on Human Rights Practices,* Algeria Chapter, Washington D.C., January 30, 1997.

28. 1998 and 1999 editions of *World Press Freedom Review.*

29. U.S. Department of State, *1999 Country Reports on Human Rights Practices,* Algeria Chapter, Washington D.C., January 25, 2000.

30. *1999 Country Reports on Human Rights Practices,* Algeria Chapter, Washington D.C., February 25, 2000.

31. Reporters Sans Frontiers, "Five Journalists Still Missing," Paris, July 10, 2000.

32. U.S. Department of State, *1999 Country Reports on Human Rights Practices,* Algeria chapter, Washington D.C., February 25, 2000.

33. www.elwatan.com (2002).

34. Reporters Sans Frontiers, "Five Journalists Still Missing," Paris, July 10, 2000; and U.S. Embassy Algiers, Media Directory Algiers, November 2002; and interview with Algerian official, March 2003.

35. September 12, 1999 TV speech quoted in *1999 World Press Freedom Review,* Algeria section.

36. Cited in I. William Zartman, *Government and Politics in Northern Africa,* New York: Praeger 1963, pp. 73–75.

37. Interview No. 6, Tunisian journalist, Tunis, May 3, 1973.

38. Interview No. 7, Tunisian journalist, Tunis, May 4, 1976.

39. U.S. Department of State, *1998 Country Reports on Human Rights Practices,* Tunisia chapter, Washington D.C., February 26, 1999; U.S. Department of State, *1999 Country Reports on Human Rights Practices,* Tunisia Chapter, Washington D.C., February 25, 2000.

40. *1999 World Press Freedom Review,* Tunisia section.

41. State Department, *1999 Human Rights Report,* Tunisia Section, February 25, 2000; and *Gulf News,* May 28, 2002.

42. Henry Ladd Smith, *Journalism Quarterly,* 31/2 (summer 1954), p. 333.

43. Interview with Dr. Sami Aziz, professor of journalism, Cairo University, May 8, 1973.

44. Interview No. 22, Cairo, May 10, 1973.

45. C. Wilton Wynn, "Western Techniques Influence Party Newspapers of Egypt," *Journalism Quarterly,* 25/4 (December 1948), pp. 391–94.

46. Interview No. 17, Egyptian journalist, Cairo, May 8, 1973.

47. Ainslie, op. cit., p. 143; Adnan Almany, "Government Control of the Press in the United Arab Republic, 1952–1970," *Journalism Quarterly,* 49/2 (summer 1972), pp. 342–43.

48. Tom J. McFadden, *Daily Journalism in the Arab States,* Columbus: Ohio State University Press, 1958, p. 88.

49. Interview No. 106, Egyptian journalist, April 1973.

50. Don Peretz, "Democracy and the Revolution in Egypt," *Middle East Journal,* Winter 1959, p. 37.

51. Law for the Organization of the Press (qanun tanzim al sahafah), sections 1, 3, 6, 7, and 8. This law is described and analyzed by an Egyptian expert in Gamal

al 'Utaifi, *Huriyyit al Sahafa,* Cairo: al Ahram Commercial Press, 1971, pp. 39, 59, and 87.

52. A few Egyptian weeklies, all in private hands, were allowed to function outside this system because they were not politically significant: *Journal d'Egypte,* and the Copt-owned *al Watani;* interview no. 18, Egyptian journalist, Cairo, May 9, 1973.

53. Interview with Gamal al 'Utaifi, *al Ahram* editor and People's Assembly member, Cairo, May 9, 1973.

54. Al 'Utaifi, p. 40; and interview with Gamal al 'Utaifi, *al-Ahram* editor and People's Assembly member, Cairo, May 9, 1973.

55. Al 'Utaifi, pp. 41, 43, 63, 73, 76.

56. Editorial "A Thought," by Ali Amin, published in *al-Ahram* on May 3, 1965, the day he left *al-Akhbar.*

57. President Sadat cited these three principles often, e.g. his speech quoted in *al-Ahram,* June 27, 1977.

58. Sadat's speeches, *al-Ahram,* September 29, 1973, *al-Ahram,* May 4 and July 17, 1977.

59. Sadat's speeches *al-Ahram,* September 29, 1973, and September 28, 1975.

60. Musa Sabri, *Akhbar al-Yawm,* October 4, 11, and 18, 1974; Mamduh Rida and Anwar Za'luk, in *al-Ta'awun al-Siyaasi,* April 7 and May 1, 1977, respectively. See also Fu'ad Matar, *al-Nahar* (Beirut), February 4, 1974.

61. President Sadat, *al-Ahram,* February 8, 1974 and May 27, 1975.

62. *Al-Ahram* February 8, 1974. Examples of editorial discussion: On Nasserism: Bathi and Gawdat in *al-Musawwar,* March 14–28, 1974; on parties: Sa'dah and Ali Amin in *Akhbar al-Yawm* August 24, 1974 and August 21, 1974; on press freedom: Mahfuz in *al-Akhbar,* February 22, 1974; on corruption: *Akhbar al-Yawm,* July 3, 1976, August 20, 1976, and September 14, 1976.

63. Following a disagreement over the March issue, the editor of *Tali'a* was fired by al Ahram Publishing House, which then converted the magazine. The changes at *Rose al-Yusif* were made in April.

64. James Napoli and Hussein Y. Amin, "Press Freedom in Egypt," chapter 9 in Festus Eribo and William Jong-Ebot, Eds., *Press Freedom and Communication in Africa,* Trenton, NJ: Africa World Press Inc, 1997, pp. 193–94.

65. U.S. Dept. of State, *Country Reports on Human Rights Practices,* 1996 and 1999, chapters on Egypt, January 30, 1997, and February 25, 2000.

66. President Sadat's speech at Mersa Metruh, *al-Ahram,* August 9, 1977.

67. One example among many was in his speech to the ASU Central Committee on July 22, 1978, reported in all Cairo newspapers the next day.

68. A fourth party, the New Wafd, which emerged in early 1978, dissolved itself the same year without having started to issue a newspaper.

69. Napoli and Amin, op. cit., p. 194.

70. Napoli and Amin, p. 197, who cite an example of the soft treatment of *al-Wafd* compared to harsh treatment of *al-Shaab.*

71. Sonia Dabbous, "Egypt," in Kamalipour and Mowlana, op. cit. pp. 71–72.

72. Dabbous, pp. 63–64.

73. Interview with Ibrahim Nafie, Chief Editor of *al-Ahram,* Washington D.C., Spring 2000.

74. For example, Salama Ahmad Salama in *al-Ahram,* June 8 and 12, 1995.

75. *Al-Ahram International,* May 18–24, 2000; and *Middle East International,* May 19, 2000 pp. 14–15 and June 2, 2000 p. 15.

76. For example, in 1993 they arrested not only two journalists but also Labor Party Chairman and Vice Chairman because of articles accusing Mubarak of rigging the October 4 referendum, but no charges were filed; U.S. Dept. of State, *1993 Country Reports on Human Rights Practices,* chapter on Egypt, January 31, 1994.

77. Committee to Protect Journalists, letter to Mubarak February 24, 1996, published by Africa News, May 1996; see also *World Press Freedom Review,* 1998 and 1999.

78. "Heated trial leads to fist-fight," *al-Ahram International,* July 16–24, 1998, p. 4.

79. Andrew Hammond, in *The Washington Report on Middle East Affairs;* June 2000, p. 25; *1999 World Press Freedom Review.*

80. *Al-Ahram International,* May 18–24, 2000.

81. "Soapbox" column, *al-Ahram International,* June 8–14, 2000, p. 9.

82. *Middle East International,* May 19, 2000, pp. 14–15 and June 2, 2000, p. 15; interview, Ahmad Musallami, journalist, Abu Dhabi, January 19, 2003.

83. *1999 World Press Freedom Review.*

84. Interview by Shaden Shehab in *al-Ahram International,* January 6–12, 2000 p. 3.

85. Shaden Shehab in *al-Ahram International,* June 17–23, 1999.

86. Shaden Shehab in *al-Ahram International,* September 2–8, 2000, p. 2.

87. Shaden Shehab in *al-Ahram International,* April 16, 1998.

88. U.S. Dept. of State, *1999 Country Reports on Human Rights Practices,* chapter on Egypt, February 25, 2000.

8

Offshore Pan-Arab
Print Media

A significant development in Arab media during the 1990s has been the growth of newspapers and broadcasting stations that have their main editorial offices outside of the Arab world but at the same time consider their target audiences as being within the Arab world. In fact their potential audience is in all of the Arab countries, so they are in effect regional media, or as one observer calls them "transnational."[1] Here we call them "offshore" to distinguish them from those print and electronic media that have their headquarters and most of their audiences within one Arab country. They are also characterized by their focus on reaching a pan-Arab readership rather than catering to readers in a single country, and this affects their editorial policy.

Offshore media are not entirely new. Arab newspapers and magazines have been published in Europe for more than a quarter century, the majority of them moving to London and Paris from Beirut at the time of the Lebanese civil war. Yet the phenomenon has outlasted the original impetus of the Lebanese crisis, and even expanded substantially, for several reasons.

This chapter describes and analyzes offshore print media. Two chapters on the developments in Arab television after 1990 that follow include discussion of offshore Arab TV stations.

BACKGROUND

The Lebanese civil war had a powerful negative impact on the Lebanese press. When the conflict began in 1975, the dangers associated with writing and publishing in the midst of the fighting persuaded some newspaper owners to move their operations to London, Paris, or Rome. Previously Lebanon had been a haven for Arab publishers and journalists of all political persuasions but then it became unsafe. Many journalists also left the country and found employment in the newly established offshore enterprises. Non-Lebanese Arab financial interests also became involved, and a new phenomenon of offshore Arab newspapers emerged.[2]

Several Arab newspapers established themselves in Europe to benefit from the fact that there were professional Lebanese journalists living there, in London, Paris, and Rome. They left Lebanon because of the civil war and went to Europe, or they were willing to relocate to Europe as Arab newspapers were established there, because of its proximity to the Middle East and because they were fluent in English and/or French. Some Lebanese newspapers relocated to Europe and then moved back later, such as the weekly *al-Hawadis;* others moved but were unable to survive, such as the weekly *al-Dustur* that moved to London and died there. The pro-Iraqi newspaper *al-Tadamun* edited by Fuad Matar, was published in London until 1990 when Iraq invaded Kuwait and Iraqi subsidies stopped. The weekly *al-Mustaqbal* moved to Paris and survived for about ten years under the editorship of Nabil Khoury but it then closed.[3]

During the 1980s and 1990s, Saudi Arabian businessmen became the major investors in Arab offshore print media. They were motivated by opportunities they saw to invest in media that would add to their prestige and might be commercially beneficial, and they were encouraged to base their operations in Europe where press freedom prevailed rather than in Saudi Arabia which maintained formal and informal restrictions on publishing. Although publishing in London was expensive, wealthy Saudi businessmen were able and willing to cover these high costs more than others and they sought to control pan-Arab publications. Because their publications were well funded, they attracted some of the best talent among Arab professional journalists. The same phenomenon helped promote Arab satellite television in the 1990s as wealthy Saudis also invested heavily in that too (see next chapter). After the initial Saudi investments in Europe-based media, others followed.

During the 1990s, the number of offshore Arab newspapers expanded further, encouraged by satellite technology allowing easy and fast distribution to the Arab world, plus the presence of Arab professional journalists. Some small publications by Arab dissidents living in exile also emerged. In 1998, with the decline in oil prices and resulting financial pressures, some publications cut costs and reduced staffs, and newspapers such as *al-Hayat* relocated part of their operations into the Middle East to reduce costs, but the advantages of having a base in Europe kept most of them there. By the beginning of the twenty-first century, all of the important Arab offshore papers had concentrated in London, which journalists found more hospitable than other European cities. These publications were reaching an estimated thirty million readers in the Arab world and elsewhere.

STRUCTURE AND OWNERSHIP

By 2003 there were three major publishing houses with headquarters in London which produced publications for a pan-Arab audience: the Saudi Research and Marketing group, al-Hayat and al-Quds al-Arabi. In addition there were several small-circulation independent Arab publications that reached readers in only a few countries.

Saudi Research and Marketing Group

In 1977, Saudi Research and Marketing group began publishing a daily newspaper called *al-Sharq al-Awsat* (The Middle East), which was edited in London and printed there on modern equipment. It was originally flown daily to Arab countries but later transmitted by satellite to printing plants in Saudi Arabia. It was the first Arab newspaper to use this approach. This use of technology is common today, but at the time it was unusual. The official publishers are Hisham and Muhammad Ali Hafez, sons of a well-known Saudi publisher who had built the newspaper *al-Madina* into a respectable daily, which still exists today in Jidda. They had been publishing an English language daily *The Arab News* in Jidda since 1974. The first editor of *al-Sharq al-Awsat* and an initial shareholder was Jihad al Khazen, an experienced Lebanese journalist who had been editor of the Beirut newspaper *Daily Star,* and who during the Lebanese civil war had moved to Jidda to become editor of *The Arab News.* Other staffers in London were mostly Lebanese and Palestinian, but its content was respectful of Saudi sensitivities.

Since *al-Sharq al-Awsat* started in 1978 during the oil boom, it had a strong financial position, although that weakened in later years. After the paper started up, Prince Ahmad bin Salman, the son of Riyadh Governor Prince Salman bin Abdal Aziz, one of the kingdom's most prominent leaders, became the paper's main financial supporter. Prince Ahmad reportedly bought an 80% share of the paper, leaving the Hafiz brothers with 20%, but then in 1999 other investors including Shaikh Salih Kamel, bought out the Hafiz brothers. Later, when Prince Ahmad died, his brother Prince Faisal bin Salman became chairman. The paper was not able to cover costs from advertising so it required subsidies from its investors. Shaikh Kamal Adham, the former head of Saudi intelligence, was reportedly also an investor until his death in 1999.[4] Kamal Adham reportedly invested in it because he wanted Saudi Arabia to have a stronger voice in the Arab world.[5]

The paper has made full use of the available technology, and by the end of the century, it was being printed simultaneously in the three main Saudi cities (Jidda, Riyadh, and Dhahran), plus four major Arab cities (Kuwait, Cairo, Beirut, and Casablanca), and four Western cities (Frankfurt, New York, Marseilles, and London). It is the only such paper printed in Saudi Arabia. *Al-Sharq al-Awsat* also maintains bureaus in most Arab countries, and using satellite technology it is printed in of them in order to ensure timely distribution. After the fall of Saddam Hussein's regime in Iraq in 2003, the paper began a special edition for Iraq and established a sizeable readership inside that country.

This publishing house also puts out seventeen other publications for the Arab world. One is the weekly *al-Majalla,* a seventy-page news magazine that reports in depth on social and cultural issues, and also deals with current affairs, economics, and science. It takes a moderate editorial line. It depends heavily on advertising revenues. Others include a weekly newspaper *al-Muslimoon* (the Muslims); the popular women's magazine *Sayidaty;* the men's magazine *al Rajal;* the children's magazine *Basim;* and a TV guide in Arabic. Although Saudi Research and Marketing publications are made available throughout the Arab world, their primary readership is in Saudi Arabia. Approximately two thirds of the circulation of *al-Sharq al-Awsat* is in Saudi Arabia, for example.[6]

Al-Hayat

A second Arabic daily newspaper to use the technique of multisite printing from a European base is *al-Hayat.* The original *al-Hayat* was a prominent and respected Lebanese newspaper founded by Kamal Mrowe in 1946. It had been managed by him until his assassination in 1966, and then continued after that, maintaining its readership throughout the region. It had to cease publication in 1976 because of the civil war, after being the target of thirteen bombing attempts against the paper. When it reopened in London in 1986, it took advantage of the presence there of Arab journalists. The family started it up again in 1987 in London, and later hired Jihad Khazen as its chief editor. In 1990, Saudi prince Khalid bin Sultan, a son of the Saudi defense minister (and known in the West as the Saudi military commander during Desert Storm), invested in *al-Hayat,* giving it some financial security, although it reportedly runs an annual deficit of $10 million, and lost $160 million between 1986 and 2002. In 1991 because of editorial differences, Jamil Mrouwe sold his shares in the paper to Prince Khalid and Jihad Khazen also sold his, leaving the prince as sole owner.[7]

Al-Hayat has a staff of about 300 and more than 20 bureaus and correspondents in most Arab capitals, and because its editors consider the paper a pan-Arab one, and they claim it is more independent of local politics or restrictions placed in local papers. *Al-Hayat* was restructured to make it more appealing to Arab readers outside of Lebanon, and it no longer devoted the first two or three pages to Lebanese news. *Al-Hayat* was at first distributed in Saudi Arabia from a printing facility in Bahrain and shipped to the kingdom, but now it is printed for Saudi readers in Riyadh, Jidda, and Mecca. It also prints editions in London, New York, Frankfurt, Cairo, Beirut, Bahrain, Dubai, and Saudi Arabia. Its editorial page has often reflected Arab nationalist views, for example criticizing what it saw as American hypocrisy and a double standard.[8]

In January 1997, the New York, Washington, London, and Riyadh offices of *al-Hayat* were the targets of letter bombs. The perpetrator and his motives were never officially identified, but the former editor believes they were the work of the Egyptian radical Islamist Ayman Zawahari, who later became notorious as a partner of Usama bin Ladin's.[9] In any case, it is clear that *al-Hayat* has gained a special place in Arab media as a favorite of Arab intellectuals throughout the region, who like its thoughtful editorials, which present issues from a wide variety of perspectives. Readers tend to seek it out for its views more than for its news, although *al-Hayat* also does carry a full menu of news.

In 1992, the al-Hayat Publishing House also began publishing the eighty-page Arabic magazine *al-Wasat* that covered Arab and international events. Edited in London and distributed throughout the Arab world, at its peak it claimed a circulation of 76,000 copies, and competed with *al-Majalla,* focusing on current affairs and politics and taking a conservative editorial line. For financial reasons however, it was converted into a supplement to *al-Hayat* and only its editor remained.[10] Then in 2002, *al-Hayat* struck a deal with the Lebanese Broadcasting Company (LBC) to open a jointly-operated television news channel based in a London studio. This combined *Hayat*'s strong news base and extensive correspondent resources with LBC's solid TV presence (see Chapter 10).

Al-Quds al-Arabi

The third important pan-Arab daily is *al-Quds al-Arabi* (Arab Jerusalem), published in London. It's content has a Palestinian flavor and it has strong Palestinian connections. It carries few commercial ads and seems to have limited financial support. Its editor is a Palestinian from Gaza, Abdel Bari Atwan, formerly with *al-Majalla* of the Sharq al-Awsat group. The newspaper's senior editors, like their counterparts at the other two large London Arab publishing houses, have gained prominence among Arab audiences by their appearances on satellite television. Atwan is frequently a guest on al-Jazeera and BBC, while political editor Khalid al-Shami often appears on MBC and CNN. The editorial focus of *al-Quds al-Arabi* is events in the Arab world with special attention to Arab-Israeli issues. It uniquely includes a daily page of translations from the Israeli press. Editorially it tends to be stridently Arab nationalist on foreign affairs issues and frequently attacks U.S. Middle East policy. The paper carries little or no advertising and apparently has no Saudi funding but it does receive financial backing from other sources in the region.[11]

Al-Quds al-Arabi has a small staff of around fifteen people, and relies heavily on news agencies. It is printed in London, New York, and Morocco and distributed in most of the Arab countries plus Europe. It carries summaries of the Egyptian press and Arabic translations of some of the Israeli press. It suffers financially from low advertising revenue, and depends heavily on subscriptions and subsidies; its headline and news coverage have tabloid characteristics.

Other London-Based Newspapers

Several other Arabic publications are edited in London and intended for the Arab world. Two dailies are *al-Arab*, and *al-Zaman*.

Abdal Munim al Hawni, who is a former Libyan Information Minister, publishes *al-Arab* and the paper tends to reflect official Libyan views, leading to the supposition that it has Libyan funding. It is run as a family business; the owner is also editor in chief, and one son is managing director and another writes editorials and handles public relations. It has few full-time staff members and relies heavily on news agencies. It is in the form of a tabloid and does not cover issues in as much depth as the leading pan-Arab newspapers. It is printed in London and Tunisia and is distributed throughout the Arab world.[12] In several countries, however, it has been banned because of its content.

Al-Zaman is published by Said al-Bazzaz, an Iraqi national who had been head of Iraqi television under Saddam Hussein but fled Iraq in 1992 after Desert Storm and from London he became a critic of the Iraqi regime. It tended to be highly critical of U.S. policy, and its circulation was largely limited to the Gulf states and the U.K. It carried very few commercial ads and reportedly was subsidized by Iraqi businessmen. After the fall of Saddam Hussein's government, *al-Zaman* was able to be distributed in Iraq, so it opened offices there and started publishing a special Iraqi edition with more local news, and it quickly became the leading daily in the country, claiming a large circulation in the tens of thousands. The paper however maintained its head offices and most of its staff in London. Al-Bazzaz says that it has a "pluralist" orientation, giving voice to all political opinions.[13]

There are also several weekly newspapers published in London in addition to those mentioned above. *Al-Mushahid* (The Witness) is a sixty-six-page political magazine originally established by the BBC Arabic service in 1996 but it became independent in 1999 when it was purchased by a group of Gulf businessmen. It is printed in London and shipped by air to the Arab world. Its editorial line is generally moderate but critical of U.S. policy. *Al-Hawadith* (The News) is a seventy-eight-page magazine that was first established in Lebanon in 1908, and then moved to London in 1975. It reports on major events and provides commentary on current affairs, with a focus on Lebanon, Syria, and the Middle East. It carries an occasional extended feature on defense news. Advertising is a major source of funding.

Al-Mustaqilla (The Independent) is a twelve-page weekly that covers mainly current affairs and does not deal with financial issues, the arts, or sports. Editorially it follows a moderate Islamic line. It has limited financial resources and little advertising, but receives subsidies from some Arab countries. *Al-Fajr* (Dawn) is a twelve-page weekly newspaper whose focus is on the horn of Africa, mainly Sudan and Eritrea. Its editorial line favors Ethiopia and Eritrea and opposes the Sudan. *Al-Shahid* (The Martyr) is a twelve-page weekly newspaper that editorially supports the Sudanese

TABLE 8.1   Selected Offshore Pan-Arab Print Media (2003)[14]

Name	Headquarters and date established	Estimated circulation (2003)	Owner	Chief editor
Dailies				
al-Sharq al-Awsat (The Middle East)	London 1977	60,000	Pr. Faisal b. Salman	Abdal Rahman Rashid
al-Hayat (Life)	London 1988	40,000	Pr. Khalid b. Sultan	George Samaan
al-Quds al-Arabi (Arab Jerusalem)	London 1989	15,000	Palestinians	Abdal Bari Atwan
al-Arab (The Arab)	London 1977	10,000	Ahmad el-Houni	Ahmed el-Houni
al-Zaman (The Times)	London 1977	5,000	Saad al-Bazzaz	Saad al-Bazzaz
Weeklies				
al-Majalla (The Magazine)	London	20,000	Pr. Faisal b. Salman	Abdalaziz Khamis
al-Mushahid (The Observer)	London 1996	8,000	Gulf businessmen	Hisham al-Diwan
al-Hawadith (The Events)	London 1975	25,000	Gulf businessmen	Milham Karam
al-Mustaqilla (The Independent)	London 1993	5,000	Muhammad Hashimi	Muhammad Hashimi

government and is moderately Islamic. It covers current affairs, business, and arts. It has a small staff and relies mainly on news agencies.

Finally, there have been a few small London-based publications which are little more than information bulletins put out by dissident groups each with a single-issue focus, and circulated primarily in the U.K. One example is *al-Ittihadi al-Dawlia* (The International Unionist), an eight-page daily paper established in 1995 and published by the Sudanese National Movement. Most of them however were focused exclusively on Iraq in opposition to the regime of Saddam Hussein, and the collapse of his regime in 2003 affected their existence. Two of those moved into Iraq in 2003 to take advantage of the new publishing opportunities there: *al-Mutamar* (The Congress), an eight-page weekly established in 1995 and published by the Iraqi National Congress; and *Baghdad*, a sixteen-page weekly paper in English, established in 1991 and published by the Iraqi National Reconciliation Party. Two others, however simply disappeared from London in 2003: *Sawt al-Iraq* (Voice of Iraq), a twelve-page monthly paper established in 1980 and published by the al-Da'wa Islamic Party; *Free Iraq,* an eight-page weekly paper in English, established in 1996 and published by the Iraqi Liberal Council.

Content and Political Role

Al-Hayat carries one of the most famous names in Arab publishing, from the daily Lebanese newspaper established by Kamal Mrowe, and it continues to aspire to play a leading role in Arab journalism. When Prince Khalid bin Sultan became the major investor in the paper, he did not substantially change its editorial direction. Some close observers noticed its Lebanese style, due to the fact that most of its staff have remained Lebanese. One however says that *al-Hayat* does not have a clear "identity," and for that Saudi readers regard it as a Lebanese paper because of its staff, while Lebanese readers regard it as a Saudi paper because of its financial backing. After Desert Storm, Prince Khalid took a more prominent role as owner. It has well-known and respected writers, and good contacts in Arab governments who provide access to useful information. In its early days, *al-Hayat* was widely considered the best pan-Arab daily paper, but some readers say that lately the quality of the paper declined somewhat and it has faced serious financial problems. However, Prince Khalid reportedly continues to subsidize it because of the prestige it brings to him and to his country.[15]

Al-Hayat has always been somewhat cautious about sensitivities in the various Arab countries. In 1995 its managing editor said self-censorship was necessary, explaining: "Our main concern is not to be banned in Saudi Arabia because most of the advertising comes from the Saudi market. From time to time we have to take into consideration Saudi censorship."[16] Despite the Saudi backing of *al-Hayat,* the Saudi government has occasionally banned it from entering the kingdom, an example is for criticizing the Saudi Information Ministry. Also *al-Hayat* showed its independence in August 1990 by reporting the Iraqi invasion of Kuwait before some of the Gulf newspapers did. Its editorial page has often been critical of American hypocrisy and a double standard.[17]

Al-Hayat's editors insist that the princes who own the paper do not interfere in editorial decisions, but that they do come to the paper's defense if it is criticized.[18] In 2003, *al-Hayat*'s leading columnist and former chief editor has said that there is more press freedom today than in the past, especially for the offshore publications. Yet financial considerations are still important. It is more expensive for *al-Hayat* to publish in London than in the Middle East, but press freedom is somewhat greater. Nevertheless, since the London-based newspapers must be distributed in Arab countries in order to generate advertising revenue, they must take Arab government censorship rules into account, at least to some extent. An offshore newspaper that is completely free and ignores all of those rules will be stopped and not reach its audience. *Al-Hayat* editors want their newspapers to be distributed throughout the Arab world but they are particularly interested in Saudi Arabia because that is the most lucrative advertising market. Saudi censors reviewing incoming newspapers are more tolerant of political subjects than of articles and commentaries which touch on religion, or on subjects considered socially or culturally sensitive, such as cloning, or even women driving. For virtually all Arab countries, *al-Hayat* must be careful not to violate the taboo against directly criticizing the ruling family, whether the country is a monarchy or a republic.[19]

Al-Sharq al-Awsat is a highly-regarded pan-Arab newspaper but on key issues it tends to respect Saudi rules, because of its Saudi ownership, although it is not as conservative as newspapers published inside the kingdom. The editorial line is conservative on political affairs and very cautious in reporting on internal matters in Saudi Arabia and other Gulf countries, to an extent because its advertising revenue comes largely from the Saudi market. It includes editorials and op-eds by prominent Arab and Western writers. It carries detailed reports on international affairs and has supplements on economics and finance.[20]

The editor in chief of *al-Sharq al-Awsat* acknowledges that distribution in the Arab world necessitates respecting the local laws in those countries, and consequently there are limitations on what it can say. Unlike many newspapers based inside Arab countries, however, it does not give special priority to news about Arab leaders. The editor says that the owner, although a Saudi prince, does not interfere in editorial policy and only involves himself in the financial aspects of the paper.[21]

Journalists who have worked for *al-Sharq al-Awsat* say that the paper's editors feel pressures on their editorial policies not only from Saudi Arabia but also from other Gulf states.[22] Some conservatives in Saudi Arabia and elsewhere regard the paper as too pro-American, and too critical of Arafat.[23] One observer says that *al-Sharq al-Awsat* does respect Saudi taboos including the royal family and economic performance, but it is more liberal than Saudi-based papers, for example it will print photos of movie stars which the Saudi daily *al-Bilad* will never do, and it won't put a photo of the cabinet meeting on page one unless the cabinet actually does something important. *Al-Sharq al-Awsat* has different editions for different countries but this is primarily for market reasons to meet local interests rather than local censorship. For example the Moroccan edition will front-page Moroccan news but other editions won't.[24]

One observer says that both *al-Hayat* and *al-Sharq al-Awsat* are different from newspapers published inside Saudi Arabia, although they all depend on Saudi money; and *al-Hayat* is more independent and *al-Sharq al-Awsat* is more dependent on Saudis. Another agrees that *al-Hayat* is freer than *al-Sharq al-Awsat,* for example on social issues such as the role of women, and on political issues like the role of Syria in Lebanon, which it is more willing to criticize because it has Lebanese Maronite backing. It still has the image of an elite newspaper, and part of its image is because of its long history and reputation. Another journalist says that *al-Sharq al-Awsat* is better quality than *al-Hayat* with better news coverage and just as many good editorials.[25]

Al-Hayat tends to focus somewhat more on political and current affairs than *al-Sharq al-Awsat.* Its readership includes intellectuals, academics, and politicians. Its news reporting is considered fairly objective except for some caution with respect to issues that are sensitive in Saudi Arabia.[26] Unlike most Saudi domestic newspapers, however, *al-Hayat* occasionally crosses the line of what the Saudi authorities regard as acceptable, for example Saudi censors banned the October 23, 2003 of *al-Hayat* for printing a letter by sixty-seven American intellectuals on terrorism.[27]

Both newspapers are editorially quite critical of U.S. Middle East policy, (as are most Arab newspapers) but their style and tone differ. *Al-Hayat*'s criticisms are normally quite strong, while those in *al-Sharq al-Awsat* are often tempered with reference to American rationales, perhaps because, as one observer says, its chief editor, Abdul Rahman al-Rashid, is "an unabashed supporter of the United States."[28]

Al-Sharq al-Awsat has a higher circulation than *al-Hayat,* in part because of its strong Saudi readership, and in part because it has sister publications which it sells along with the newspaper. Differences between the two papers are also in part due to the fact that the top posts in *al-Sharq al-Awsat* and all of its sister publications are headed by Saudis, while there are no Saudis in comparable *al-Hayat* positions.

The third major offshore newspaper is *al-Quds al-Arabi.* Its focus is on events in the Arab world with special attention to Arab-Israeli issues. It uniquely includes a daily page of translations from the Israeli press. Editorially it tends to be stridently Arab nationalist on foreign affairs issues and frequently attacks U.S. Middle East policy. The paper carries little or no advertising, and apparently has no Saudi funding so it is not financially strong, but it does reportedly receive financial backing from other sources in the region, including reportedly the Palestine Liberation Organization, Sudan, Iraq, and possibly Qatar.[29] Because of the paper's strong connections with the Palestinians and the PLO, and its editorial content, one analyst views the paper as an instrument that PLO Chairman Arafat has used to criticize Arab regimes when they do not support Palestinian causes sufficiently. Also the paper reportedly has received funding from the governments of Syria, Libya, and the Sudan which encourage editorials critical of Kuwait for example. Its editorials are more likely to criticize Saudi Arabia and the other Arab gulf states than *al-Sharq al-Awsat* and other pan-Arab newspapers do. Governments in the Gulf and Egypt ban its entry from time to time because it has a number of good writers.[30]

Al-Quds is not a wealthy paper; it has few ads, few correspondents, and a limited circulation and it is often banned by various Arab governments, but it is read because it has a different editorial slant. Because it aspires to be a pan-Arab paper and is published outside the region, *al-Quds* does have more latitude to criticize Arafat and the Palestinian Authority than do Palestinian newspapers published in the West Bank and Gaza. One of its features which attracts readers is its daily page of translations from Israel's Hebrew press.[31] More than the other two leading offshore papers, *al-Quds* has the style of a contentious opposition newspaper, for example interviewing the outspoken Saudi Prince Talal when *al-Sharq al-Awsat* reportedly refused to do so.[32] It has tended to be critical of the Syrian, Saudi and Algerian governments, which have banned it occasionally. Nevertheless, *al-Quds* tends not to be so harsh on some Gulf countries, leading readers to believe that it may receive subsidies from that region.

Al-Arab and *al-Zaman* have often been critical of U.S. policy. *Al-Arab* has tended to reflect the views of Libya, pan-Arab anti-Westernists, and moderate Islamists. *Al-Zaman,* prior to 2003, devoted extensive coverage to Gulf affairs especially to Iran and Iraq, and was critical of Saddam Hussein, but its criticism was measured rather than strident, focusing on the suffering of the Iraqi people. Since the demise of Saddam Hussein it has devoted more space to Iraqi internal matters because it is widely distributed inside that country and has reporters there. Both as an exile publication and since 2003 it has sought to avoid taking sides with any of the several opposition factions.[33]

The publishers of offsite pan-Arab newspapers claim that they are independent of Arab government influences and controls, and generally speaking they do enjoy a degree of freedom greater than that of newspapers published in the region. However, close observers conclude that these newspapers still are influenced by the political environment in the Arab world because the publishers have strong financial and political connections in that region and most importantly, they seek to distribute their newspapers widely there. Most of their readership and their advertising revenues came from the Arab world, and this inevitably influenced editorial policy. For example, if a paper strongly criticized the Saudi regime, it would have difficulty being distributed in Saudi Arabia, no matter whether it was published in Beirut or London.[34]

One observer says that there is a new alliance in the Arab world in which the moneyed class including Saudi princes and wealthy businessmen and politicians like Rafiq Hariri of Lebanon, are involved in publishing (or broadcasting) as an investment to promote a certain political line, buy influence, or for prestige. He says this is a new phenomenon in the Arab world where publishers previously were motivated by family tradition or other reasons. This also applies to the establishment of the new satellite television systems (see below).[35]

Distribution can be affected by editorial content because national governments can prohibit entry of newspapers. Editors of offshore newspapers have also admitted that they are not entirely free and that self-censorship exists, but they usually explain that it is necessary in order to retain Arab advertising, especially from large markets such as Saudi Arabia.[36] The pan-Arab newspapers try to deal with the problem of distribution in different ways. *Al-Sharq al-Awsat* for example has a special edition for Saudi Arabia, and occasionally prints special editions for other countries. All of its editions have some Saudi flavor, and Saudi officials sometimes favor it with exclusive interviews. The special editions cater to local interests and sensitivities, for example giving prominence in news coverage to the activities of political leaders.[37]

Why do the offshore newspapers retain their publishing headquarters outside the Arab world? In fact, some professional journalists argue that they should leave Europe and "move back" into the region, arguing that because of improvements in technology, the newspapers can just as easily be published from the region, where they would be closer to their audience and probably find lower costs.[38]

It had been assumed that these papers enjoyed more editorial freedom because they were based in Europe, and that is why they stayed there. Some observers however argue that in fact, moving their headquarters into the region would have little effect on their editorial freedom because these offshore papers already respect Arab taboos and restrictions, because they need to be distributed in the Arab world. One commentator says, ". . . the experience of the offshore Arab media has demonstrated the feebleness of their claim to be 'operating freely' in Europe. . . . An inescapable structure of ownership and patronage has asserted itself." He says they do "address all Arab issues, offering a wider perspective than those of national media in the individual Arab states," but they are not entirely free.[39]

On the other hand, offshore Arab newspapers do have a margin of freedom because they are published outside the region. Arab journalists in London enjoy working for Arab publications that operate in an atmosphere of somewhat greater freedom, and have a pan-Arab focus. In fact, readers often buy them believing they provide news and comment from a somewhat different perspective. After 1997, for example, *al-Hayat* tried to increase its circulation in Saudi Arabia by devoting more space to Saudi issues and news, but circulation in fact declined because many Saudis were reading it for its pan-Arab content.[40]

NOTES

1. Jon B. Alterman, *New Media, New Politics; from Satellite Television to the Internet in the Arab World,* 1998, Washington D.C.: The Washington Institute for Near East Policy, Policy Paper No. 48, 1998, p. ix.

2. Some of this information is from Alterman, op. cit., pp. 7–14.

3. Interview, Hisham Milhem, Washington D.C., May 2001.

4. Alterman, p. 8; and interview with Abdallatif al Mennawi of *al-Sharq al-Awsat,* Cairo, February 9, 2001.

5. Interview with an Arab journalist, Cairo, February 9, 2001.

6. Alterman, p. 9.

7. Alterman, pp. 7, 10; Todd Richissin in the *Baltimore Sun,* October 5, 2002. Interviews with Jamil Mrouwe in Abu Dhabi, January 20, 2003, and with Jihad Khazen in London, January 22, 2003.

8. Anthony Shedid, *Jerusalem Post,* July 26, 1995; interview with Saudi journalist, Washington D.C., May 2002; and Todd Richissin, "Al Hayat, the Respected Daily," *Baltimore Sun,* October 5, 2002.

9. Alterman, p. 11; Jihad Khazen, in an interview in London, January 22, 2003 said Zawahari was angry because *al-Hayat* failed to publish an interview with him.

10. Alterman, p. 11.

11. Interview, Abdallatif al-Mennawi, of *al-Sharq al-Awsat,* Cairo, February 9, 2001; Alterman, p. 12.

12. U.S. Embassy London, "Profile of Arabic Media in London," 2002.

13. Reporters Without Borders, "The Iraqi Media Three Months After the War: A New But Fragile Freedom," Report, July 22, 2003 (http://www.rsf.fr).

14. Circulation figures are informal estimates provided by informed observers and should be considered rough orders of magnitude rather than exact.

15. Interview with Wafa'i Diab, Deputy Chief Editor, *al-Anba* newspaper, Kuwait, May 29, 2002; interview with Abdallatif al-Mennawi, Egyptian correspondent for *al-Sharq al-Awsat,* Cairo, February 9, 2001.

16. *Rocky Mountain News,* July 30, 1995, quoting then managing editor of *al-Hayat,* Khayrullah Khayrullah.

17. Dawood al-Shirian, quoted in Associated Press report March 23, 2002, by Donna Abu-Nasr. Todd Richissin, in *Baltimore Sun,* October 5, 2002.

18. Interviews with Abdal Rahman Rashid, Chief Editor of *al-Sharq al-Awsat;* George Samman, Chief Editor of *al-Hayat;* and Abdallwahab Badrkhan, Deputy Chief Editor of *al-Hayat,* all in Abu Dhabi, January 20, 2003.

19. Interview, Jihad Khazen, London, January 22, 2003.

20. *Profile of Arabic Media in London,* op. cit.

21. Interview, Abdal Rahman Rashid, Abu Dhabi, January 20, 2003.

22. Abdal Bari Atwan, quoted in the *Jerusalem Post,* July 26, 1995.

23. Interview with Saudi editor, Washington D.C., September 23, 2002.

24. Interview with Saudi journalist, Washington D.C., May 2002.

25. Interviews with Saudi journalist, Washington D.C., May 2002; and with an Arab journalist, Cairo, February 9, 2001, and with Wafa'i Diab, cited.

26. *Profile of Arabic Media in London,* cited.

27. *Profile of Arabic Media in London,* cited, and *Washington Post,* October 24, 2002, p. A26.

28. Mamoun Fandy, in the *Washington Post,* 2001, p. B2.

29. Alterman, op. cit., p. 12.

30. Interview with Arab journalist, Cairo, February 9, 2001.

31. Interview with Abdallatif al-Mennawi, Egyptian correspondent for *al-Sharq al-Awsat,* Cairo, February 9, 2001.

32. Interview with informed Arab observer, London, January 22, 2003; also see www.azzaman.com.

33. *Profile of Arabic Media in London,* op. cit.; interview with informed Arab observer, London, January 22, 2003.

34. Interview, Hisham Milhem, Washington D.C., May 2001.

35. Milhem interview, cited.

36. Khairallah interview, cited.

37. Interview with Wafa'i Diab, cited.

38. *Middle East International,* April 7, 2000, p. 22.

39. Khaled Hroub, in *Middle East International,* April 7, 2002, pp. 22–23.

40. Interview, Abdalwahab Badrkhan, Deputy Chief Editor, *al-Hayat,* Abu Dhabi, London, January 20, 2003.

9

Arab Radio and Television Prior to 1990

Radio and television in the Arab world have for the most part been monopolies under direct government supervision. There have been exceptions in the early years, and then private broadcasting has grown since 1990, but the rule for many years has been direct government operation and ownership of radio and TV. Thus organizational patterns for these media are much less complex than for the print media, and they are more uniform throughout the Arab world. In this chapter, we will review the development of Arab electronic media systems up to 1990. After 1990, although radio systems changed very little, television changed substantially and that will be analyzed in subsequent chapters.

There are several reasons for the predominance of government-owned broadcasting systems in the Arab world. First, the minimum cost of establishing a radio or television system is much higher than the minimum cost of establishing a newspaper, and thus it is far beyond the capability of nearly all private persons in these developing countries. Secondly, this high cost encourages the pooling of resources, or a monopoly, and because these media reach beyond borders and literacy barriers, the government has a much greater interest in controlling them or at least keeping them out of hostile hands. Anyone with a printing press has the technical capability of reaching the literate elite, and while this is seen by the government as a potential threat, it is not nearly as great a political threat as a radio or television station broadcasting to millions. Radio and television, which have the potential of reaching every single person in the country, and many outside it, instantaneously, are regarded by Arab governments as too important to be left to private interests. There has been very little argument in the Arab countries against this basic claim of government.

Third, radio and television developed more recently than print media, and the trend toward greater authoritarian control over all media that we have seen in our discussion of the print media has affected these newer media more because they have no tradition of independence to uphold. Television, which was not established under Arab control anywhere until after 1956, arrived in an era of declining press diversity, when even newspapers were being standardized and mobilized. Radio, which began in the West around World War I and in a few Arab countries shortly after that, did not really develop in many Arab countries until after World War II. In some places, radio began during a period of press factionalism, diversity, and relative independence, and at that time radio too had a large degree of independent, private influence. But it developed and expanded in a period when governments were encroaching on press freedom, and this made governmental control of radio that much easier.

Individual countries had different experiences with radio and television because of unique local factors that influenced these media. But many of the Arab countries first acquired these media when the country was still under European colonial influence. The British and French colonial administrators tended to put them under governmental control from the start, both because they sought to use them as instruments of colonial rule, and because their experience at home in France and Britain had been with government-sponsored electronic media. When these colonial powers departed, they usually turned over broadcasting facilities to the newly independent governments, that were content to maintain them as governmental institutions.

There are also other, minor reasons for governmental control of the electronic media, such as the scarcity of broadcast frequencies and the difficulty of finding and training qualified personnel. But the main factors are the intense government interest in the media as political instruments, the high cost, the lack of tradition as independent entities, and in some cases the precedents set by colonial administrators. The authoritarian approach to broadcasting in the Arab countries is further seen in the general lack of concern for the size, nature, and interests of the audience. Arab radio and television stations rarely conduct any research into listening or viewing audiences. Programs are not shaped to fit precise needs and desires of the audiences but rather they are designed by broadcasting personnel and government officials who decide what the public should have. Listener and viewer mail gives them some flavor of the public reaction but even that is not a determining factor in program decisions.

Advertising is carried on radio and television broadcasts throughout the area, but it is quite restricted and commercial broadcasting exactly as conducted in the United States does not exist. The most common arrangement is for the radio or TV program to carry a cluster of advertisements at specific times, carefully placed between programs to avoid interruptions, and without any sponsorship connection. These advertisements do bring revenues which help cover broadcasting budgets, but usually the government had to provide the bulk of the station's income from receiver license fees or other sources.

A handful of stations in the Arab world depend almost entirely on advertising revenues. The United Arab Emirates for example has both commercial radio and commercial television stations, which derive their incomes from advertisements and which exist alongside the government-operated, noncommercial ones. Bahrain's television was established as a commercial venture under contract with an American firm, although now the Bahrain government operates it directly. And several of Egypt's eleven radio services carry advertisements, including the Middle East Radio whose light programming and abundance of ads make it resemble American programming in some ways. Finally, both of Lebanon's television stations have been operated on a commercial basis; these will be discussed separately below. Some countries like Tunisia and Saudi Arabia allowed no advertising at all at the beginning but then permitted it later. Saudi newspapers have for many years carried ads but Saudi broadcasts only included commercials starting in the 1980s. In both print and electronic media, Saudi ads are strictly controlled to conform to social and religious norms, for example prohibiting immodest dress for women or the selling of alcohol. Oman, Algeria, and Libya have continued to prohibit advertising on either radio or television.

Despite the fact that most Arab radio and television systems are under direct control of the government and therefore exhibit similar organizational characteristics, there are some differences among them in the political roles they played prior to 1990. For purposes of analyses, systems that existed in the Arab world prior to 1990 can be divided into three groups. Seven countries, Algeria, Egypt, Iraq, Syria, Libya, South Yemen, and the Sudan, treated radio and television in a manner similar enough to put them into one group. These seven governments have pushed their development as instruments of political communication most strongly, and which we will call strict-control systems. The style and tone of programming in these countries, while not the subject of detailed objective surveys, seems to differ from those of the second major group, which we will call loyalist systems. These two groups include all of the other Arab states except Lebanon, which is a special case, and will be discussed separately.

STRICT-CONTROL SYSTEMS

The seven Arab states mentioned above controlled broadcasting more strictly, and have tended to give higher priority to the development of the electronic media than have other Arab states with comparable resources. They have shown greater appreciation for radio and television as instruments to reach and mobilize the mass of the population which is still largely illiterate. They have devoted a greater share of their resources to radio, and have been earlier to establish television systems.

Radio

When the revolutionary regimes came to power in these seven countries, they devoted a great deal of attention to radio, promoting its expansion so that it could be used as a political tool to mobilize the masses and propagate the official line.

Egypt has developed the most extensive and powerful radio broadcasting system in the Near East and Africa. In the 1970s more than 2,000 program personnel and 2,500 engineering staff, working in 43 studios in the broadcast building in Cairo put out more than 1,200 radio hours each week in fourteen services, 8 of them for domestic audiences. Powerful transmitters made these programs audible all over Egypt and in most of the Arab countries as well, even on medium wave. This system was built essentially after the revolutionary regime came to power in 1952 and decided to stress radio broadcasting as an instrument in support of policy. A private firm had started radio in Egypt as a purely commercial venture in the 1920s and the monarchy had not devoted much attention to it for political purposes. In 1934 the government gave the Marcony Company an exclusive contract to run radio but then in 1947 the government terminated this contract and put radio under a government ministry.[1]

Even when the government ended the private contract with Marconi in 1947 and increased government intervention somewhat, this was done primarily because of nationalist pressures; the control of radio was given to a semi-autonomous board of governors whose supervision was relatively loose.[2]

The new Egyptian leadership that seized power in 1952 found only a modest 72 kilowatt medium wave radio facility, with no short wave and a small broadcasting staff. The new regime began immediately to build up this capability and ensure control over it, putting radio under the new Ministry of National Guidance which invested large sums to boost signal audibility and expand programming. It also abolished the monarchy's receiver license fee to expand the audience by removing this cost barrier.[3] In less than a decade, the government increased transmitter power 28-fold, providing good reception throughout the country and abroad. During the 1950s, programming expanded to include not only the General Service but also the "second" program of cultural fare for intellectuals, and "With the People" aimed specifically at workers and peasants to provide political indoctrination as well as practical information. The "European Program" was developed in six foreign languages along with the "Sudan Corner" and "Voice of the Arabs;" later the Koranic, music, youth, Hebrew, Palestine, and Middle East Broadcasting programs were added to reach other special groups in Egypt or abroad. Programs designed for domestic audiences alone increased from 18 hours per day in 1952 to 72 hours by 1960 and more than 120 hours in the late 1970s, when 85 percent of urban adults reportedly listened to the General Service alone.[4]

The Egyptian government also developed radio as a powerful instrument for reaching foreign audiences, but radio expansion was primarily caused by a desire to communicate government policy more effectively to all Egyptians. The regime promulgated broadcasting law that required the Egyptian Broadcasting Corporation to "strengthen the national consciousness . . . participate in the educational campaign among the people . . . deal with social problems and exhort adherence to moral and ethical values."[5] The effort had a political and social purpose.

Similarly, the other six countries discussed in this section also expanded their facilities relatively rapidly after revolutionary regimes came to power there and took over more direct control of radio. In Syria, the government through its Broadcasting and Television Corporation established radio transmitters all over the country in the 1950s, boosting power from 13.6 to 150 kilowatts, and in subsequent years increased that even further. Its Home Service grew to more than 18 hours daily, and other services were promoted also. In Iraq, real expansion of radio broadcasting took place immediately after the July 1958 revolution, when the new regime was engaged in propaganda battles with Egypt and Syria, and was trying hard to make Iraqis and other Arabs understand its point of view.

The pattern repeated itself elsewhere. When the Sudan became independent in 1956, the new regime transferred control of broadcasting from a semi-autonomous committee of leading Sudanese personalities over to a governmental department. This department devoted considerable effort to turning a low-power station reaching only 11,000 of the country's 11 million people 8 hours daily into a nationwide network on the air 17 hours each day. In Algeria and South Yemen, the revolutionary groups which forcibly replaced the European colonial regimes in the 1960s gave high priority to making the radio facilities more effective and more controlled. These groups had fought battles over the radio stations themselves during the liberation struggles, and then immediately after independence the facilities were rebuilt and expanded under tight supervision of the ruling National Liberation Fronts. In Libya, the Libyan Broadcast Service has been under direct government control since 1962. The group of army officers which seized power in 1969 from the Libyan monarchy immediately made the Libyan Broadcasting Service responsive to direct orders from the new Revolutionary Command Council and began planning for increased listener coverage.

Television

Television, too, was promoted more energetically prior to 1990 by the regimes in these seven countries than elsewhere in the Arab world, when differing resource levels are taken into consideration. These countries have tended to establish television systems earlier than other Arab countries because their governments were especially anxious to exploit the new medium for political purposes. Table 9.1 shows that except for Lebanon (a special case, see below), most of the seven states inaugurated national, Arab controlled television systems before the rest of the Arab world did. Only South Yemen and Libya lagged behind the group, and this was because their revolutionary regimes did not come to power until 1967 and 1969, respectively.[6]

The first Arab-controlled television system was opened by Iraq in May 1956. This was a modest facility of 500 watts with a program devoted largely to entertainment for the Baghdad audience. When the revolutionary government replaced the monarchy two years later, it boosted the station's power and increased the political content of the programs, drawing partly on the support of the Communist countries for this. New transmitters were built throughout the country, allowing the audience to grow considerably: by 1961 there were 50,000 receivers and by the mid-1970s there were 350,000.

Egypt and Syria began their television systems in 1960 as separate entities after attempting without success to launch a joint enterprise under the

TABLE 9.1   Inaugural Dates of National Television Systems

Iraq	1956
Lebanon	1959
Egypt	1960
Syria	1960
Algeria	1962 (French 1956–1962)
Kuwait	1962
The Sudan	1962
Morocco	1962
Saudi Arabia	1965
Tunisia	1966
Libya	1968
Dubai	1968
Jordan	1968
South Yemen	1969 (Britain 1964–1967)
Abu Dhabi	1969
Qatar	1970
Bahrain	1972
Oman	1974
North Yemen	1975

aegis of their short-lived political union. The Egyptian government expanded coverage during the 1960s to major populated areas by building twenty-nine transmitters and subsidizing the purchase of communally owned receivers in many poorer locations. As with radio, the Egyptian government built television facilities on a grand scale, fitting out eleven TV studios in Cairo with the latest equipment and hiring 2,500 program staff and more than 1,000 technical staff.[7] Meanwhile the Syrian government was busy erecting transmitters outside Damascus in Horns, Aleppo, and then in other provinces in order to reach the bulk of the population. The number of TV receivers in Syria grew as a result to 42,000 in 1961, 425,000 by the mid-seventies, and over one million by 1986.

The nationalist revolutionary groups which ended colonial rule and came to power in Algeria and South Yemen also promoted television and turned it to their own political uses. The nascent Algerian television system which the French had operated since 1956 in Algiers was heavily damaged by both sides during the course of the liberation struggle, but the new regime in 1962 immediately began to rebuild it and to redirect its content politically. French extremists destroyed the Oran transmitter to prevent the Algerians from hearing de Gaulle, but in 1963 the Radio and Television Authority (RTA) asked the French ORTF to help them rebuild. In South Yemen, the regime that came to power with the hasty departure of the British in 1967 found the modest British-run TV station so badly damaged, and its own financial situation so weak, that it took nearly two years to begin telecasts again. But a deliberate expansion took place in this country under tight political control of the new government, so that three transmitters served more than 21,000 receivers in the mid-seventies. The South Arabian Broadcasting Service, established in 1954, began TV in August 1964, and by 1966 there were 16,000 TV receivers in the country; by 1986 there were over 50,000 in South Yemen. The Sudanese government, also facing financial problems and a vast geographic territory to cover, nevertheless pushed ahead with television in 1962 under the Abboud military regime, that had a political purpose in doing so. Abboud was out in 1964, but television received another impetus after President Numeiri came to power in 1969. The government improved service to the Khartoum-Omdurman area so that by the mid-1970s more than 70,000 receivers were in use there including many in clubs and other organizations; and a special effort in the Blue Nile area with transmissions and government-supplied receivers boosted viewing there too.

Finally in Libya, the monarchy had for years not felt any need to build a national television system even though thousands of Libyans could watch foreign TV programs from the American base at Wheelus or from Italy or Tunisia. The monarchy only started television modestly in 1968 and in less than a year the revolutionary group which seized power made television one of its priorities as an instrument of control and mobilization. Colonel

Qaddafi and his Revolutionary Command Council expanded transmitter capacity and politicized programming, while in 1970 he presided over the closure of the American Wheelus air base and its TV system, that had been broadcasting programs for resident U.S. military personnel that were seen by some Libyans.

Programming

The regimes in these seven countries generally made more effort than governments elsewhere in the Arab world to have radio and television programming convey political messages to the masses of the population. The government uses television to get messages across to citizens and to mobilize and control public opinion when major issues arise. The politicized programming generally had revolutionary overtones, advocating substantial and rapid change at home or abroad, and was open and explicit such as the Libyan Information Ministry's published statement on broadcast objectives: "To embody the Arab revolutionary objectives of freedom, socialism and unity and to permeate such objectives in the minds of the people; . . . to bind the Arab struggle for liberation of the occupied territories with the cause of liberation and freedom in the Third World."[8]

For example, Sudanese television and radio tended to devote large portions of their newscasts to the latest achievements of the government and to its activities, followed by interviews or other features documenting the benefits that such changes have brought. Then on special occasions, such as Sudanese National Day (May 25), these media began weeks ahead of time drumming up enthusiasm for the event by rebroadcasting highlights from previous such events interspersed with slogans taken from standard socialist rhetoric. Plays with political lessons—such as the perfidy and evil of the capitalist, the threat of the imperialist, and the urgent need to oppose Israel—were broadcast using the best acting talent available. Such programming was carried out with varying degrees of intensity and skill in all seven of the countries being discussed here.

Probably the most effective, subtle and well-executed political programming of this sort was done in Egypt, where radio and TV personnel seem to have had a much lighter touch than in Iraq, for example. The Egyptian regime first concentrated on radio in the 1950s, building powerful internal and external services, then it turned in the 1960s to TV as a supplementary means to reach Egyptians. President Nasser used both to evoke enthusiasm for the social, political, and economic changes he was promoting and contempt for the domestic and foreign enemies he was fighting. Regular listeners understood quite clearly from news and commentaries, and from features, drama, and music programs what direction his policy was taking and who his friends and enemies were. To cite one domestic example, radio and television between October and December 1965 broadcast the lengthy trial and confessions of the eighteen Muslim Brotherhood members who had plotted against the regime, and the presentation clearly drew the moral for the audience that the regime wanted to show. As for foreign affairs, the electronic media launched numerous campaigns against "imperialism" in the form of the Baghdad Pact, Glubb Pasha, the Suez Canal Company, Israel, and for Arab unity and socialism.

Egyptian broadcasters in both media, but particularly in radio, at times displayed excessive zeal in promoting the official line, and credibility suffered—especially at the time of the June 1967 war—so that these media subsequently became more restrained. But the Egyptian leadership has made it clear that radio and television, like the press, are to continue "to participate along with all the organs of the state in educating men capable of shouldering the burdens of the new stage" of the revolution. The small amount of program material that does carry criticism of governmental policies is usually couched in humor or innuendos for which the Egyptians are famous.[9]

Each of the seven countries discussed in this section aggressively used the electronic media to convey political messages, usually in support of leftist, anti-imperialist Third World themes. These were usually the countries that have provided the bases for Palestinian nationalists to broadcast their political appeals for support among Arabs for the liberation of their homeland. Despite the similarity in name of the Palestinian program, usually called the "Voice of Palestine," these programs were broadcast over national transmitters and are carefully monitored by the host government. Consequently their content conforms to the policy requirements of the host, and when they step out of line they go off the air.

Politically motivated programming tended to be most obvious and pervasive on Iraqi and South Yemeni radio and television. Algerian, Syrian, and other broadcasters were similar but generally not in quite so strident a manner. Some of the material was acquired from Communist sources, but much was locally generated and all was shaped to fit local conditions and government policies. In all of these countries, however, at least half of the material carried on the electronic media in normal times had no immediate political implications. Then all acquired nonpolitical entertainment films and tapes from many sources, especially American, and they broadcast these alongside political material that was often hostile to the United States. Thus it was a common experience for audiences in these countries to watch an evening TV newscast laden with political reports deliberately putting America in a bad light, and then view a Hollywood film or TV series such as *Little House on the Prairie* or the very popular *Dallas*.

Nevertheless, the governments in these seven countries tended to be more concerned about alien political ideas reaching their populations via the airwaves. The Ministries of Information made certain that all of the imported foreign films used on the mass media are nonpolitical or politically acceptable, and they even tried to block listening to some foreign radio broadcasts, even by means of jamming signals.

LOYALIST BROADCASTING

Except for Lebanon, radio and television in the other ten Arab states tended to be slower to develop, and the programming style was less intensely and aggressively political. The major reason for the difference was that the governments of these other Arab states (Morocco, Tunisia, Jordan, Kuwait, Saudi Arabia, Bahrain, Qatar, the United Arab Emirates, Oman, and North Yemen) seem to have been less interested in active social engineering of the masses and therefore they were less intrigued with the media as tools for social change than are the regimes in the seven countries just discussed. These ten governments, including six monarchies, showed some awareness of the political importance of the electronic media for reaching the masses, so they have seen to it that radio and television were in government hands. But they generally did not push as hard as the "revolutionary" regimes to expand the reach of radio and TV as a priority matter, nor did they explore all the possibilities of program politicization. They devoted relatively more attention to other development projects.

Radio

The first Arab radio broadcasting in any of these countries began in the 1940s, and in most of them it started much later. The Jordanian government in 1948 took over the Ramallah transmitters built by the British in Palestine but it did not expand these facilities substantially until the mid-fifties when it found itself under attack by broadcasts from Cairo because of the Baghdad Pact and Glubb Pasha. This radio war helped encourage Jordan to build new transmitters in Amman in 1956. The loss of the West Bank including Ramallah to Israel in the 1967 war undercut Jordan's radio capabilities, however, and the government has not given broadcasting a very high priority in the distribution of its scarce resources. Skilled Jordanian broadcasters have also left the country, further weakening the system as they sought better-paying jobs in the Arab states of the Persian Gulf.

North Yemen also began radio broadcasting shortly after World War II, and it too lacked the money to invest in the medium and it was also totally lacking in trained personnel. The government showed little positive interest so that still in the mid-seventies this country had only a rudimentary broadcasting system and only 90,000 receivers distributed among more than five million people. The other states of the Arabian Peninsula have had the financial means to devote to broadcasting but they have been relatively slow to do so. When Saudi Arabia opened its first radio station in 1948, it was only audible in the Jidda-Mecca area. The Saudi government, conscious of its international role as protector of the Islamic holy places, developed its short wave radio capability aimed at Muslims in Indonesia, Pakistan, and elsewhere, but it did not push domestic radio particularly strongly. It did not open a radio station in Riyadh, the capital, until 1963, or in Dammam for Eastern Province audiences until 1967.

In neighboring Kuwait, radio broadcasting began in 1952 but it was only heard 2 1/2 hours per day and this increased very little until the country was fully independent nine years later. After 1961 the program and audience did grow substantially, a fairly easy task in such a city state with abundant oil revenues. Further south, in the small Arab emirates of the Persian Gulf and in Oman, there was no Arab controlled broadcasting before the late 1960s except in Bahrain which opened a modest facility in 1955. The British, responsible for foreign affairs and defense in the area until 1971, operated a radio station from Sharjah starting in 1966 but the Arab rulers saw no pressing need to have radio stations for their own people. Then in 1968–1969, anticipating full independence and competition for international attention, the oil rich states of Qatar and Abu Dhabi opened their own radio stations. The new federation of the United Arab Emirates took over British radio facilities in 1971 and Ras al-Khaimah, one of the constituent states, expressed its independence from the federation by opening its own station in 1974. Oman had no radio station at all until after 1970 when the new sultan deposed his reactionary father and opened the country up to the outside world.

Thus it was primarily external pressures of competition among neighboring states, manifesting themselves after the British departure, which induced these small states to invest some of their oil wealth into radio facilities. These rulers purchased large transmitters and fancy studio equipment, and they imported radio talent, not so much to communicate government policies on specific issues to their own populations as to convey to the world the image of independence, sovereignty, and national identity which they felt their small countries needed. The rulers saw them as external symbols of power more than as internal instruments of communication and certainly not agents of social change.

In North Africa, the leadership in Tunisia and Morocco also did not push government-controlled radio as much as Arab revolutionary regimes did. Morocco was fully independent in 1956, but it was not until 1959 that the government closed the private commercial radio stations and took over control of all broadcasting to create a national network. The Tunisian government which took over at independence in 1956 put radio under a government department but gave it some autonomy. Not until 1964, when President Bourguiba had a member of the Tunisian ruling party's Political Bureau appointed director of Radio Television Tunisienne did the government clearly show its concern for tight policy control. The government did expand radio facilities somewhat, but a survey in 1973 showed that as

many as twenty-five percent of urban Tunisian adults still did not listen to
radio even once a week.[10]

Palestine was a special case. The British started radio in Palestine in
1936, but after Israel was established in 1948, and the East and West
banks were unified under Jordan, Palestinian broadcasting was under non-
Palestinian control until the 1990s (see next chapter).

Television

Arab-controlled television did not come to any of these ten countries
until after 1961, and it generally lagged behind TV development in the
other states. The Kuwaiti government, which had oil revenues to spend on
the medium, was the first of the ten to go into it. But the newly independent Kuwaiti government at first allowed a wealthy private entrepreneur
to establish a small television station and only after this had begun operating did it take over and start to develop a government-run system. With
abundant resources and ideal geographical conditions the government was
able to provide a good signal for all 900,000 inhabitants of this country
without any difficulty.

The government of Saudi Arabia began television broadcasts only in
1965 after some delays, and the five major urban areas were not covered by
the network until November 1969. The Saudis had sufficient funds to do it
sooner, but conservative elements strongly resisted introduction of the new
medium altogether, and the government hesitated to push because of
unpredictable social consequences. Finally, however, the government saw
that television might be a substitute for public cinemas (which were and
still are banned), and it accepted as inevitable a medium that other countries had enjoyed for years. The decision to inaugurate Saudi television was
also spurred by international broadcasting considerations. Cairo radio
broadcasts were at the time critical of the Saudi government and widely listened to by Saudis, so television was seen partly as a self-defense measure.
And when the Saudi government in 1969 opened the largest antenna in the
Middle East in Dammam with a pair of 12.5 kilowatt transmitters, its
motive was not so much to give Eastern Province Saudis a better TV picture
as to reach Kuwait, that had had television for nearly a decade.[11]

Saudi television first allowed advertising in January 1986. In 1977 and
1979 McCann of UK surveyed ads through the Middle East Marketing
Research Bureau, Cyprus, when Bahrain and Qatar were allowing ads on
TV. Prior to 1986, the Saudi Arabian Government had allowed ads in
newspapers, magazines and billboard, but delayed on TV for 23 years for
religious reasons. A study by al-Khereiji 1986–1989 found Saudi TV ads
allowed no alcohol or tobacco, and women appear only if directly relevant
to the ad and they are modestly dressed in hijab.[12]

Similarly, the other Arab states on the Persian Gulf felt this same urge to
compete with electronic media. In 1968, before any of the small lower gulf

emirates had television themselves, many people were buying TV receivers to watch Kuwaiti and Aramco (Dhahran) television. Bahrain at that time had an estimated 7,500 receivers for that purpose, while Qatar had 2,500. This cross-border competition helped encourage Dubai, Abu Dhabi, and Qatar to use their surplus oil revenues to open showcase television stations in 1968, 1969, and 1970, respectively. In the UAE, Dubai TV began transmission in color on December 2, 1974, and in 1978 it became the first Arab station to have a channel exclusively in English (channel 33).[13] The governments of neighboring Bahrain and Oman, not so wealthy, had other priorities and did not open their TV stations until 1972 and 1974; also, the former was a private commercial venture for the first three years. Finally, North Yemen, the poorest state on the Arabian Peninsula, opened its television system in late 1975 but then only because the Abu Dhabi government offered to finance the entire enterprise. The Yemeni government itself had shown no urgent desire to invest in television.[14]

In Morocco and Tunisia, too, the governments were encouraged to install local television systems because of TV growth in neighboring countries, rather than because of any urgently felt need to create a domestic information channel. Both countries became independent in 1956 but did not establish television until 1962 and 1966, respectively. Tunisian television began as a private enterprise but then it was taken over entirely by the government, which censors all broadcasts. For years Tunisians and Moroccans living in Mediterranean coastal areas had been able to tune in to European broadcasts, and after 1962 some could see Algerian TV as well. The Tunisian and Moroccan governments could not lag far behind in promoting this most modern symbol of statehood.

Finally, the Jordanian government in 1968 opened its own television system after the Jordanian population had acquired more than 10,000 TV receivers in order to see programs from several neighboring countries. Jordan Television began in 1968, and in 1985 radio and TV were merged into a single organization Jordan Radio and Television Corporation. In 1972 a second TV channel began and in 1974 it went to color. As with most of these conservative governments, the impetus to begin TV came from external pressure rather than from any internal concerns or an ideological propensity to create an instrument to reach and mobilize the population for social change. The latter does not seem to exist in these states.

Programming

The content and style of radio and television broadcasting in these ten states tended to be characterized by less politically motivated programming, with more entertainment and popular culture. The newscasts and public affairs features consistently presented evidence of the latest achievements of the government, and extol the virtues of the top personalities. And the Ministries of Information provided the editors with guidance on political programming that is followed. But the guidance was often of a negative variety, instructing editors to ignore sensitive issues rather than to exploit certain themes for their propaganda value. Editors who carefully avoided taboo subjects were given more freedom to do programs the way they wished. With the exception of President Bourguiba during the first dozen years of Tunisian independence, the national leaders in these countries tended not to exploit the electronic media for direct personal communication with the masses the way the leaders in the revolutionary states do. Nor was it common for these radio and TV stations to launch aggressive campaigns promoting political themes in commentaries, features, drama, and song. Programming is much more bland and the vast majority of it is nonpolitical.

Because of the prevailing political atmosphere in these countries (discussed previously), the broadcast personnel were cautious about anything political, preferring to avoid all problems with the government. Since nearly all of these countries lack formal opposition organizations open political opposition and antiregime views are not generally reflected in broadcast programming at all. Even in Kuwait and Morocco, where some political opposition functions in public, it had only limited access to radio and television—far less than to the press. Also, these government-operated facilities tended to be more careful about criticizing foreign governments than do the media in the other Arab states.

For example, the Saudi Arabian government established its television system with modest educational and entertainment motives in mind, rather than political programming. When it proved difficult to fill the many hours of TV time with appropriate educational programming, editors turned to imported entertainment footage. The Saudi government prohibits anything on radio or television that offends Islam, advocates non-Muslim religion, or refers to alcohol and sex.[15]

Even Jordanian electronic media are relatively low in political content and tend to stress entertainment, despite the fact that Jordanians and Israelis—at war since 1948—can see and hear each other's radio and television. It is simply not characteristic of the Jordanian government to politicize its media radically in order to mobilize the population for change.

The constraints on broadcast programming in these ten states are in many cases cultural rather than political. In Saudi Arabia, for example, Saudi women even in the eighties still do not appear on television, because social custom requires that they wear veils in public. They are allowed to speak on radio, but both media observe other social and cultural taboos, too, such as drinking alcohol, eating pork or criticizing Islam. Similarly, broadcast editors in the other countries are careful not to violate local social customs and mores. They generally rely heavily on imported films and tapes, especially entertainment material from the West, but these are all carefully checked before use for social and cultural taboos as well as political suitability.

LEBANESE BROADCASTING

Lebanon is a special case among Arab broadcasting systems, as it is among Arab print media systems (see Chapter 5). Lebanese media institutions do not fit the model of the third world (public sector ownership, usually by a government agency) or of the West.

Lebanese broadcasting has been at least partially private and partially owned and operated by the government. Since radio was established in 1938 by the French Mandatory authorities, who insisted on controlling it completely, the newly independent Lebanese government had no difficulty in taking it over completely as a monopoly when the French withdrew from the country in 1946. The French established the precedent of governmental radio, so the Lebanese officials were able to retain it.[16]

Control of radio was exercised at first by the Ministry of Interior, then by the Information Ministry, but the Lebanese government was relatively slow to push expansion of the medium. During the first years of operation by the Lebanese government the number of radio receivers remained below 50,000, or fewer than the UNESCO standard of 5 per 100 inhabitants. The government did not devote the necessary funds to transmitter expansion until the early 1960s, when finally the signal reached the entire country and listenership was able to grow substantially.

The Minister of Information and his Director General of Information control editorial policy of Lebanese radio directly. They assure that politically important programming conforms to governmental guidance. However, newscasts prior to 1975 generally did not follow any discernibly consistent policy line, and usually they presented issues in a straightforward and balanced manner. Also, most of the program time was devoted to entertainment and features that reflected no particular political coloration.

Television in Lebanon, like the print media, began as a private enterprise. Until 1978, Lebanon was the only Arab country whose TV networks were wholly owned and operated by private commercial interests.

Lebanese TV was started by businessmen who saw the enterprise in business terms and gave little attention to its social implications. The first attempt at TV was in 1954 when two Lebanese businessmen Wissam Izzedine and Alex Arida applied to form a TV company, and after two years of negotiation they signed an agreement with the government and in August 1956 received a license for La Compagnie Libanaise de Television, SAL (CLT). The CLT was a commercial enterprise established by Lebanese businessmen with some French shares. The agreement with CLT stipulated that it could not broadcast programs that would threaten public security, morals, or religious groups, or enhance the image of a political personality or party, but it was required to broadcast free of charge news and bulletins provided by the Information Ministry and it was subject to all press law restrictions. It was allowed to devote up to twenty-five percent of air time to advertising. When CLT started broadcasting on May 18, 1959, it was the first commercial TV station in the Arab world.

The CLT did not retain a monopoly. In 1959, another company founded by another group of Lebanese businessmen asked the government for permission to establish Compagnie de Television du Liban et du Proch-Orient (Tele-Orient). It received an identical license in July 1959 and began broadcasting May 6, 1962. This company also extended its geographic coverage rapidly, and expanded programming from one to two channels. After several years during which both companies had difficulty selling air time, they agreed to coordinate their marketing and scheduling, and before the civil war began in 1975 they were making large profits. In 1974 the Council of Ministers renewed the CLT license for nine years, but required that CLT allow government censors to be present in the station and also transmit a one-hour program in the evening prepared by the government. It also required CLT to pay six percent of its net ad revenue to the government, and reduced ad time to fifteen percent.[17] By the 1970s, television coverage included Beirut, some of its suburbs, and Tripoli, and had expanded from its original two channels to four. Both networks broadcast throughout the evening and offered a choice of programs in Arabic, French, and English. The number of television receivers grew accordingly from 60,000 in 1961 to more than 400,000 in the mid-seventies.

Both CLT and Tele-Orient depended on advertising income, and commercials took up proportions of air time comparable to American TV although the scheduling was different. Advertising in Lebanon, as in Europe, tends to be grouped together before and after programs rather than interrupting them; also, firms tend not to be allowed to sponsor specific programs as they do in the United States. The Lebanese government did have the authority to issue broadcast licenses for television, and under the terms of the licenses it could set editorial policy guidelines for news and special events coverage. The government, however, tended to exercise this right only as a veto power over sensitive issues in times of political crisis. The news was written and edited by TV editors, using local reporters and international news services rather freely. They were careful to avoid favoring one group over another, or criticizing a foreign power, so their political material tended to be much more bland than the press.[18]

The bulk of their programming was nonpolitical, and nearly three-quarters of it is usually imported film or videotape. Foreign interests did not diminish over the years, either. The French supplied considerable material to CLT and their role in that station became so important that license agreements were negotiated directly between the French and Lebanese governments. Tele-Orient, for its part, was more dependent on American and British support and a major shareholding interest of Lord Thompson of Fleet Street, London. The CLT used the French SECAM color technique, while Tele-Orient used the German PAL color system.

Lebanese civil strife, which plagued the country for more than a decade, starting in 1975, affected the structure and content of Lebanese radio and television. The various Lebanese factions became increasingly interested in the electronic media for explaining their views as lines hardened geographically and the partisan newspapers were unable to circulate freely. One new radio station began broadcasting from a clandestine location, calling itself Voice of Lebanon and clearly supporting one of the major protagonists in the struggle, the right-wing Christian Phalange Party. Another new clandestine station went on the air calling itself Voice of Arab Lebanon, which attacked the "fascist Phalange" while supporting leftists and Palestinians.

At first the factions did not attempt to take over the broadcast stations by force, just as they had at first left the newspaper offices alone. Then on March 11, 1976, when Brigadier General Abdal Aziz al-Ahdab announced seized power in Lebanon from President Sulaiman Franjieh, the regular Lebanese radio and television systems were split into two competing sections. General Ahdab took over the medium wave and FM radio transmitters, and also saw to it that the CLT television company, located in the Tallat al-Khayyat area of Ras Beirut which he controlled, broadcast pro-Ahdab Arabic newscasts each night. Meanwhile, supporters of President Franjieh, who refused to resign the presidency, continued to control the main medium- and short-wave radio transmitters in the predominantly Christian area north of Beirut. The Franjieh group was also able to control the Tele-Orient TV facilities because they were located in the Beirut suburb of Hazmia that was under Christian control since the beginning of the crisis. The Tele-Orient version of the evening news was clearly biased in favor of Franjieh and thus contrasted sharply with CLT's news.

By the end of May 1976, General Ahdab had resigned, and "his" radio and TV stations had taken on the political biases of the Lebanese Arab Army (LAA) which controlled the area. For the next six months, Lebanon had radio and television stations separately supporting the LAA and Franjieh factions. By the end of 1976, however, a new Lebanese president was installed in office, the security situation was improved, and the opposition elements had lost control over the main radio and television transmitters.

Yet the Lebanese situation, despite everyone's hopes and efforts, did not remain stable, and the electronic media, like all other Lebanese institutions, were soon affected again by political and military events. During the following decade seven unauthorized radio stations belonging to different political factions became fixed elements in Lebanon, in competition with the government-run Lebanese Radio. The Voice of Lebanon was continued and strengthened by the Phalange Party, and the rival Voice of Arab Lebanon was operated by the Muslim leftist independent Nasserite movement (Murabitun). In addition, the Lebanese Forces' Christian militia went on the air with Radio Free Lebanon, while the Christian militias in South Lebanon operated their own independent Voice of Hope, and when former

President Franjieh split with the Lebanese Front in 1978 he started the Voice of United Lebanon.

Then in 1984 the Islamic Charitable Society started Voice of the Nation, and Druze leader Walid Jumblatt's Progressive Socialist Party (PSP) began broadcasting over its own Voice of the Mountain. All of these stations continued to operate in the mid-1980s despite a decision by the National Unity Government (in which Jumblatt, for example, was a minister) that they should all go off the air and return Lebanese Radio to its monopoly. Moreover, Lebanese Radio was itself affected by continued turmoil. When the battles in early 1984 for control of West Beirut between the Lebanese army on one side, and the Shiite Amal Movement and the PSP on the other resulted in the takeover of the area by opposition militias and the predominantly Shiite 6th army brigade, the victorious forces made sweeping personnel changes in the Ministry of Information and radio facilities located there. Lebanese radio news programs thereafter clearly supported Amal and PSP political views.

As for television, in 1978 the two commercial stations, CLT and Tele-Orient, having been buffeted by recurrent crises, came to agreement with the Lebanese Government on a three-way merger into a single broadcasting company for all of Lebanon called Tele-Liban. The two original commercial entities each controlled twenty-five percent of the shares while the government controlled fifty percent, bringing the latter directly into what had been, at least legally, a privately controlled television system. Yet the content of Lebanese television programming did not change a great deal, with channels 1 and 2 carrying Arabic and English programs, and channel 3 carrying French, the English and French material coming mostly from the West.

Then the takeover of West Beirut in early 1984 by opposition military units led to personnel and program changes in television as it did in radio. Tele-Liban's previously unified news staff was split and moved, primarily according to religious affiliation, so that the newscast from channel 7 in West Beirut was written entirely by Muslims, while the simultaneous newscast from channel 5 in Hazmiyyah was written by Christians, and audiences could easily tell the difference. Since both programs were in Arabic, audiences could choose the news according to their preferences.

Thus the continuing bitter factional feuds in Lebanon helped maintain diversity in its media, but at the price of even greater bias by individual broadcasting units.

NOTES

1. James Napoli and Hussein Y. Amin, "Press Freedom in Egypt," chapter 9 in Festus Eribo and William Jong-Ebot, Eds., *Press Freedom and Communication in Africa,* Trenton: Africa World press, 1997, pp. 198–205.

2. Douglas A. Boyd, "Egyptian Radio: Tool of Political and National Development," *Journalism Monographs* vol. 48 February 1977: 3–5.

3. Douglas A. Boyd, "Development of Egypt's Radio: 'Voice of the Arabs' Under Nasser," *Journalism Quarterly*, vol. 52, no. 4, Winter 1975, p. 645.

4. Boyd, "Development of Egypt's Radio," pp. 645–53, and Sydney W. Head, ed., *Broadcasting in Africa*, Philadelphia: Temple University Press, 1974, p. 19.

5. Head, p. 19; Boyd, *Journalism Monographs* vol. 48 February 1977, pp. 13–23.

6. Limited-range TV stations were established in Dhahran, Saudi Arabia, in September 1957 by Aramco, at Wheelus in December 1954 by the U.S. military channel USAFRTS, and in Algiers in 1957 by the French government, but these were not indigenous systems.

7. Head, p. 24.

8. Quoted in Head, p. 29.

9. The quote is from Information Minister Dr. Kamal Abu al-Magd, cited in *al-Ahram*, June 30, 1974, p. 4.

10. USIA, Office of Research, Report no. E-7-74, p. 6.

11. Douglas A. Boyd, "Saudi Arabian Television," *Journal of Broadcasting* vol. 15 no. 1 Winter 1970–1971: 74–78.

12. Douglas A. Boyd, Safran al-Makaty, S. Scott Whitlow, and G. Norman Van Tubergen, "Advertising in Islam," *Journal of Advertising Research*, vol. 36, no. 3, May/June 1996, pp. 16–26.

13. U.S. Embassy Abu Dhabi telegram "Television in the UAE" November 9, 1994.

14. *Al-Thawra* newspaper, Sanaa, December 9, 1975.

15. Department of State, *1999 Report on Human Rights*, Saudi Section, February 25, 2000.

16. Nabil H. Dajani, "The Press in Lebanon," *Gazette*, vol. 17, no. 3, 1971: 172.

17. Nabil H. Dajani, "The Changing Scene of Lebanese Television," TBS issue no. 7, fall/winter 2001.

18. Interviews in Beirut, May 29, 1973, Lebanese journalists.

10

Arab Television Since 1990: Structure

A revolution has taken place in Arab television since 1990. Prior to that time, Arab television in each country was watched almost exclusively by the domestic audience in that country. Some television broadcasts could be seen outside their country of origin, but only in nearby parts of neighboring countries because these were terrestrial television signals that only traveled short distances, mostly by line-of-sight, normally not more than fifty miles. The advent of satellite television in the 1990s changed that.

This chapter will describe changes in the structure of Arab television since 1990 with emphasis on the impact of Arab satellite television. The next chapter will discuss changes in program content of Arab television since 1990.

The focus of this chapter is on television because Arab radio has not changed much since 1990 from what was described in Chapter 9. It is true that some Arab entrepreneurs have invested in radio for a pan-Arab audience as a result of developments described in the following, for example the Lebanese businessman and political figure Rafiq Hariri started al-Sharq Radio based in Paris, but most of the efforts by Hariri and others like him have been devoted to satellite television.

The advent of Arab satellite television was important because it brought to the Arab world a new style in news coverage and in political discussion programs. News reporting was more aggressive and thorough. Talk shows explored topics new to Arab television that had only been dealt with previously in private conversations or to some extent in Western broadcasts like

CNN. Now, with Arab satellite television, they were being discussed in the media in Arabic, including call-ins, on a pan-Arab level so the content was by Arabs and for Arabs. That was new.

The first important satellite television channel was established by private businessmen seeking a pan-Arab market and they chose Europe for their headquarters. Because the content of private Arab satellite TV broke new ground, and because it crossed borders, it influenced the content of the existing terrestrial television channels that were controlled and restricted by governments. Also, during the 1990s, it helped persuade most Arab governments to establish their own satellite channels.

Therefore by the early twenty-first century, there were three distinct types of Arab television system side by side: the original government-controlled terrestrial systems, plus the new private and governmental satellite systems. In this chapter we will examine the post-1990 status of terrestrial TV in the Arab world, and the advent of Arab satellite TV and its impact.

CHANGES IN THE STRUCTURE OF GOVERNMENT-CONTROLLED TERRESTRIAL TELEVISION SINCE 1990

The structure and ownership pattern of the existing terrestrial radio and television systems did not change a great deal after 1990 but they have remained essentially the same as developed in earlier decades and described in the previous chapter. Every Arab state has a government-controlled radio and television organization. Moreover, in the majority of Arab countries, the state or state agencies (such as the Ba'th Party in Syria) own and operate all television and radio as a government monopoly. In fact, prior to 1994, no private television companies existed in the Arab world except unauthorized ones in Lebanon and Palestine, but since then private television has been legalized in those countries plus Morocco, Egypt, and Qatar. In those five countries, private television channels exist alongside governmental ones. In addition, structural changes have taken place since 1990 in the government-owned broadcasting organizations in Qatar, and the United Arab Emirates.

Lebanon

Lebanon has remained unique among Arab countries, both because of the variety of broadcasting systems that exist there, and because of the changes that have taken place in participating broadcasters over short time periods.

During the Lebanese civil war (1970–1989), the monopoly of the government-owned television Tele-Liban had been broken de facto by the emergence of a number of illegal TV stations. Then in the 1990s, private television stations continued to proliferate in Lebanon. The first illegal station and the most successful of them was the Lebanese Broadcasting

Company (LBC). The Lebanese Forces Militia established it in August 1985, and viewers considered it from content to be a Maronite Christian channel. LBC quickly overtook Tele-Liban in audience share and advertising revenues. At first it operated out of the Christian town of Junieh, but during the fighting it was often forced to move about and broadcast from a mobile van.[1]

Tele-Liban continued to function in the 1990s but it was weakened financially by the competition from so many other broadcasters that its quality suffered and it was near collapse. A major reason was that it is not as interesting as other channels because its news broadcasts focus primarily on the activities of the president, the prime minister, and the government.[2]

The Taif Agreement of 1989, which ended the Lebanese civil war, led to a reorganization and expansion of television. A large number of businessmen applied for licenses to broadcast, and by the end of 1991, ten new TV stations were on the air. In 1991 the government said that TV could only be owned by Lebanese citizens and only broadcast on VHF. In 1992 the government required all TV owners to apply for new licenses.[3]

In 1989 a group of Lebanese officials founded al-Mashriq (East) television, in competition to LBC, and it gained a wide audience because it showed popular Arabic films. In 1991 the Communist Party started MTV but it had no discernible communist content and soon a group of businessmen bought it out. Then, also in 1991, Hizbollah started "al-Manar" (Landmark) Television. Groups of businessmen started Sigma TV and Kilykia TV—Kilykia is associated with al-Nahda organization and the al-Diyar (Home) newspaper—but they carried no news and were mostly entertainment. In East Beirut the Lebanese Forces operated C33 TV which offers mostly Western movies. Murr TV was established by former Defense Minister Michael Murr. Independent TV (ITV) was established by a Maronite priest Henry Sfeir, and a group of Maronite priests established al-Mahaba TV.

In 1991 a new TV channel "TeleLumiere" was established in Lebanon by the Assembly of Catholic Patriarchs and Bishops in Lebanon. It claimed not to be political or commercial, as well as nonprofit, and aimed to support peace, human rights, and openness, and to oppose violence, fanaticism, and discrimination. It expressed respect for all religious ideologies, and refused to broadcast any political news.[4] In 1993, Rafiq Hariri, a prominent businessman who was then between tours as prime minister, founded al-Mustaqbal (Future) Television.

On November 10, 1994, parliament passed Law No. 382 on the media. This law in effect legalized the end of the state monopoly on television, and put the state broadcaster Tele-Liban in competition with private firms, each of which was linked to a prominent politician or religious group. The purpose of the law was to provide some regulation of the private broadcasters which had emerged uncontrolled during the civil war. It carried over some media restrictions from the previous press law and the penal code. It said that no one individual could own more than ten percent of any TV company, and it abolished the time limit on commercial advertising.

After passage of the 1994 law, the Council of Ministers, which had the authority to grant licenses, gave licenses to only six broadcasters but denied them to others; some of the latter shut down but others continued illegally. The director general of the Information Ministry admitted that the selection of licensees was largely a decision made on political grounds, rather than for technical reasons. In 2000, after Rafiq Hariri left office, additional licenses were granted.[5]

In 1996, the Lebanese government declared that only four private TV stations were licensed to operate: LBC, Future TV, MTV, and NBN. The distribution of licenses revealed a balance among religious groups since LBC was owned by Maronite Christians led by former president Sulaiman Franjieh, Future TV was operated by Sunni Muslims led by then Prime Minister Hariri, MTV was owned by Greek Orthodox Christians led by the then interior minister, and NBN was owned by Shia Muslims led by Parliament Speaker Nabih Barri. In addition a few other TV stations continued to operate without licenses, including al-Manar owned by Hizbollah, and Tele-Lumiere owned by a Christian group.

Moreover, a decree of 1996 added new restrictions to the 1994 law, requiring "objectivity in the broadcasting of news and reports" in order to "safeguard supreme national interests," and to distinguish factual news from propaganda and advocacy. It also prohibited live broadcasts of demonstrations without prior approval of the government.

In Lebanon there are in fact multiple layers of censorship including unwritten restrictions which journalists respect. For example a presenter on Future TV admitted she would not interview the prime minister who was then Selim al-Hoss and a rival of Future owner Hariri.[6] Lebanon continued to have many radio stations, some of them representing specific interests. For example, since 1996 the Catholic Church maintained the Voice of Charity with headquarters in Jounieh, which carried broadcasts aimed at all parts of the country. Its declared purpose was "Christian, social, and cultural, serving man and society."[7]

Other Structural Changes

Qatar and the UAE undertook significant structural changes in their television systems in the 1990s.

In Qatar, Shaikh Hamad bin Khalifa al-Thani became ruler on June 27, 1995, taking over in a bloodless coup against his father. He then announced an end to media censorship, abolishing the censorship office and even abolishing the Ministry of Information itself. At the same time, however, he nevertheless created a new General Association for Radio and television to supervise the government-owned terrestrial broadcasting facilities. The Qatari government continued to own all radio and television except al-Jazeera (see below). In 1993 private cable TV was introduced but it is censored.

In the United Arab Emirates, in 1995 the government created the Emirates Broadcasting Corporation (EBC), to make radio and television more efficient and more competitive with the new satellite channels but all radio and television are government owned. Then in January 1999 the government reorganized radio and television, establishing Emirates Media Incorporated as an autonomous organization attached to the Information Ministry. As the Minister of Information Shaikh Abdullah bin Zayid described the change, "the Government has relinquished formal control over the country's largest media group. Emirates Media Incorporated now enjoys editorial and administrative independence. It remains somewhat dependent, however, on government funding, while ownership is still officially vested in the government." He added: "EMI now has an administrative structure based upon transparency, effectiveness and flexibility . . . (which) has permitted it to move towards privatization and to rely increasingly upon the revenues it raises itself." He said EMI only covered forty percent of its costs with advertising revenue. He explained the change by saying that Arab government broadcasting is facing a new situation, saying: "The international communications industry offers more and more choice to an increasingly educated public that is able to make its own judgments. We owe it to the public to tell them the truth, or at least the truth as we see it, for if we do not they will no longer listen to us."[8]

According to UAE senior officials, following the creation of the EMI, the Ministry of Information no longer gives policy instructions to the broadcasters as it did in the past.[9] In fact, the EMI does have considerable autonomy and freedom to operate, despite the fact that the Minister of Information is chairman of its board, and legally it is still a government entity, receiving subsidies from the public budget.

Meanwhile, the Dubai, Sharjah, and Ajman emirates within the UAE continued to have their own separate television channels, theoretically controlled by the UAE federal government but in practice controlled by the emirate governments in each case. Each emirate has a license to broadcast, while EMI represents the federal government.[10] In 1992, Dubai TV became the first channel in the Arab world to broadcast 24 hours a day.

Other Mixed Systems

In Egypt, the Egyptian Radio and Television Union (ERTU), established in 1971, was reconfirmed by law no. 13 of 1979 and law no. 223 of 1989 as the sole authority over all radio and television in the country. Its several channels focus on different parts of the country. Broadcast censorship remained based on a 1975 law, banning anything conflicting with religion, national security, or government positions on issues such as foreign or economic policy.[11]

The ERTU expanded its television activities considerably especially after the mid-90s. During 1999–2001, ERTU started six new "thematic" digital TV channels, presenting news and current affairs, arts and culture, drama, sports, music, and children's programming. The news program included live coverage of the Egyptian parliament, which attracted a considerable audience, and what the producers called Western style chat shows. Because of the expansion, ERTU added younger staff personnel. In early 2001, a channel for women, called "Nefertiti" started in Egypt. By 2001, Egyptian government-owned TV had two main channels plus six local governorate ones and three satellite ones, and was preparing to launch its second communications satellite, Nilesat 102.[12]

In the 1990s, Egyptian businessmen sought to establish private TV stations. In 1997 for example the chairman of the American Chamber of Commerce, Shefiq Gabr, publicly called for private TV which had been unthinkable only a few years earlier. This effort was reportedly blocked by Information Minister Safwat Sherif, who said on the TV program *Good Morning Egypt* on January 1, 1997 that "The Egyptian media are not ready to compete in the era of open airways." In 2000 the Minister repeated his opposition to private television.[13]

By 2003, however, the government allowed the emergence of private TV channels. One was called "Dream Television," that started in 2001 and offered two channels of entertainment and drama, but also included political programming that dealt with sensitive subjects, although usually in a restrained way. Another new Egyptian TV station, al-Mihwar, was established in January 2002 by businessmen Hassan Ratib and Hani Surur.[14]

In Palestine, broadcasting emerged somewhat from under Israeli control during the 1990s. Prior to that, Palestinian media professionals had been working in Syria, Iraq, Egypt, Tunisia, and Algeria and other Arab countries under the auspices of the governmental broadcasters in each location, which required them to respect local regulations. As of 1993, there was no Palestinian-controlled radio or television in the Israeli-occupied West Bank or Gaza, although other Arab radio and TV and broadcasts including Jordanian, could be seen or heard throughout those areas.[15]

Then the Oslo Accords, negotiated between Israel and the Palestinians in 1993, led to the emergence of the Voice of Palestine controlled by the Palestinian Authority (PA) and private broadcasting stations and gave the new Palestinian Authority (PA) some limited rights to control radio and television in the West Bank and Gaza. At first the Accords only permitted the PA to use one medium-wave and ten FM radio frequencies, plus some limited television. The PA created a Palestinian Broadcasting Corporation (PBC) with headquarters in Ramallah on the West Bank, and built a

100 kilowatt radio transmitter which reaches audiences throughout the West Bank and Gaza plus Syria, Saudi Arabia, and Egypt, and it set up eleven low power TV transmitters in the West Bank and Gaza. The PA subsidized the broadcasts which also obtained revenues from some commercial advertising. In addition to these approved transmitters, however, several unauthorized radio and television transmitters appeared in that area. The Authority began television broadcasting in 1995 and put it under the PBC. By the early twenty-first century, the Authority was operating two television stations including one satellite channel.[16]

Broadcast media in Palestine underwent considerable change and stress during the 1990s, however. For example, in February 1998, the PA closed a private TV station in Bethlehem, and in December it closed others. In April 1999, the PA closed al-Amal TV in Hebron for three weeks after it broadcast a controversial program on Islam. In May 1999, the PA closed al-Ru'ah television in Bethlehem after the security chief Jabril Rujub said it insulted Christians and could harm Christian-Muslim relations. The following month fifty journalists held a sit-in demonstration at PA headquarters in Bethlehem to protest the closing. In September 1999 the PA arrested a talk show host, Maher Adisouki in Ramallah for criticizing the PA's policy on Israel.[17]

In May, 2000, the PA closed several radio and TV stations. When it ordered Omar Nazzal, director of the al-Watan private TV station in Ramallah to cease broadcasting, it gave no reason but observers said it was because a caller on a talk show criticized Arafat for attacking Hizbollah in an interview with Israeli channel two TV. On May 23, 2000, the PA allowed al-Watan to resume broadcasting because it had not violated any laws. This was the fifth closure of al-Watan since it began in 1996. On May 30, 2000, PA intelligence (CID) agents raided the offices of the private television station al-Nasser and its sister radio station al-Manara in Ramallah, for criticizing secret talks in Stockholm between the PA and Israel. Al-Nasser's director Ammar Ammar and human rights groups denounced the harassment. On June 1, 2000, the CID closed down al-Mahed television station in Bethlehem and arrested its owner Samir Qumsiya, who is also director of the Union of Private Television and Radio Station owners. Earlier the PA police arrested Fathi Barqawi, chief news editor of the Voice of Palestine, the official PA radio station, for "incitement and vilifying the Palestinian leadership" after he criticized the Stockholm talks.[18]

Palestinian broadcasting also came under Israeli pressure and restrictions. The new Palestinian radio and television broadcasts were monitored very closely by the Israeli government, which from time to time was critical of their content. In October 2000, Israeli military forces hit the VOP transmitters in Ramallah with missiles which stopped broadcasts but only temporarily.[19] On January 18, 2002, during the al-Aqsa intifada, the Israeli military destroyed the Voice of Palestine in Ramallah, the main communication institution of the Palestinian Authority. To do so, they blew up a five-story building which had housed the studios and administration offices of VOP. The PA then resumed some VOP transmissions from a secret location elsewhere in the West Bank or Gaza, and VOP director Radwan Abu Ayyash denounced the attack.[20] Then in April 2002, during the height of their incursion into the West Bank, Israeli military forces partially or totally destroyed the al-Nasser and al-Watan Palestinian television stations, and al-Manara, Ajyal, and Love and Peace radio stations.[21]

In Morocco, the government continued to operate the official television channel Radio-Television Marocaine (RTM). In 1989 it had allowed a second TV channel to begin broadcasting as a joint venture between the government and private investors, as the first commercial television in Morocco and the first that allowed some private control. Called "2M International," two thirds of the capital for this new station came from private commercial interests and the rest from the state. It allowed commercial advertising and also part of its broadcast day was scrambled and accessible only by paid subscriptions. In 1996 the government bought a seventy percent majority share of 2M to save it from bankruptcy. The Minister of Communication is chairman of the board, and a government-appointed committee monitors broadcasts. It announced in 1998 it was preparing to privatize 2M, but that did not happen. The government clearly is in control of 2M, for example in April 2000 it fired the chief editor of the station after it reported on an interview with Polisario leader Muhammad Abdalaziz in New York.[22]

The other private station operating in Morocco is Radio Mediterranee Internationale (Medi-1) which began broadcasting in Tangier in 1980 under agreement with a French firm and as of 2003 continues to function. The Moroccan government stated in 2002 that it intended to privatize the electronic media, but as of 2003 it had not done so.[23]

Stable Terrestrial Systems

Most Arab countries have maintained their terrestrial television stations with little change from before 1990.

In Jordan, Jordanian Television (JTV) remained as the only authorized television broadcaster. It is partially funded by a license fee but also from commercial revenues. All news bulletins and most other programs are produced in house. Jordan's terrestrial television can be seen in Syria, Northern Saudi Arabia, Israel, the West Bank and Gaza, and South Lebanon.

In 1999, King Abdullah of Jordan announced plans to change the structure of television by putting it under joint public-private ownership instead of entirely governmental ownership. In August 2000, the Jordanian House of Representatives approved the establishment of private broadcasting stations by Jordanian foreign companies, as long as they "respect the objectives and values of the Jordanian state." This ended the state monopoly on broadcasting, although since 1998 Jordan has allowed the non-Jordanian private channels MBC, BBC, and Monte Carlo radio to broadcast on local FM frequencies. The parliament established a new broadcasting regulatory board on which nine of the thirteen members are government appointees.[24]

In Saudi Arabia, the Broadcasting Service department of the Ministry of Information, continues to have a monopoly over all public broadcasting. Saudi Information Minister Fuad al-Farsi, when asked in 1999 about privatization of radio and television, said that would be impossible because they were "a manifestation of sovereignty." The Saudi government censors remove from all foreign-produced radio or TV programs any reference to politics, religions other than Islam, pork, or sex, and locally produced programs respect these taboos. However, in 1996, Saudi TV responded to competition from abroad by introducing some program changes, including a new weekly live political talk show "Face to Face," in which ministers and other senior officials answer questions from the host and from viewers calling them or faxing them in. Yet resistance to change is strong. In 1998, a Saudi Muslim preacher speaking to worshippers in Mecca warned of the "poison" of satellite television, indicating it was having an impact.[25]

In Bahrain, the government made Bahrain Radio and Television a public corporation in 1993, which according to a senior official in the government gave it "administrative and financial independence." She acknowledged that this was partly due to satellite TV, saying, "With the availability of global satellite channels to the general public, intensive efforts are directed towards providing good local programming to ensure the competitiveness of local channels which reflect the culture of our society."[26] The basic structure remained the same, however.

In Iraq, until 2003, the government continued to own all broadcasting media and to operate them as propaganda outlets. No opposing views were permitted. The government regularly jammed incoming foreign broadcasts. The Iraqi government also tightly restricted the use of satellite dishes to only a few authorized individuals. It periodically warned the public that violations were punishable by heavy fines and two years in prison. In 1999 the government promised to ease the ban but it did not do so. Between 1991 and 2003, however, when Northern Iraq was under independent Kurdish rule, independent Kurdish stations operated which broadcast programs hostile to Baghdad.

When the U.S.-led attack on Iraq in March 2003 led to the collapse of the regime of Saddam Hussein and the establishment of a U.S.-British occupation government, all of Saddam's tightly controlled broadcasting ceased. Iraqis immediately began buying satellite television dishes and many started watching al-Jazeera, al-Arabiya, LBC-Hayat and other TV channels that had previously been banned.[27]

The occupation authorities permitted private radio and television stations to function, and several began transmission using available equipment. The

Kurdish stations were the first to be heard after the fall of Saddam's regime, and the non-Kurdish broadcasting was much slower to start up than newspapers, to a large extent because of cost and lack of equipment. Non-Iraqi radio broadcasts from the neighboring countries and elsewhere however were audible on FM and AM channels.[28]

When the occupation authorities set up the "Iraqi Media Network" (IMN), that U.S. administrator L. Paul Bremer said in June 2003 was an interim body intended to replace Saddam's Information Ministry, it opened a new television channel and two radio stations. These stations employed Iraqi professionals who returned from exile, plus some Iraqis who had worked for Saddam's information ministry. They were used to carry occupation authority announcements, but policy control over content was fairly light.[29]

In Kuwait, radio and television suffered catastrophically in 1990 when Iraqi forces occupied the country. The Iraqis forcibly removed most of the important production and control equipment, taking it back to Iraq, and they began broadcasting a surrogate service they called "Television of the Provisional Government of Free Kuwait," which claimed to represent the Kuwaiti people, but it was in fact Iraqi controlled. After liberation in early 1991 in Desert Storm, Kuwait rebuilt its facilities which were fully operational by 1993. Audiences in Eastern Saudi Arabia, Bahrain, Qatar and at times the UAE can see Kuwaiti terrestrial television broadcasts, and Kuwaitis can usually see Iraqi and Iranian TV.[30]

In Tunisia, the government continues to own and operate all broadcasting through the Tunisian Radio and Television Establishment (ERTT), and news is taken directly from the government agency TAP. Bilateral agreements with France and Italy allow viewers to see France 2 and Rai Uno but in October 1999 the government stopped France 2 because of its critical coverage of the election and said it would not resume because it wanted more local coverage.[31]

In Libya, the state still owns and controls broadcasting through the People's Committee of the Great Jamahiriya Television, and supervised by the People's Committee for Information of the Information Ministry. It does not permit broadcast of opinions contrary to official policy.[32]

In Algeria, broadcasting remains under government control, although different administrations have treated it with varying degrees of strictness. After 1989 when the new constitution ended the one-party system, government supervision of broadcasting was somewhat reduced for a while, but then in 1992 after President Chadli Benjedid resigned and the military took over, broadcasting again became a closely managed mouthpiece of the government. This remained the case during the presidency of General Liamine Zeroual 1994–1999 and since the election of president Abdalaziz Bouteflika in 1999. A new information law passed in Algeria in 1990 allowed for private TV but as of 1993 none had been established. Broadcast media are very careful with political subjects. On the eve of the April 15, 1999, Algerian presidential elections, for example, when five of the six candidates withdrew, leaving Abdulaziz Bouteflika uncontested, radio and TV failed to report that.[33]

In the Sudan, the government still controls all broadcasting directly and requires content to reflect policies of the government and of the National Islamic Front. A permanent military censor at TV ensures compliance.

The audience for terrestrial television remains primarily a domestic one in each country because the signal has a limited range. Nevertheless during the 1990s, a number of Arab governments increased the power of their terrestrial transmitters in border areas in order to be able to reach at least some audiences in neighboring countries. For example by the early twenty-first century, audiences in Bahrain, Qatar, and the UAE could normally watch telecasts from up to seven other countries even without cable.

As for the structure of radio broadcasting, it has not changed much since the 1980s. Lebanon has about fifteen radio stations operating, a result of the civil war in which they proliferated. One of them is al-Noor Radio, owned by Hizballah. Most other Arab countries have just one government-monopoly radio system.

DEVELOPMENT OF PRIVATE ARAB SATELLITE TELEVISION

Satellite TV technology was available before 1990 for Arab satellite television but neither Arab governments nor private individual entrepreneurs took advantage of it immediately. Arabsat, the Arab satellite, was launched in 1985, but it was underutilized. Several factors then converged at the beginning of the 1990s which led to the creation of a series of new Arab satellite broadcasters, and this radically changed the nature of Arab television.[34]

First, improvements in technology opened satellite TV to many more viewers, as the better antennae became accessible and affordable. When Arab TV began using satellites in 1985, the dishes were large and expensive, so only the wealthiest viewers installed them. The newer technology made smaller and cheaper dishes possible. A satellite dish can be purchased for under $200 and if necessary one can serve several houses in the neighborhood.[35] Secondly, when CNN covered the Kuwait crisis of 1990–1991 around the clock, Arab leaders and businessmen who watched it realized that CNN was far more sophisticated and interesting than the existing local Arab TV broadcasts. Many of them had seen American TV broadcasts as students or visitors to the United States, and they realized how effective television could be in covering major events in the Middle East. Although only a limited number of Arabs had access to CNN's 24-hour coverage of that crisis, some Arab entrepreneurs saw it and recognized how powerful it could be as a political and commercial vehicle. They regarded CNN as having a Western bias and decided that it might be possible to create a similar TV channel that was controlled by Arabs and reflected Arab perspectives. Shaikh Walid Ibrahim, who created the first private Arab satellite television channel, reportedly got his inspiration as a student in the United States.[36]

Technically, Egypt was the first Arab country to start a satellite TV channel. Egypt, which had been excluded from Arabsat (because of the Arab boycott related to the peace process), launched its own satellite, "Nilesat," partly motivated by a need to convey Egyptian official policy on the 1990–1991 Kuwait crisis. Thus Arab Satellite TV first came to the Arab world on December 2, 1990 when Egypt began its broadcasts. The content of the programs, however, was at that time identical with the content of Egyptian terrestrial television. But a second satellite channel, Middle East Broadcasting Corporation (MBC), immediately followed in 1991, and it was the first truly pan-Arab station in content and purpose, and unlike the Egyptian channel it was privately owned. MBC was followed by other private stations and by government-owned satellite channels so that by the twenty-first century nearly all Arab countries had satellite TV transmissions, three of which (al-Jazeera, ANN and al-Arabiya) were all-news channels. The main impact of this change was to introduce an approach to content, a presentation which was quite new to the Arab world.

Before satellite television came to the Arab world, many Arabs had turned to Western international radio broadcasting in Arabic—primarily from the BBC, Radio Monte Carlo, and Voice of America—in order to hear the style and type of news and commentary that was not available from local Arab media. Listening to Western radio broadcasts in Arabic was especially popular in times of crisis or tension, and it reflected a degree of dissatisfaction with the local broadcasts which were government-controlled or influenced. Arab satellite television was also different in content from terrestrial television.

When Shaikh Salih Kamel and Shaikh Walid Ibrahim of Saudi Arabia, founded the Middle East Broadcasting Center (MBC) in 1991, based in London, it was unique because it was the first private Arab satellite channel. Both men had strong ties to the Saudi royal family. (Shaikh Walid's sister is married to King Fahd and is the mother of Fahd's favorite son Abdulaziz.) He also came to the MBC project with some international media experience, since he bought the faltering United Press International (UPI) some years earlier, and subsidized its operation to keep it going. It is assumed that the royal family quietly supported this MBC venture financially for political reasons, in order to support a pan-Arab media channel which would be friendly to Saudi Arabia. Many in the region in fact consider it to be the king's channel. MBC received an audience boost for reporting on the 1994 Yemeni civil war which was bigger than any other TV channel, including CNN. One observer says the king paid a large percentage of the startup costs.[37]

Between 1991 and 1998 MBC had strong financial backing and good advertising revenues which allowed it to grow, expanding the London staff to 150 and opening bureaus in most of the Arab countries. Since 1998, however, the fall in oil prices and problems in management persuaded MBC to reduce staff and move the headquarters to Dubai in 2001 to cut costs, yet it remained a major Arab TV channel.[38]

Competition from other pan-Arab satellite television quickly emerged during the 1990s. In 1994, Shaikh Salih Kamel sold his 37.5 percent share of MBC and joined with Saudi Prince al-Walid bin Talal in founding a new TV station they called "Arab Radio and Television Network" (ART). Kamel said he started it to combat Western-style programming coming into the area.[39] Originally, based in Rome, it later moved to Cairo. Prince al-Walid is related to the king and he is also one of the world's wealthiest men, owning shares in many major international companies including Citicorp and Eurovision.

Also in 1994, the Saudi business group of al-Mawarid founded "Orbit" a pan-Arab satellite TV channel based in Italy. (In 2000, it moved its headquarters to Bahrain.) Orbit was the Arab world's first fee-based coded-signal television channel. Al-Mawarid is controlled by Prince Khalid bin Abdullah, son of the Saudi Crown Prince. At the beginning, Orbit was operated as a joint venture with the BBC Arabic Service, producing an all-news and documentary program. However, the partnership ran into difficulties when the BBC approach to journalism clashed with the approach of the Saudi sponsors. This agreement lasted only twenty months. When Orbit carried a BBC-produced "Panorama" program which the Saudi leadership did not like, Orbit management was persuaded to cancel the BBC contract. Orbit then made new arrangements with Rupert Murdoch's Sky TV and others, and from then on avoided program content offensive to its Saudi benefactors.[40]

As one observer noted, after everyone saw the impact of CNN during Desert Storm, the Saudis were quick to recognize that satellite television was a powerful tool which they could invest in. After the Saudis took that step, others followed.[41]

During the 1990s, four private satellite TV channels emerged in Lebanon. Lebanese Broadcasting Company (LBC), a private TV station owned by Lebanese Maronite Christians (see above), created an Arab satellite channel called "LBC International" in April 1996, reportedly with some financial assistance from Shaikh Salih Kamel.[42] In 1993, the wealthy Lebanese businessman Rafiq Hariri founded "Future Television" (al-Mustaqbal), and it started satellite broadcasting in 1995. Hariri also, in 1993, bought Radio Orient, a commercial radio station based in Paris with transmitters in Lebanon. In 2001, he joined with others to establish Zayn Television, based in Dubai, which specialized in programs for children.[43]

In 2000, Hizbollah, a Shia political group, received a license to start a satellite station called "al-Manar."

A fifth Lebanese station National Broadcasting Network (NBN) started satellite transmissions in 2000. NBN had been founded by a Lebanese Shia group led by Lebanese politician Nabih Barri, speaker of the Lebanese parliament. It offers news and entertainment, but the news gives special priority to Nabih Barri and his allies. It is sometimes nicknamed the "Nabih Barri Network."[44]

Although Saudis and then Lebanese led the way, others soon joined in the competition.

In 1997 a group of businessmen headed by Syrian businessman Sawmar al-Assad founded the "Arab News Network" (ANN), broadcasting from London. At the time, al-Assad was only twenty-six, but his father Rifaat was then Vice President of Syria, and his uncle Hafiz was President of Syria. (In 1998 Rifaat left his position and in 2000 Hafiz died and was succeeded by his son Bashar.) ANN is a 24-hour all-news channel. It has fifty employees in London and reporters in most Arab countries. In 1999 a Tunisian named Mohammed al-Hachimi, publisher of the weekly newspaper *al-Mustaqilla,* established al-Mustaqilla Television based in London. Hashimi was originally a strong critic of the Tunisian government and then he softened his criticism somewhat. As of 2003 it was suffering from limited financial resources and was broadcasting only eight hours a day.[45]

The success of al-Jazeera's all-news format encouraged some others to increase their news content. Abu Dhabi satellite television increased its news to eight hours per day, and LBC in 2002 agreed to join with *al-Hayat* newspaper to produce jointly a television program with more news content. In 2002, an Algerian businessman named al-Khalifa established al-Khalifa Television based in Paris. It is an all-news channel which gives priority to North African Arab interests that are ignored by other channels, but he also uses it to promote his own business interests. Then in February 2003 another all-news satellite television channel named al-Arabiya began broadcasting from its headquarters in Dubai. It was created by Shaikh Saleh Kamel, owner of MBC, who joined with businessmen from Saudi Arabia, Kuwait, and Lebanon. According to its director general, it was intended to compete with the all-news al-Jazeera channel, but without engaging in the sensationalism of some of al-Jazeera's programs.[46]

AL-JAZEERA TELEVISION

The most unique, controversial and influential new Arab satellite television station is al-Jazeera, based in Qatar. In 1996, it was founded as a nominally private enterprise which received start-up funding for five years from the Qatari government. Its uniqueness comes from the style and content of its programming.

Establishment of al-Jazeera

In January 1996, the Qatari government issued a decree establishing al-Jazeera as an independent television station, and it began broadcasting on November 1, 1996. The Qatari leadership's decision to establish al-Jazeera as a significantly new kind of television network seems to have been motivated by several reasons. First, it was founded soon after the Ruler, Emir Hamad bin Khalifa al-Thani seized power from his father in a bloodless coup d'etat in June 1995. Creating al-Jazeera was one of several innovative decisions which Shaikh Hamad took in the first years of his administration which could be considered part of a pro-active and somewhat liberal trend in the country's leadership. He also abolished the Ministry of Information in March 1998 and he sponsored municipal elections a year later even allowing women to vote. As one observer noted, "Sheikh Hamad belongs to a new generation of Arab leaders more open to political and social ideas familiar in the West." Shaikh Hamad had mentioned the idea of a private TV station as early as August 1994, when he was still crown prince, so it was in the planning stage for some time.[47] Others agree that he took the decision on al-Jazeera in the context of his overall policy since taking over in 1995, saying "He has sought to liberalize and open up Qatari politics by increasing political transparency and public participation. Women have been given the right to vote . . . and he plans to have . . . an elected majlis and support a free press."[48] The al-Jazeera chairman explains the network as part of the same trend in Qatar that includes democratic elections and a more liberal approach to the media, including the abolition of the Information Ministry.[49]

Secondly and relatedly, the Qatari leadership established al-Jazeera probably to gain some favorable publicity for Qatar in the region and in the world for their country under new management. Qatar is one of the world's smallest countries, little known outside the Middle East, and not given much attention even by its neighbors. Although it has one of the largest natural gas reserves on earth, and has developed significant military cooperation with the United States, most Westerners and even most Arabs know nothing about it. Putting his country "on the map" was clearly one of the emir's motives in founding al-Jazeera. One Qatari official expressed his government's strategy regarding al-Jazeera as the government's instrument of political self-defense in its competition with Saudi Arabia, which indirectly controls MBC, ART, Orbit, and al-Sharq al-Awsat.[50]

Third, Qatar's foreign policy in recent years, even before Shaikh Hamad became emir, has been characterized as following a course that is sometimes deliberately different from that of its neighbors, particularly Saudi Arabia. Previously Qatar had been politically and socially so indistinguishable from its big neighbor that it looked a bit like a small Saudi appendage, but the Qataris recently have taken pains to show that they are independent. When the Qatari leaders saw Saudis successfully invest in pan-Arab satellite television to the extent that they had become the dominant players in that market, this caught the attention of the Qatari leaders who decided to try the same themselves.

For al-Jazeera, it was fortuitous that at the time of the decree which established it, a number of highly qualified Arab professional broadcasters with BBC Arabic Service experience became available because the collapse of the BBC-Orbit agreement in 1996 put them out of work in London. According to the managing director, he hired seventeen or eighteen professionals from the BBC to be the core of the new al-Jazeera station, and about ten of them remained in leading roles there.[51] By 2001, most of al-Jazeera's staff of about 450 was from Arab states other than Qatar, although the top management and seventy percent of its technical staff were Qatari.[52] As a consequence of the fact that most of the reporters and presenters have no roots in Qatar, the style and character of al-Jazeera is pan-Arab rather than Qatari.

The Qatari leadership sought from the beginning to make the new station different. According to the Board Chairman, Shaikh Thamar bin Hamad al-Thani, they decided to concentrate almost exclusively on news and current events, since the other Arab satellite channels carried a variety of programming which contained a great deal of entertainment, and there was no all-news channel in Arabic. This approach was risky because news and commentary programs can carry material sensitive to one government or another, but the Qataris decided to take that chance.[53]

Growth and Development of al-Jazeera

Al-Jazeera's growth and development was rather dramatic, facilitated by some good luck as well as hard work. Soon after it started broadcasting, al-Jazeera began covering news stories in a way that other Arab television stations had not tried before.

When it began, al-Jazeera management sought to concentrate on Arab and Islamic news so it opened offices in key Arab and Muslim cities, starting with Gaza and Ramallah in Palestine, plus Iraq, Pakistan, Iran, and Afghanistan. It is the only Arab channel with a regular correspondent inside Israel, although others have reporters in Palestine who occasionally interview Israelis there. In Iraq, few other television networks had any representation. In December 1998, when the conflict between Iraq and the U.S.-led coalition escalated to the point that American aircraft were carrying out strikes against Baghdad in Operation Desert Fox, al-Jazeera was there covering the event while Western networks were not. Al-Jazeera management regards this as the milestone event that brought it to the international attention of many Arab viewers and also to international prominence, because many international networks depended on Al-Jazeera for coverage, much as they had depended on CNN for coverage in Baghdad of the beginning of desert storm in 1991.[54] Then a few weeks later, on January 5, 1999, Saddam Hussein selected al-Jazeera for exclusive coverage of his Army Day speech, in which he called for an uprising against Arab monarchs, a major news event that again turned the spotlight on the new network. In addition, al-Jazeera interviewed senior Iraqi officials Taha Hussain Ramadan and Tariq Aziz.[55]

Al-Jazeera had already covered the Israeli elections in depth, and its reporters had conducted interviews with Israeli leaders Ehud Barak in 1998 and with Shimon Peres. When the Palestinian al-Aqsa intifada began in October 2000, al-Jazeera had reporters in the West Bank, Gaza, and Israel, covering the story as it evolved. It carried graphic footage of Palestinian civilians being killed, or made homeless. As the intifada continued, al-Jazeera attracted a wide audience throughout the Arab world because it was reporting in Arabic and dealing in detail with issues and events that were of importance to Arabs, unlike CNN or any other Western station. Also in October 2000, Libyan leader Muammar Qaddafi selected al-Jazeera for an exclusive statement on Palestine.[56]

Meanwhile in 1999, when the Taliban regime invited four news organizations, CNN, Reuters, AP Television News, and al-Jazeera to open offices in Afghanistan, al-Jazeera accepted the offer, because it is an Islamic country which it wanted to include in its coverage. The other three news organizations declined, apparently regarding Afghanistan as insufficiently important.[57] As a result, al-Jazeera was able to achieve several major scoops. On June 10, 1999, it became the first network to interview Usama bin Laden, and on January 9, 2001 it covered the wedding of Usama's sons, events which attracted considerable attention in the Arab world although not a great deal in the West. It provided exclusive coverage of the Taliban destruction of the Buddha statues in March 2001, which gave it some brief notoriety.[58]

Then after the September 11, 2001 attack on the United States, the West also became very interested in Afghanistan and Usama bin Laden, so al-Jazeera's exclusive broadcasts from Kabul by its reporter, Tayseer Allouni, were carried on television networks worldwide. After 9/11, the Taliban expelled all journalists except those from al-Jazeera, so it was the only network to cover the U.S. bombing of Kabul live and other events at the beginning of the war. On September 26, 2001, it broadcast the only pictures of the Taliban attacking the U.S. embassy in Kabul. After 9/11 it also rebroadcast the 1998 interview with bin Laden with English subtitles. On October 7, November 3, and December 27, 2001, it broadcast exclusive footage of statements by bin Laden, all of which brought the network worldwide attention because they were used by CNN and many other broadcasters.[59] During the U.S.-led invasion of Iraq in 2003, al-Jazeera's coverage of the fighting from an Arab perspective made it widely popular in the Arab world. In September 2003 it broadcast the first film footage of Usama bin Laden that had been seen for many months, reinforcing al-Jazeera's reputation worldwide as a leading newsgathering organization.

Immediately after 9/11, CNN quickly made arrangements with al-Jazeera to share material on an exclusive basis. This arrangement lasted until January 31, 2002, when CNN broadcast al-Jazeera's October 21 interview with bin Laden without permission and al-Jazeera terminated the agreement. Meanwhile, on November 13 the network's Kabul office was destroyed accidentally in a U.S. attack and by then other news agencies were gaining access to the country. On October 10, the major U.S. networks agreed to a request by the U.S. government not to broadcast bin Laden statements live, on the grounds that he was getting too much air time, but this did not affect al-Jazeera. When al-Jazeera started broadcasting in 1996 it had been for only six hours each day, but because of its success it soon went to twelve and then since January 1, 1999 it has been on the air 24 hours daily. By the end of 2001 it had nearly five hundred employees, including fifty foreign correspondents in thirty-one countries.[60]

CONTROL AND FINANCING OF THE NONGOVERNMENTAL SATELLITE CHANNELS

During the 1990s, therefore, a number of nongovernmental Arab television channels emerged, all seeking to reach a pan-Arab audience. By 2003 there were fourteen private satellite systems, including three all-news channels (al-Jazeera, al-Khalifa, and al-Arabiya).

All of these new satellite TV channels were started as nominally private undertakings, although their owners all had strong connections to various Arab political leaders.

The founders of these new satellite channels had to make a basic choice between free-to-air commercial broadcasting, which would carry advertising and derive revenue from that source, or fee-based subscription broadcasts using encoded signals and decoders rented by audience members. The majority of the new channels—MBC, LBC, ANN, Future, al-Jazeera and others—are free-to-air and commercial, while ART and Orbit are subscription services. Orbit was the first Arab channel to use a fee-based subscription system; ART began as free-to-air but started a subscription service in 1997 alongside the free-to-air one.[61] Depending on commercials as the free-to-air channels did was also risky because of the weak economic base that exists in the region for media, as noted in previous chapters. On the other hand, it was also financially risky offering a subscription service with an encoding system because that type of arrangement was virtually unknown in the Arab world.

As it turned out, none of the Arab satellite stations has been able to cover costs by advertising revenues. Analysts agree that this is due to several

TABLE 10.1   Nongovernmental Arab Satellite Television Networks

Name	Owner's nationality	Date established	Free-to-air or subscription	Base
MBC	Saudi	1991	free	Dubai
ART	Saudi	1994	subscription	Cairo
Orbit	Saudi	1994	subscription	Rome/ Manama
Future	Lebanese	1995	free	Beirut
LBCI	Lebanese	1996	free	Beirut
Al-Jazeera	Qatari	1996	free	Doha
ANN	Syrian	1997	free	London
Al-Manar	Lebanese	2000	free	Beirut
Al-Mustaqilla	Tunisian	2000	free	London
NBN	Lebanese	2000	free	Beirut
Dream TV	Egyptian	2001	free	Cairo
Zayn TV	Lebanese	2001	free	Dubai
Al-Mihwar	Egyptian	2002	free	Cairo
Al-Khalifa	Algerian	2002	free	Paris
Al-Arabiya	Saudi	2003	free	Dubai

factors: the region as a whole is not wealthy; the advertising market is weak; audience research is difficult to do, so advertisers do not know much about their audience; many companies advertise in Western outlets; and politics steers ads to regime-loyal outlets such as for example Saudi TV in preference to al-Jazeera. Arab satellite TV therefore helps build prestige more than income. One estimate is that an Arab satellite television channel costs about $40 million annually, and only LBC is close to covering that expense. A 1999 study showed that only three Arab satellite television companies, LBC, Future, and MBC, were covering their costs with advertising revenues, while al-Jazeera was generating relatively little money from advertising.[62]

The most lucrative television advertising market is Saudi Arabia. More than $270 million was spent on advertising in Saudi Arabia in 1995, the highest in the Middle East. Ad spending on Saudi TV was $26 million in 1990, $58 million in 1992, leveled off at $56 million through 1994, fell to $48 million in 1995; the decline was caused by competition from the pan-Arab satellite stations as MBC, ART, and Egypt took 62% of the $186 million spent on pan-Arab media ads.[63] Generally speaking, however, Middle East advertising is "woefully underdeveloped" according to one analyst. In 1996 advertisers gave satellite TV only a little over $100 million, and in 1997 it was $200 million, with $300 million to terrestrial TV, which are low figures. Audience ratings are unreliable. Also digital technology applied to communication satellites has increased the number of channels substantially (Nilesat 101 launched in April 1998 has over eighty channels, far more than earlier ones, and the new Arabsat of 1999 has even more). This fragmented the market and further increased competition for advertising money.[64]

Moreover, costs at first inhibited audience expansion. The cost and availability of satellite dishes has been a constraint on viewing of Arab satellite TV. Dishes have also been restricted by law or even banned in some Arab countries. In the 1990s, in Saudi Arabia and Iraq, the production, importation, sale, or use of dishes was a criminal offense. In 1992 the Saudi government ordered a halt to dish importation at the request of religious authorities and in 1994 banned their use altogether. The Saudi ban was widely ignored, and the number of dishes in Saudi Arabia increased from under 200,000 in 1994 to over one million in 1998. The Iraq ban was very strictly enforced until 2003 when Saddam's regime collapsed, after which satellite television viewing became legal and the public eagerly bought receiving dishes so they could watch several regional and international channels. As for cost, in the mid-1990s household dishes were expensive; later, costs have been reduced, but financial constraints have restricted the numbers of audience members for satellite TV, which are still smaller than for the old-fashioned terrestrial kind. Cable subscriptions in Lebanon, for example, are relatively inexpensive.[65]

Reliable audience statistics for Arab satellite television are unavailable because independent surveys cannot be conducted everywhere in the region. There is some data on what audiences watch but very little on what motivates their watching habits.[66] By one estimate, however, as of 2002 the ownership of satellite dishes in the Arab countries was reasonably widespread, ranging from 20% to 60% in most countries, but lower in Egypt because of low income levels there. It was estimated that as many as 78% of the Palestinians had at least some access to satellite television. By 1998, 70% of Egyptian households had television receivers. By 2001, one estimate was that in wealthy Arab states satellite dishes were found in every fourth home.[67] But another estimate in late 2001 was that only 10% of Arabs have satellite dishes.[68] Most of the Arab middle class would like to have access to satellite TV, but even by 2001, much of this class was unable to afford the price.[69]

Because of the high cost of the new medium, the new investors in these first Arab satellite TV channels were among the region's wealthiest people. The first Arab satellite TV stations were created by wealthy Saudis who had close connections with the Saudi royal family. Just as wealthy Saudis in the previous decade had established offshore newspapers designed to reach a pan-Arab audience, so now others sought to make use of the new satellite technology for political and commercial purposes. Their personal resources enabled them to cover the high initial investment and to provide ongoing subsidies. Also the support they enjoyed from powerful political leaders helped assure that they would have sufficient funding to sustain the venture even if advertising revenues were limited. Their connections also helped ensure that they would have political support if they needed it to protect them from criticisms that might come for their new ventures.

The investments which the founders made in the new satellite TV chan-nels were undoubtedly considerable, although it is very difficult or impos-sible for outsiders to find out with any certainty how much they cost. One observer estimates that MBC was started with an initial investment of 3 billion pounds sterling, and that Orbit cost $2.3 billion to start up, but that ANN began with an initial investment of only $100 million for five years.[70] The amount of the five-year start-up funding which the Qatari government provided to al-Jazeera was five million rials ($137 million) annually, according to the station's management, which said that after four years they managed to cover 64% of their expenses with revenues from advertising and sales of news footage.[71]

All of these networks of course sought to generate revenue, either from advertising or (for ART and Orbit) from subscriptions, but the subsidies were very important to the success of these ventures.

Members of the al-Saud family of Saudi Arabia are apparently silent partners behind Orbit and ART, the two leading pay-TV channels, and they have personal and business links to Lebanon's LBCI and Future TV. In this way, influential Saudis, with strong Saudi government connections, control several leading satellite TV outlets, including MBC, ART, and Orbit, and they may have links also to ANN. Among the major ones, only al-Jazeera is completely outside Saudi influence. All of them are losing money and must be subsidized, and they continue the subsidies for essen-tially political reasons.[72]

Finally, one economic factor that influences program decisions is the fact that talk shows and game shows, which most of the private satellite channels thrive on, are less expensive to produce, and they have been wel-comed by audiences, especially in countries where people have less chance to express their opinions.[73]

GOVERNMENT SATELLITE TELEVISION

After the private entrepreneurs established satellite stations, most Arab governments followed suit during the 1990s. Satellite TV channels were cre-ated by the governments of Egypt in 1990, Kuwait in 1991, Tunisia and Dubai in 1992, Jordan in 1993, Morocco in 1994, then followed by Algeria, Qatar, Iraq, and others, with Lebanon coming on the list in the year 2000. Their purpose was essentially to take advantage of the new technology and also to compete with the private ventures that were emerging at that time.

In December 1990, because of the Gulf crisis caused by Iraq's occupation of Kuwait, the Egyptian Radio and Television Union (ERTU) began broad-casting television programs via Arabsat to the Arab world on a 24-hour basis, and called it the Egyptian Satellite Channel (ESC). This was the first Arab satellite transmission, and then Egypt opened its second satellite channel, Nile TV, in October 1993, in English and French, designed primarily to promote tourism. The Kuwait Space Network started transmissions on December 8, 1991. The Jordanian Arab Space Channel started on February 1, 1993. Bahrain and Qatar placed their main channels on Arabsat which went directly to the Arab world, while Dubai's satellite channel was the first to be seen as far as the United States. Dubai television began in 1994 to broadcast around the globe via satellite, using Arabsat, Eutelsat, and Galaxisat, covering Europe, Africa, North America, and the Far East. Dubai satellite TV also has a Business Channel, half in English and half in Arabic, whose dual mission is to bring global news and information to Dubai for UAE and other businessmen, and at the same time to give the world business news from an Arab perspective.[74] In January 2000, Abu Dhabi Television was relaunched as a satellite channel, that subsequently became one of the most popular of all channels in the region.

The Jordanian government started the Jordan Satellite Channel for television in February 1993, and it is carried on Arabsat 2 that covers the Middle East and south Europe, but JSC is also carried on Orbit which reaches Europe and North America.

Governmental involvement in satellite television is now almost universal in the Arab world, promoted primarily by political motivations. The tiny emirate of Ajman started terrestrial television on February 1, 1996, and only two years later, on February 1, 1998 it started satellite transmission. The director of satellite TV in Sharjah, another small emirate, said its purpose was to "play a leading role in promoting the national image worldwide with its educational, religious, cultural, and social programs."[75]

In 1999, Iraq began satellite broadcasting, inaugurated by Saddam Hussain. In 1990, because of its invasion and occupation of Kuwait, Iraq was expelled from Arabsat. Arabsat readmitted Iraq in 1994 but refused to allow it to use the facility until it paid a $2 million debt, and several Arabsat members remain politically opposed to Iraq's using it. In 1996 Iraq tried to gain access to a satellite transponder in Turkey but the UN committee overseeing sanctions on Iraq vetoed that proposal. Iraqi radio services including Voice of the Masses and Radio Mother of Battles were forced off the air during Desert Storm hostilities but by 1996 they were back on the air.[76]

MEDIA CITIES AND FREE ZONES

An outcome of the changed TV environment has been the creation of several "media cities" or "media free zones," primarily for television broadcasting. One reason was cost. Every channel requires thousands of hours of programming annually. Programs can be purchased from foreign suppliers but locally produced programs are more culturally appropriate and cheaper. As television channels increased, therefore, production centers were started in the Arab world because they provided Arab satellite stations with lower cost production. The centers emerged where talent was concentrated or could be attracted with local government subsidies.[77] Also, some Arab governments supported them because they believed that having media enterprises would attract needed foreign investment.

Egypt was the first Arab country to seek to attract Arab media institutions when in 1995 it announced the creation of Egyptian Media Production City (EMPC), billed as "Hollywood of the East." Located in October 6th City, 30 kilometers from downtown Cairo on 3.5 million square meters of land near the Nilesat earth station, its plan called for TV studios, satellite stations, printing presses, news agency offices, and other facilities. But construction was slow and by 2000 its use by media organizations was limited. Then in 2000 Egypt decided to establish a Media Free Zone near EMPC, which would offer private satellite TV stations tax and customs exemptions under investment law no. 8 of 1997. In April 2000, al-Jazeera signed up, after Egypt agreed that it would not impose censorship on production, although this did not prevent some official Egyptian complaints about al-Jazeera programming. Orbit also opened a production center there.[78]

In 2002, MBC moved some of its production to EMPC from Europe, such as the popular *Who Wants to Be a Millionaire*. Several Egyptian channels, such as Mihwar, Tamima, Dream TV (Egypt's first private TV network), and Tabiba were also there.[79] One respected Egyptian journalist however expressed disappointment in the project, saying it had sounded like a harbinger of liberalization in Egyptian media policy which did in fact not materialize, and that concerns about Egyptian censorship had prevented some media organizations from coming there.[80]

Jordan also sought to attract media organizations with a free zone. Shaikh Saleh Kamel created the Jordanian Media City Company in Amman in 2001, established a production center for TV companies there, and began using it for his ART. It includes TV studios, transmission stations, and satellite receivers. It operates as commercial free zone, meaning companies there can import goods tax free and pay no uplink taxes.[81]

In January 2001, the Dubai government opened the Dubai Media City, a 500-acre facility offering 100% foreign ownership and tax exemptions to media organizations including broadcasters, print media, advertising and public relations agencies as well as individual journalists. Within a few months, in 2001, MBC had moved its television production headquarters from London to Dubai, although it also maintained production facilities in Beirut and Cairo. Zayn TV (partly owned by Future TV), Reuters, and CNN also went to Dubai, along with Saudi Research and Publishing Company which relocated from Jidda. MBC executives explained that their move from London was to save money and to be closer to their "core audience," and to have better access to Arab talent. An MBC official claims his costs were reduced by 30 percent by moving from London to Dubai.[82]

The Dubai government reportedly invested $800 million in its media city, for reasons of both commerce and local pride. Dubai Crown Prince Shaikh Muhammad bin Rashid said at the inauguration that it was intended to "attract international and regional media businesses" and "to serve as a media hub for the region" and to reinforce Dubai as "the crossroads of the Middle east." He said "I guarantee freedom of expression to all of you and the right to be completely objective in your views and reporting" but he added: "Let us do so responsibly, objectively and with accountability and in the spirit of the social and cultural context in which we live." Observers said there would be limits set not only by libel laws as in the West, but also by conservative social norms such as those involving sexual content.[83]

Subsequently, the DMC did establish a code for tenants which said there could be no pornography, no broadcasters owned by political parties, no preaching of religion other than Islam, and no defamatory content.

In short, the development of Arab satellite television systems during the 1990s, primarily led by Saudi investors and the government of Qatar, has been a major development on the Arab media scene. It has had some impact on the structure of Arab television generally, but the greatest impact has been on the content of television programming, which will be explored in the following chapter.

NOTES

1. Mahmoud M. Hammoud and Walid A. Afifi, "Lebanon" chapter 11 in Yahya R. Kamalipour and Hamid Mowlana, Eds., *Mass Media in the Middle East: A Comprehensive Handbook,* Westport, CT: Greenwood Press, 1994, pp. 166–68; Nabil Dajani lecture at Georgetown University April 25, 2000.

2. Magda Abu Fadil, Lebanese American University, interview, Beirut, June 5, 2001.

3. Dajani lecture April 25, 2000.

4. www.telelumiere.org.lb.

5. Naomi Sakr, "Optical Illusions: Television and Censorship in the Arab World," Transnational Broadcasting Studies electronic journal (hereinafter TBS) no. 5, fall/winter 2000.

6. Naomi Sakr, "Optical Illusions," op. cit.

7. www.radiocharity.org.lb (2002).

8. Shaikh Abdullah's speech April 2001 in Dubai, published in Emirates Bulletin No. 80, April 30, 2001.

9. Interview with Ibrahim al Abid, UAE Ministry of Information, June 6, 2000.

10. Douglas A. Boyd, *Broadcasting in the Arab World,* Ames: Iowa State University Press, 1999 (hereinafter "Boyd, *Broadcasting*"), pp. 193–94.

11. U.S. Department of State, *Country Reports on Human Rights Abuses 1993,* January 31, 1994, Egypt section.

12. "High Hopes for Egyptian Media Production City;" and "Producers Look to Globalization at CAMAR," TBS report no. 7, fall/winter 2001.

13. Steve Negus, "TV Wars," in *Middle East International* January 10, 1997, p. 9; Naomi Sakr, *Satellite Realms: Transnational Television, Globalization and the Middle East,* New York and London: I. B. Taurus, 2001, p. 107.

14. Interview with Hala Sirhan, *TBS* no. 8, spring 2002.

15. Orayb Aref Najjar, "Palestinian Media" chapter in Kamalipour and Mowlana, op. cit., pp. 221–23.

16. Boyd, *Broadcasting,* pp. 107–111; and *New York Times,* October 24, 2000.

17. U.S. Department of State, *Country Reports on Human Rights Practices, 1998 and 1999,* February 26, 1999 and February 25, 2000, Occupied Territories section, and *1999 World Press Freedom Review,* Palestine section.

18. Khaled Amayreh, *al-Ahram International,* June 8–14, 2000, p. 4.

19. *New York Times,* October 24, 2000.

20. *al-Ahram Weekly,* January 24–30, 2002, p. 6.

21. *al-Ahram Weekly,* May 2–8, 2002, p. 4.

22. Boyd, *Broadcasting,* pp. 257, 266; and U.S. Department of State, *Country Reports on Human Rights Practices, 1999,* February 25, 2000 Morocco section.

23. U.S. Embassy Rabat, Morocco Media Directory, January 2003.

24. Naomi Sakr, "Optical Illusions."

25. U.S. Department of State, *Country Reports on Human Rights Practices, 1993, 1996 and 1999,* January 31, 1994, January 30, 1997 and February 25, 2000, Saudi Arabian section.

26. Dr. Hala Umran, U/S for TV and Broadcasting in the Ministry of Information, quoted in *Moneyclips,* UK, January 22, 1995.

27. Reporters Without Borders, "The Iraqi Media Three Months After the War: A New But Fragile Freedom," Report, July 22, 2003 (http://www.rsf.fr).

28. BBC Monitoring Media Services, "Iraq: The Media in Post-war Iraq," July 15, 2003 (http://www.ifj.org); many that claimed to be dailies in fact appeared less frequently.

29. Reporters Without Borders, "The Iraqi Media Three Months After the War: A New But Fragile Freedom," Report, July 22, 2003 (http://www.rsf.fr) equipment. The occupation authorities also sponsored a television station through their "Iraq Media Network" organization.

30. Boyd, Broadcasting, op. cit., pp. 138, 140, and Mohammed El-Nawawy and Adel Iskandar, *Al Jazeera: How the Free Arab News Network Scooped the World and Changed the Middle East,* Cambridge, MA: Westview, 2002, p. 18.

31. Abdallah Hidri, "Tunisia" chapter in Mohammed El-Nawawy and Adel Iskandar, *Al Jazeera,* Cambridge, MA: Westview, 2002, pp. 278–79.

32. Kerim Mezran, "Libya" chapter in Kamalipour and Mowlana, op. cit., pp. 180–82; U.S. Department of State, *Country Reports on Human Rights Abuses 1993,* January 31, 1994.

33. Boyd, *Broadcasting,* pp. 214, 228–29; Laid Zaghalami, "Algeria" chapter in Kamalipour and Mowlana, pp. 17–19.

34. See in particular the excellent study by John B. Alterman, *New Media, New Politics?,* Washington D.C.: Washington Institute for Near East Policy, 1998, Policy Paper No. 48, pp. 16–17.

35. Simon Henderson, "The Al-Jazeera Effect," Washington Institute on Middle East Policy, Study no. 507, December 8, 2000.

36. Alterman, *New Media,* op. cit.

37. Alterman, *New Media,* p. 22; Nawawy and Iskandar, p. 39.

38. Public Affairs Office, U.S. Embassy London, "Profile, Arabic Media in London," Summer 2002.

39. Alterman, *New Media,* op. cit., p. 30.

40. David Gardner and Ray Snoddy in *Financial Times,* April 10, 1996; *Middle East Times,* February 6, 2000.

41. Interview with Hisham Milhem, Washington D.C., May 2001.

42. Nabil Dajani lecture at Georgetown University April 25, 2000; Edmund Ghareeb, "New Media and the Information Revolution in the Arab World," *Middle East Journal,* vol. 54, no. 3, summer 2000, pp. 403–04.

43. *Gulf News* March 9, 2000; Naomi Sakr, *Satellite Realms,* New York: I. B. Tauris, 2001, pp. 76, 194.

44. Marwan M. Kraidy, TBS issue no. 5, fall/winter 2000; interview Magda Abu Fadil June 16, 2001 Lebanese American University, Beirut.

45. Public Affairs Office, U.S. Embassy London, "Profile, Arabic Media in London," Summer 2002.

46. *Washington Post,* February 11, 2003, p. A12.

47. Louay Y. Bahry, *Middle East Policy,* vol. VIII, no. 2, June 2001, p. 88.

48. Edmund Ghareeb, "New Media . . ." pp. 405ff.

49. Interview with Shaikh Hamad bin Thamar al-Thani, published in TBS issue no. 7, fall/winter 2001.

50. Interview with Khalid al-Mansuri, Director of research, Qatari Foreign Ministry, Doha, May 2001.

51. Muhammad Jasim al-Ali, interview, TBS issue no. 7, fall/winter 2001.

52. Muhammad Jasim Ali, al-Jazeera general manager, interview with the author, Doha, May 2001.

53. Interview with Shaikh Hamad bin Thamar al-Thani, TBS issue no. 7, fall/winter 2001.

54. Interview with Shaikh Hamad bin Thamar al-Thani, published in TBS issue no. 7, fall/winter 2001.

55. El-Nawawy and Iskandar, *Al-Jazeera,* op. cit., p. 167; and Ghareeb op. cit., p. 408.

56. Bahry op. cit., p. 91; Nawawy and Iskandar, pp. 3, 51; TBS issue no. 7, fall/winter 2001.

57. Mohammed Jasim al-Ali, TBS interview, published in TBS issue no. 7, fall/winter 2001.

58. Nawawy and Iskandar op. cit., pp. 22, 149, 160.

59. Nawawy and Iskandar op. cit., pp. 21, 144, 149, 153–55, 159–62.

60. Nawawy and Iskandar pp. 25, 34, 163–69; *Gulf Times,* October 10, 2001.

61. Alterman, *New Media,* op. cit., pp. 29–30.

62. Sakr, *Satellite Realms,* op cit., p. 116.

63. Reuters World Service, February 1, 1996, "Saudi TV ads."

64. Naomi Sakr, in *Middle East Report,* Spring 1999, p. 7.

65. Nabil H. Dajani, "The Changing Scene of Lebanese Television," TBS issue no. 7, fall/winter 2001.

66. Jihad Fakhreddine, in TBS no. 5, fall/winter 2000.

67. Nawawy and Iskandar pp. 46–47; *Middle East International* May 8, 1998, p. 8; Fakhreddine, op. cit.

68. Mamoun Fandy, "To Reach Arabs, Try Changing the Channel," *Washington Post,* December 2, 2001, p. B2.

69. Hussein Amin, in TBS issue no. 6, spring/summer 2001.

70. Alterman, *New Media,* op. cit., pp. 22, 29, and Edmund Ghareeb, op. cit., pp. 407, 410–11.

71. Muhammad Jasim Ali, al-Jazeera general manager, interview with the author, Doha, May 2001; Alterman, *New Media,* op. cit., p. 22 confirms the $137 million figure.

72. Naomi Sakr, "Television Censorship in the Arab World," TBS no. 5, fall/winter 2000; interview with Arab journalist, Cairo, February 9, 2001.

73. Jihad Fakhreddine, "Pan Arab Satellite Television," TBS no. 5 fall/winter 2000.

74. Hussein Y. Amin, "Actors and New Stakes in the Euro-Arab Satellite Scene" an interview with Stephen Marney, TBS issues nos. 5 and 6, fall/winter 2000 and spring/summer 2001.

75. www.ajmantv.com (2002); and Emirates Bulletin, Abu Dhabi, UAE, no. 184, September 25, 2001.

76. Najib Ghadbian, in *Middle East Review of International Affairs,* vol. 5, no. 2, June 2001; and *Middle East International* October 25, 1996, p. 10.

77. Naomi Sakr, in *Middle East Report,* Spring 1999, pp. 6–7.

78. Heba Kandil and Hussein Y. Amin, in TBS no. 5, fall/winter 2000; and Naomi Sakr, in *Middle East Report,* Spring 1999, p. 7.

79. Naila Hamdy in TBS issue no. 8, spring 2002.

80. Salama A. Salama, "Abandon Ship," *Pharaohs magazine,* March 2000, p. 24.

81. TBS issue no. 7, fall/winter 2001, "Private Sector Media City Launched in Amman."

82. TBS issue no. 7, fall/winter 2001; and *Khaleej Times,* April 28, 2002.

83. Abdullah Schleifer, in TBS issue no. 5, fall/winter 2000.

11

Arab Television Since 1990: Programs

The previous chapter has described the changes in structure of Arab television since 1990. This chapter will present highlights of program characteristics of Arab television since 1990. Programs to an extent have changed because of the structural developments, and new structures, especially private stations, have led to program innovations throughout the region.

The various Arab satellite channels offer somewhat different program content, depending to a large extent on the prevailing political environment in the country which controls the channel.

AL-JAZEERA PROGRAMS

Two features make al-Jazeera stand out: its extensive news coverage in Arabic by reporters who know what the Arab public wants, and its political discussion programs that deal with controversial subjects. Other Arab satellite stations did some of both first, but al-Jazeera went further than the others. Then after al-Jazeera started others felt obliged to imitate it to some degree, although most of them are not all-news stations and they focus heavily on entertainment.

Reportedly al-Jazeera has the Arab world's most watched newscast. The station's news coverage of the al-Aqsa Intifada, that started in October 2000, gave it a major boost in viewership. The reporters and camera crews provided live news and graphic images that were more comprehensive because their news programs were much longer, and the station promoted the story by repeating the most dramatic images such as 12-year-old Palestinian schoolboy Muhammad Durrah dying in his fathers arms after being hit by Israeli gunfire. The station also repeatedly played the new Palestinian song "Jerusalem will return to us" that mentioned Durrah's name. That presentation was much more appealing to Arab viewers than the CNN broadcasts that were in English and presented selected coverage based essentially on Western interests and concerns. Al-Jazeera established itself as the best Arab news source on Israel and Palestine. Although other Arab satellite TV stations had already started interviewing Israelis, al-Jazeera was the first one to interview top Israeli officials such as Ehud Barak and Shimon Perez. The government-run Arab terrestrial stations also covered the Intifada but not as graphically or as intensely, perhaps to avoid greatly enflaming Arab public opinion.[1]

Al-Jazeera also attracted Arab audiences because of its current affairs commentary and debate programs. These programs have caused a great deal of discussion throughout the Arab world, some of which is directed pro and con at the style of the network itself. The Chairman of the network says his news strategy is "one opinion and another" ("al-ra'y wa al-ra'i akher"), meaning that it intends to present both sides of the story,[2] and this applies also to the discussion shows.

One of the most famous and controversial programs is "opposite directions" hosted by Faisal Qassim, a Syrian journalist who has a UK education and almost a decade of experience with the BBC 1988–1996. He claims he is independent in selecting subjects that are often sensitive issues, and choosing guests who are of very different opinions, somewhat like CNN's *Crossfire*. For example, he has paired an Islamist with a feminist to discuss polygamy; an Islamist with a secularist who criticized Islam; a Jordanian opposition leader with the Jordanian deputy prime minister; and an American official with a critic of the United States on the subject of American bombing of Afghanistan. Qassim also interviewed Muammar Qaddafi in October 2001, who made news by agreeing that the United States had a right to seek revenge for the 9/11 attack. Because of this program, Qassim has become a celebrity all over the Arab world.[3]

Another program, "More than One Opinion," seems to be modeled on the McLaughlin Group as it presents divergent views in a lively manner. Other popular programs are listed in Table 11.1.

Audience

Precise audience numbers are difficult to obtain because Arab media research is quite limited. Some observers assert that al-Jazeera is the most widely watched Arab satellite television station.[4] The main focus of al-Jazeera's program content is pan-Arab as opposed to Qatar domestic issues, indicating that the management of the station see their role as

TABLE 11.1   Regular al-Jazeera Political Programs[5]

Following are the major political discussion and interview programs (all are weekly unless otherwise indicated)

Title	Host	Type
Opposite Directions (al-tijah al-mu'akis)	Faisal al-Qassim	Two guests of opposing views
More than One Opinion (akthar min ra'y)	Sami Haddad	Three guests debate the week's most newsworthy issue
Without Boundaries (bila hudud)	Ahmad Mansur	Interview of a prominent person
Islamic Law and Life (sharia wal hayat)	Mahar Abdullah	Contemporary issues from an Islamic perspective
Open Dialogue (hiwar maftuh)	Ghassan bin Jiddo	Arab intellectuals discuss a current issue
Scene of the Incident (mawqi' al-hadath)	Hussain Abdulghani	Reporter at a hot spot
Very Confidential (sirri lilghaya)	Yusri Foda	Investigative documentary (monthly)
Under Scrutiny (taht al-mihjar)	various	Examines a political or social issue
Guest and Issue (daif wa qadia)	Muhammad Kraishan	Interview on a current issue
Al-Jazeera Correspondents' World (murasilu al-Jazeera)	Muhammad Burini	Reports from around the world
Private Visit (ziyara khaasa)	Sami Kulaib	Interview of a prominent person at home
The Weekly File (al-malif al-usbu'i)	Jamal Azar	Discusses prime news of the week
Eyewitness to the Era (shahid ala al-Asr)	Ahmad Mansur	Interviews on past events
A Bit of History (shay min al-tarikh)	Ahmad Taha	Examines an event in history

providing a service for the Arab world not for local consumption. One study claims that 70% of Arabs who own satellite dishes reply primarily on al-Jazeera for news and political information.[6]

Officials claim that 40 to 50 million of the 300 million Arabs watch al-Jazeera, including 3 million in Europe and a few hundred thousand in the United States. They say that in times of crisis, their audience doubles.[7] There is no doubt that private satellite channels have had a great impact even where restrictions exist. For example, one study of TV use among Saudis in 2001 found the following: the highest ratings went to MBC 56 percent, 1st Saudi channel 45 percent, al-Jazeera 34 percent, Egyptian

satellite 31 percent, LBC 23 percent, Bahrain satellite 19 percent, al-Mustaqbal 19 percent, Dubai satellite 15 percent, 2nd Saudi 14 percent, Abu
Dhabi satellite 13 percent.[8]

Governmental Complaints

As al-Jazeera became more popular, a lively debate developed in the
Arab world and elsewhere over the network itself and the role it was play-
ing in the region. Virtually every Arab government at one time or another
complained about specific programs that it objected to.

For example, some Arab government officials objected that its talk show
comments calling on Arab leaders to do more to help the Palestinians,
combined with al-Jazeera's intensive coverage of Israeli repression of the
Palestinian intifada, unnecessarily incite their Arab citizens against them.[9]
Gulf issues also caused concern. For example, in the winter of 1998–1999,
Kuwait and Saudi Arabia were displeased that al-Jazeera gave Saddam
Hussein and other Iraqi offcials a platform to express their view and even
to denounce Gulf Arab rulers. But then the Iraqis were displeased with al-
Jazeera's less than flattering coverage of Saddam's birthday celebrations.[10]

In a number of cases, the governments showed their displeasure by closing down the network's local bureau. On November 5, 1998 Jordan closed
the al-Jazeera bureau in Amman and cancelled the accreditation of its correspondents because of a broadcast that referred to the country as an
"artificial entity" and accused the king of collaborating with Israel. It was
reopened in February after Qatar apologized. In June 1999, Kuwait closed
the station's offices and banned al-Jazeera reporters from covering Kuwaiti
stories because an Iraqi caller had criticized the emir of Kuwait on the program "Islamic Law and Life." Kuwait lifted the ban and reopened the
bureau on July 29, 1999. At other times, Kuwait has complained that the
station has a pro-Iraq bias because it regularly interviews Iraqis. On
March 21, 2001, the Palestinian Authority closed the al-Jazeera bureau in
Ramallah because of a documentary critical of Chairman Arafat, but the
bureau was reopened two days later.[11]

On May 10, 2002, Bahrain closed the station's bureau, saying it "deliberately seeks to harm Bahrain" and "represents the Zionist side in the
region." Bahraini Information Minister Nabil al-Hamr announced at that
time that he had banned al-Jazeera from reporting inside Bahrain for being
biased toward Israel and against Bahrain. Apparently Bahraini officials
were angered by al-Jazeera's reporting without permission anti-United
States pro-Palestinian protests in Bahrain.[12]

Some governments have also resorted to symbolic gestures. In July,
2000, Morocco recalled its ambassador from Qatar because it said al-
Jazeera "led a hostile campaign" against the Moroccan monarchy and
because of coverage of Moroccan-Israeli ties and Islamic fundamentalism.
The ambassador returned in October. In April, 2000, Libya recalled its

ambassador from Qatar after a program criticized Libya and called its People's Committees a mere façade for Qaddafi. Qaddafi however has himself appeared twice on al-Jazeera, because he has recognized its usefulness as a platform. In August 2002, Jordan recalled its ambassador to Qatar to protest comments on al-Jazeera that insulted the Jordanian royal family. In September 2002, Saudi Arabia recalled its ambassador to Qatar over an al-Jazeera program accusing the Saudis of betraying the Palestinians. And in December 1998 the Arab governments passed a joint resolution in the Arab States Broadcasting Union rejecting al-Jazeera's application for membership for not conforming to a "code of honor of the Arab media" that "promotes brotherhood between Arab nations."[13]

Other governments have taken legal action. When al-Jazeera on August 4, 2000, carried a story accusing Kuwaitis of killing Palestinians and Iraqis in 1991 with acid, Kuwaitis sued and a Kuwaiti court fined the station for slander. One government even used unusual means to cut off the impact of a program it did not like. On January 27, 1999, when al-Jazeera broadcast a debate between two Algerians critical of their government, the Algerian authorities cut off electricity in Algiers in the middle of the program, because so many Algerians were watching it.[14]

Official protests are frequent. The Egyptian government was unhappy with the station's coverage of Egyptian elections in 2000 and about accusations that Egypt is soft on Israel. Al-Jazeera's commentators and talk show hosts criticized President Mubarak for not doing more to help the Palestinians, and news programs showed footage of angry Palestinians burning Egyptian flags. The Egyptian information minister on October 26, 2000 made a strong public statement accusing the network of "tearing apart" Arab solidarity and threatened to close down the bureau, and some Egyptian newspaper editorials supported him, but then he reconsidered. Egypt did close the office temporarily when a Palestinian on al-Jazeera called for an Egyptian uprising against President Mubarak. The Saudi Crown Prince was reported to have complained to the Qatari emir that the TV station encouraged terrorism, discredited the Gulf states, harmed the Arab royal families, and threatened Arab stability. Saudi newspaper editorials echoed the criticism.[15]

When Arab governments have complained to the Qatari government about broadcasts, the usual response from the government has been to assert that the station is independent and any complaints should be addressed to it directly. Al-Jazeera officials, in turn, argue that they should not be accused of bias, because they have been criticized from so many different directions that the accusations cancel out. They were accused of being pro-Iraqi when they made exclusive reports from Baghdad in 1998–1999, of being pro-Israeli for interviewing top Israelis, and of being pro-Taliban and pro-bin Laden when they covered the 2002–2002 Afghan crisis.[16]

U.S. officials have also been critical of al-Jazeera, for example Secretary of Defense Rumsfeld claimed it was a "mouthpiece" for terrorists by broadcasting Usama bin Laden's messages to the world. Reportedly in

October, 2001 when he met with the Emir of Qatar, Hamad Khalifa, Secretary of State Powell asked him to tone down its anti-American content. The Qatari authorities responded that they never interfere with the news that is balanced and objective. In fact, al-Jazeera has taken pains to provide balance to bin Laden. When it broadcast the bin Laden statements on November 3, and December 27, 2001, it followed them immediately with live comments by U.S. government officials or former officials, who delivered harsh critiques of what he had said. Al-Jazeera has routinely broadcast important statements by U.S. officials.[17]

The Qatari Government

What is the al-Jazeera network's relationship to the Qatari government? In fact, the government has some influence over programming because of the subsidy and the fact that al-Jazeera chairman Hamad bin Thamar al-Thani is a cousin of the emir and also chairman of the government's radio and television system. Yet the government and al-Jazeera professionals claim it is independent. Faisal Qassim, one of the talk show hosts who had worked for years in the BBC, claims that at the BBC he only had 20% of the freedom he now has at al-Jazeera. He also defends the lack of Qatari stories by saying "nothing that happens in Qatar is worth covering."[18]

One detailed study, however, disagrees with that conclusion, pointing out that al-Jazeera does cover negative stories even about neighboring Bahrain, a country as small as Qatar, and that it has hosted opposition speakers from every Arab country except Qatar. It could for example discuss the lack of democracy in Qatar but it does not. It respects Qatari taboos because it is used as a public relations tool by the government, so that "what little coverage of Qatar is aired tends to paint a spotless image" to avoid damage to the image of Qatar as a progressive state. To name just a few examples, it treated the dispute between the ruler and his father with circumspection; it did not examine closely the ruler's 2001 decision to postpone the parliamentary elections for two years without giving a reason; nor does it look closely at Qatari foreign policy decisions. Occasionally it has touched on sensitive local topics, for example in 1997 it gave a Kuwaiti professor a platform to criticize Qatar for inviting Israel to the Doha economic summit.[19]

Other observers agree that al-Jazeera pulls its punches on Qatari sensitive subjects. One notes that such issues as the 1998 struggle between the current emir and his father, or serious critiques of Qatari foreign policy, are not carried by the station. One analyst says it generally avoids Qatari internal and foreign policy issues.[20]

Al-Jazeera officials insist, however, that there are no "red lines" and they claim to be politically even-handed, citing the talk shows that bring together Islamists and secularists, Qataris and Bahrainis, and others of differing points of view.[21] Al-Jazeera did in fact report the views of one Qatari dissident accusing the government of torture. It also reported extensively on the trial and verdict in 2001 of the men behind the 1996 coup plot. And al-Jazeera managers argue that it has on occasion even made accusations against foreign minister Shaikh Hamad bin Jasim by name, and that it did report a coup plotter had accused the police of torturing him.[22]

Even Qatari officials admit that al-Jazeera is careful in reporting on the Qatari ruling family and Qatar's "heritage," but they claim that the lack of coverage of Qatari affairs is due primarily to the fact that al-Jazeera is a regional channel and Qatar is a small country whose internal affairs are not covered by other regional broadcasters, like CNN.[23]

One analyst concludes, "Al-Jazeera's output indicates that it has been given considerable scope. Its staff prioritize stories according to their newsworthiness. . . . Along with LBC and the pay-TV provider Orbit, al-Jazeera has accelerated the trend towards live and compelling talk-show programming that has obliged the older channels to keep up with the competition."[24]

Al-Jazeera's Regional Impact

Arabs disagree about al-Jazeera's role and impact on the Arab world. One Arab scholar concludes that it "has raised the level of debate and opened the door for freer and more accurate news in the Arab world." And a detailed evaluation of al-Jazeera by two Arab-American scholars concluded that it has become a marketplace for dissent in the region. They say it has much anti-American content but it is also open to American views, and broadcasts U.S. official statements routinely. They compare it with the BBC, that has a similar autonomous relationship with its sponsoring government.[25]

Defenders of al-Jazeera argue that its presentations are balanced and helpful to the political process. The chief editor Ibrahim Hilal has denied that the station has a point of view, and he says the fact that it often carries expressions of anti-American sentiment are because that is the prevailing feeling in the Arab world and "that's not our problem."[26]

Others disagree. One scholar denies that al-Jazeera is promoting democracy, saying that a number of the talk show hosts and reporters make presentations that are biased. Another says al-Jazeera's reporters are fiercely opinionated and either pan-Arab leftist nationalists or Islamists, who present "an aggressive mix of anti-Americanism and anti-Zionism, and these hostilities drive the station's coverage," deliberately fanning the flames of Muslim outrage. He cites reports on Afghanistan presented from the Taliban point of view, and that it repeats graphic footage of Palestinian suffering as promotional material.[27] A prominent Arab journalist agrees, saying "al-Jazeera has a big problem with objectivity. . . . They are being led by the masses, they don't lead the masses. They know the taste of the Arab street and the Arab street is anti-American."[28]

The terminology used on al-Jazeera is often different from that used by Western broadcasters. For example, in reporting on the Arab-Israeli conflict, al-Jazeera will refer to Palestinian suicide bombers as "martyrs" and Israeli actions as "assassinations" while Western (and Israeli) media will use the terms "terrorists" and "targeted killings."[29] Such terms carry political implications and actually reflect basic differences in Arab and Western perceptions of Israel and the Palestinians rather than just a bias on the part of al-Jazeera.

The Washington bureau chief argues that the programming is balanced. He points out that after 9/11 he interviewed senior U.S. officials including Secretaries Powell and Rumsfeld and Condoleeza Rice and gave hundreds of hours of air time to U.S. government statements, but only a few minutes to bin Laden and the Taliban. He claims the news is uncensored. He says al-Jazeera like all media does have a cultural bias. When it shows Palestinians being killed by Israelis to an extent greater than in Western media, that it is because the Arab public wants to see it. He argues that the broadcasts reinforce Arab concern over Palestinian suffering, just as CNN in showing bodies of Americans in Somalia affected U.S. public opinion about that situation.[30]

Some Arab media columnists defend al-Jazeera even while their own governments complain about it. A respected Egyptian editor wrote that the network "threw a stone into the stagnant waters of the official and traditional media," and although some of its staff express anti-Egyptian views, the complaints are from Egyptians who are "overly sensitive and don't like criticism."[31]

In any case, most observers agree that al-Jazeera has had a major impact on the region. First, its open debates have influenced other broadcasters in the region to imitate it in some degree, and that Qatar's rivalry with Saudi Arabia has allowed it to comment on Saudi news to an unusual degree for an Arab station.[32] Secondly, al-Jazeera has "broken all the traditional taboos that prevented Arab media from tacking sensitive political, social, religious, and economic issues. . . . Critically the channel has redefined the role of television stations in the region. It has provided an open forum for those previously denied a voice in the Gulf."[33] Third, al-Jazeera has put the small state of Qatar on the political map of the Arab world, and given the country a significant political weight it otherwise could not have dreamed of.

Since the station was created by the government and financially depends on their continued subsidies, its future is uncertain.[34]

OTHER PRIVATELY OWNED CHANNELS

Middle East Broadcasting (MBC), was the pioneer in innovative programming. In September 1991, it gave Arab audiences their first experience with a new kind of Arab television. It began broadcasting from studios in London with Western-style programming and news coverage, with reports from the field and open talk shows, but its novelty was that it was in Arabic and was intended for Arab audiences. It set out to be the CNN of the Arab world. MBC made a name for itself during the first half of the 1990s because it became the leading provider of news and current affairs on Arab TV, and it captured a significant share of the Arab television audience as satellite viewing was growing. It dealt with a few subjects that had previously been taboo, but it also tended to avoid most of the traditionally sensitive issues, especially those of concern in Saudi Arabia and the Gulf. Its variety of nonpolitical content such as entertainment, sports, and films added to the attraction.[35]

MBC maintained correspondents in every Arab country except the Sudan and Libya, and it was the first to open a Jerusalem bureau. It also maintained offices in several European countries, as well as in the United States, Russia, and India. It was reportedly the first to cover the January 1992 attempted coup in Algeria, and its seven-part documentary on Desert Storm in March 1997 included presentations of Iraqi, Israeli, and Western views that were at variance with accepted official Arab versions prevalent in the Gulf, to the annoyance of the Kuwaitis.[36] Generally, MBC is regarded as having very good news coverage although it is somewhat cautious in its political commentaries.

MBC was the first Arab TV channel to give Arab audiences a systematic review of the non-Arab press when it presented the program *Press World* (alam al-sahafa) starting in 1992. Al-Jazeera then imitated this program. MBC was the first Arab TV channel to interview Israeli journalists live, starting in May of 1997, and then al-Jazeera followed.

After a few years, as other Arab satellite channels emerged with comparable news and public affairs programs, MBC decided to shift its focus to more entertainment—it carried the very popular Arabic version of *Who Wants to Be a Millionaire*—and became broad-based in order to attract the widest possible audience for the sake of the commercial advertisers. This increased its advertising revenues substantially.[37] By 1998 MBC claimed to be the most popular satellite channel among Arab viewers, with an estimated audience of two million for highly rated programs. Because of its popularity it was the most successful channel in attracting advertising revenues.[38]

Orbit, like MBC, began with the intention of becoming an all-news and documentary service, and it tried to do so in a joint venture with the BBC. However when the BBC deal collapsed, Orbit made new arrangements with Rupert Murdoch's Star TV and others, and it developed into a channel that is mainly entertainment. It is known for presenting Arab drama, music, and cultural programs, light entertainment and soap operas. Viewers however regard the programs as the most Western in style of any Arab satellite channel. It offers Hollywood films and entertainment and other programs from American television including from NBC, CNBC, CNN, and the History Channel. In October of 1996, Orbit broke a taboo by allowing Israeli

Prime Minister Netanyahu to appear for a full hour on a live call-in show. In March of 1997 it did so again when it broadcast a special on the Gulf war that included interviews with Iraqi and Israeli officials.[39]

The content of the Arab Radio and Television (ART) network, on the other hand, is and was from the beginning mostly entertainment, with several movie channels, children's programs, sports, and music. The owner describes his purpose as providing entertainment intended to compete with the Western content being carried on other channels, but suitable for Arab cultural requirements. However, it does have some political discussions programs and a few have broken taboos. Also, in 2000, ART launched the first Arab Islamic channel, Iqra, to appeal to Muslim audiences.[40]

Lebanese Broadcasting Company International (LBCI) was from the start mainly light entertainment, including music, Western and Arab films, and variety shows, and it has sought to appeal to Arab youth. At the same time it has carried some news and political commentary programs, offering relays of CNN International and ABC news, and presenting some talk shows on current political and social issues. Then in 2002 its management decided to do much more news by making a deal with *al-Hayat* newspaper in London to produce a news program jointly from a London studio. This expansion of the news content was intended to take advantage of audience interest, and to compete directly with MBC and Abu Dhabi Television which successfully combined solid news with entertainment. LBCI's reputation however has been as a light entertainment channel which employs attractive young women as presenters to appeal to a popular audience, even for example on the political program *The Night Is Yours* (Layla Laylatak). The political program *People's Talk* (Kalaam al Naas) focuses on Lebanon, while the program *Dialogue of Life* (Hiwar al-'Umr) features interviews with Arab personalities, and in 2000 for example gave a platform to Iraqi Deputy Prime Minister Tariq Aziz. Although it is Lebanese in style, it has succeeded well in attracting advertising from the Gulf, indicating a significant portion of its audience is in that region. In fact, since LBCI depends on advertisements from the Gulf, it regards the Gulf as its primary audience and is careful not to challenge Gulf sensibilities.[41]

Moreover, because LBC and LBCI are owned by Lebanese Maronite political personalities Sulaiman Franjieh and Isam Faris, its political programs tend to focus on issues of concern to Maronite Christians. In particular, it is regarded as being sensitive to Syrian concerns because of their close ties to the Syrian government. Generally the channel is regarded as professionally done. LBCI does present some political discussions on sensitive subjects, although not as much as al-Jazeera does.[42]

However, one close observer says that although LBC from the beginning was a "mouthpiece of Maronite paramilitary forces," it "has been run as primarily a commercial corporation, and only secondarily as an instrument of propaganda."[43] Another says LBC is the most popular Arab channel because it features light entertainment, attractive women, and colloquial speech.[44]

The Arab News Network (ANN), devotes a fairly large proportion of its time presenting news and social and political analysis. It too features talk shows such as "Lights in the Darkness" (Qanadil fi al-Zalam) and "Confrontation" (Muwajahat). The owner, Sawmar al-Assad, claims his purpose is to support democracy and free speech. The content is not particularly Syrian and relations with the Syrian government have fluctuated. And although he is the nephew of the former president of Syria and the first cousin of the current president Bashar, it is clear from the program content that ANN does not always respect Syrian official sensibilities.

For its first three years (1997–2000), ANN provided impartial coverage of Syria and other countries. However, when Syrian president Hafiz al-Assad died in 2000, his exiled brother Rifaat, the father of ANN's chairman, broadcast a statement denouncing the way Bashar was chosen president. This provoked the Syrian government to issue a warrant for Rifaat's arrest. ANN also gave a platform to such controversial personalities as Saddam Hussein, and made other presentations that probably made Damascus uncomfortable. It has virtually no advertisements and because it is free-to-air, it must be subsidized; there is speculation that it also has ties to Saudi Crown Prince Abdullah who is related by marriage to Rifaat.[45] Also, there is speculation that Sawmar and his father, the former Syrian Vice President Rifaat al-Assad, see ANN as an instrument for their own political purposes.

The Lebanese-based satellite television stations Future, LBCI, and al-Manar, on the other hand, represent special interests, but also seek to appeal to region-wide audiences. The first two have the broadest appeal among Lebanese satellite channels because of their effective use of entertainment.

Future Television, owned by Lebanese politician and businessman Rafiq Hariri, a Sunni Muslim, broadcasts 24 hours a day and carries a great deal of entertainment but it also carries news and public affairs programs including interviews and commentaries. It claims to provide family programming that is a combination of Oriental and Western, with "an optimistic view of the future."[46] The content of its political programs reveals that it enjoys a certain degree of freedom, but also it gave prominence to the owner. One analyst says the channel is a "cheerleader for Hariri," and points out that the priority news item is usually about Rafiq Hariri and his sister Bahia, who is a member of parliament. Future also careful not to offend Gulf sensibilities, partly because it derives considerable advertising from that region.[47]

Al-Manar (Landmark) Television, is clearly a political instrument of its owner, the Hizbollah or Party of God. Hizbollah is a militant political movement dedicated to confronting Israel, and it is also a social welfare organization and a legal political party in Lebanon with seats in parliament. It uses al Manar for political purposes and viewers can easily recognize its political coloration. Female presenters dress very modestly, and male presenters usually wear beards. Newscasts give highest priority to the intifada against Israel, and its reporters—unlike their counterparts at several other Arab satellite stations—refuse to interview Israelis. It is the only Arab TV channel broadcasting in Hebrew, that it started in 1996. It carries ads but none about alcohol or featuring women. It takes credit for helping to force Israel to withdraw from South Lebanon. Al-Manar's director, Naif Kurayyim, has said, "the aim of our message is to encourage the Jews' reverse immigration. . . . they can be sent back to other areas of the world with counter-propaganda." Al-Manar tends to broadcast graphic footage of wounded and dying Palestinians on the West Bank and Gaza, and interviews suffering Palestinians, to make negative points about Israel.[48]

Finally, it is particularly significant that most Arab satellite stations have correspondents in Palestine, equipped with mobile phones, who provide live eyewitness accounts of the Intifada and Israeli actions in the West Bank and Gaza. As one observer said, satellite TV has brought the war into the living room of most Arab families outside of Palestine and has been the most important factor in generating Arab popular anger and protest against Israel and the United States. Al-Jazeera's live hour-long phone-in show "Under Siege" carries a great deal of that popular anger, some of it directed at Arab governments for failing to help the Palestinians. And Hizbollah's al-Manar regularly announces public protests and calls on the people to join them.[49]

During the second Intifada, Arab TV channel reporters from al-Jazeera, Abu Dhabi TV, and Nile News were in Jerusalem, the West Bank, and Gaza alongside reporters from CNN, BBC, AP, Reuters, and other news agencies. Abu Dhabi television before the Intifada had had correspondents covering Palestinian events from Jerusalem, Ramallah, and Gaza, and when it began more reporters were sent to cover it. Abu Dhabi Television's Jerusalem executive producer Jasim al-Azzawy was expelled from Jerusalem by Israeli authorities in April 2002 after he had been reporting on events in the West Bank during which he had interviewed several Palestinians, and showed film of Israelis killing Palestinian police. Israel said the expulsion was because of his biased coverage, but he said it was because of Israel's unhappiness with the channel's earlier satirical broadcast entitled "Irhabiyaat" (terrorisms), shown during Ramadan that portrayed Prime Minister Sharon as a bloodthirsty terrorist, and which Israel protested. After the expulsion, Abu Dhabi broadcast an April 3, 2002 BBC program in which Azzawy and an Israeli spokesman Daniel Seaman appeared together to discuss the incident.[50]

CONTENT OF GOVERNMENT SATELLITE TV

The program content of the government-owned satellite television channels tends to be fairly similar to that of the older government-owned terrestrial stations, meaning that they carry a great deal of nonpolitical programming and the political material generally is respectful of sensibilities of the country of origin and its government.

However, the regional competition for viewers has encouraged even these stations to expand both news and political commentary programming because the audiences they aim for are regional rather than local. The program content of existing terrestrial TV stations has in fact been influenced by the development of Arab satellite television, because the former have been forced for the first time to compete for audiences. Because the satellite channels tend to challenge taboos much more, this has, to some extent, loosened up the older stations and they have tried some of the new news and public affairs programming approaches. As one Egyptian TV talk show host says, pressure from the satellite stations has made "more space for freedom" in his and other telecasts by regular Egyptian TV.[51]

Abu Dhabi Television is an example of that trend. It expanded its news coverage significantly and developed a network of correspondents throughout the Arab world and beyond, and started a series of political commentary programs that deal with subjects in a sophisticated manner. Abu Dhabi TV is semi-autonomous from the government and although it is more restrained than the free-wheeling al-Jazeera, it has gained considerable respect from viewers and media professionals around the region. In fact, competition from al-Jazeera has helped push Abu Dhabi television to expand its news coverage and offer political commentary programs that present contrasting views.[52]

For example, Abu Dhabi TV produced a political discussion program "Confrontation" (muwajiha) that observers regard as a copy of al-Jazeera's "Opposite Direction." Its programs also deal with sensitive issues such as Bahraini political prisoners and the suffering of Iraqi children, but unlike some of al-Jazeera's shouting matches, they are done in a more restrained manner. In the 1990s, Abu Dhabi TV relied almost exclusively on Western news agencies for news, but during the following years it made a deliberate effort to produce its own news reports, and present the news and events through Arab eyes, because management felt Western agencies were giving the reports an "Anglo-centric or American slant." The station hired more than 220 new employees and dispatched its own correspondents abroad and that changed.[53]

Egypt's government-owned television has also changed. By the turn of the century, Egyptian channels had joined the regional competition with new political programs like *Editor in Chief* (ra'is tahrir), *The Red Line* (al-khatt al-ahmar), *In Depth* (fil umq), *The Third Opinion* (al-ra'y al-thaalith),

Roundtable (da'irat al-hiwar), *Behind the Scenes* (wara al-ahdath) and
Without Censorship (Bidoon riqaba), among others. These programs have
raised topics that were previously taboo on Egyptian TV, such as female
genital mutilation, gender discrimination, religious discrimination, unemployment, and dual citizenship. Hamdi Qandil, the host of *Editor in Chief,*
has said that the new liberalization resulting from competition is healthy.
The presenter Farida al-Zummor of *A Word of Truth* (kilmit haqq) denies
that there is any censorship over what she presents, but observers point out
that few of the Egyptian shows are live, giving the authorities an opportunity to control them better. Moreover, self-censorship still exists as journalists follow unwritten rules.[54]

Egyptian TV does not present a wide variety of views, however. For
example, the picture it tends to present of Israel only involves the political
leadership and its military actions, ignoring opposition voices. Egyptian
radio and television almost never criticize government policies or reports
on human rights abuses, and political parties do not have access to them
even during elections campaigns. On the other hand, when Egyptian government television and a private channel carried a serialized Ramadan
drama in November 2002 that referred to the "Protocol of the Elders of
Zion," that Jewish groups and the U.S. government protested as anti-
semitic, the Egyptian information Minister and some newspapers defended
the program on the grounds of freedom of expression.[55]

Officials of the Egyptian government satellite channel admit that "There
are a lot of taboos because it represents the government's policies and politics." They say its policy is to be the "media ambassador of Egypt," and
that it will not be privatized because "you can't allow a council of businessmen, regardless of their prominence, to represent Egypt" because the
satellite channel "must reflect Egypt's national strategy." They concede
that it respects taboos regarding content, especially related to "sex and
violence, and a conservative dress code."[56] Many Egyptian viewers who
have access to satellite television, prefer non-Egyptian broadcasts over
Egyptian ones, even after Egypt started its own satellite channel, because
they regard its programs as "lackluster."[57]

There are a few other signs of liberalization. Tunisia's ERTT terrestrial
TV began broadcasting a live public debate program "Face to Face" in
1998 featuring ordinary citizens to debate public issues with government
officials.[58] Generally speaking, however, government-controlled terrestrial
channels remained under government pressure to conform to official policy. For example, in Algeria, on the eve of the April 15, 1999, presidential
elections, when five of the six candidates withdrew, leaving Abdulaziz
Bouteflika uncontested, radio and TV failed to report that.[59]

Saudi television follows even more conservative guidelines on content,
which say: "The female figure is to be restricted to ads relating to home
and child affairs. Modesty in voice, appearance, and movement is to be

observed," and "The main principles governing the concept of commercial advertising on Saudi TV consist of the true observation of the Islamic faith." Advertisements never show drinking or eating using the left hand. Saudi TV programs are not allowed to mention Hizbollah because it is so closely associated with Iran and Shiites, but the Lebanese resistance (muqawama) can be mentioned. Saudi taboos also include showing people drinking alcohol or even holding wine glasses, women in revealing clothing such as miniskirts or bathing suits, and stories in which animals are the dominant subject. Saudi TV does not show graveyards.[60]

In Algeria, the government controls all broadcasting, and as of 1996, opposition political party officials had some access to broadcasting but only in a small fraction of total air time. Algerian audiences tend to prefer foreign broadcasts by satellite over the local broadcasts because the content is heavily dominated by uninteresting government reports, including half an hour of TV news devoted to the activities of the president.[61]

Even Lebanese television, that taken as a whole is the most open and diverse system, has a few taboos. Themes that advocate cooperation among different sectarian groups in order to unify society are almost completely absent. One authority says, "Lebanon has extreme pluralism and deep divisions, fragmented along sectarian," but ". . . no serious program, to date, has been produced to deal with the sectarian conflict that plagues the country."[62]

Terrestrial television in Qatar, (as distinct from Qatar's satellite al-Jazeera) is still rather conservative. It has however also broken taboos, for example in January 1996, it broadcast an interview with Mansour al-Jamri and Shaikh Ali Salman, two exiled Bahraini opposition people who called for democratic reforms in Bahrain. This was an unusual event because previously Arab Gulf states refrained from giving a media platform to opposition voices from other Arab gulf states.[63]

In Syria, television remained constrained and very respectful of the Syrian leadership even after Bashar became president, although it made a few gestures toward liberalization, for example, the social satire *Mirror Stories* (hakaya al-maraya) broadcast in December 2001, that dealt with the normally taboo subjects of corruption and the security police.[64]

In Iraq, until 2003 the government used its satellite channel as an aggressive instrument of policy. For example in January 2002, in order to silence an Iraqi dissident living in London who had appeared on al-Jazeera and criticized Baghdad, Iraqi TV showed footage of his relatives and warned him that his sister would pay for his "mistake."[65] After Saddam Hussein's regime collapsed in 2003, the Iraqi government monopoly over broadcasting ended. The U.S.-British occupation authority, the Coalition Provisional Authority that assumed power in Iraq started its own radio and television services, but on a temporary basis; the CPA also set rules for Iraqi broadcasters but the prohibitions were limited, and confined essentially to banning incitement.

Finally, the two television stations owned by the Palestinian Authority, one of which is a satellite channel, give priority attention to portraying the suffering of the Palestinian people under Israeli rule, by showing graphic footage of Israelis killing Palestinians, and destroying their homes, and even the subtexts under talk shows report the latest such acts of violence.[66]

CONCLUSION

During the 1990s, therefore, program content of Arab television including satellite and terrestrial, private and government, has changed. The impetus for the change was the advent of privately controlled channels based in Europe, followed by Qatar-based al-Jazeera, that were less inhibited than the older government-controlled terrestrial channels. But many of the governments were persuaded to start satellite broadcasts and also to modify the programs on their terrestrial channels, in the face of competition that was crossing borders and coming into their countries that they could not prevent.

Satellite broadcasting bypasses the two key barriers, illiteracy and government control. In the ten year span of 1991–2001, journalism changed with the advent on TV for the first time of free-ranging public affairs interview and call-in shows. Because satellite television ignores national borders, censorship is declining in the Arab world. He also says Arab public opinion is now more important and Arab governments must give it more attention.[67]

Satellite channels can be more relaxed about restrictions and advertisers are pleased with that because commercials undergo less editing and are therefore cheaper. Nevertheless all Arab satellite channels have needed supplemental revenue to continue. Talk shows and game shows, that most of the private satellite channels thrive on, are less expensive to produce, so they save the stations money. Moreover, they have been welcomed by audiences, especially in countries where people have less chance to express their opinions.

Internet use in the Arab world is constrained by low literacy, moral and political censorship, lack of English, and cost of personal computers. But satellite TV is spreading rapidly, with the benefit of financial subventions of various kinds.

The impact on terrestrial television has been varied. At one extreme, until 2003 Iraqi TV was not affected because of the government's tight control over domestic and incoming programs, so competition is shut out. With the fall of Saddam Hussein competition was permitted and programs differed in content. Other government channels such as the Saudi one have been slow to change but even they have adopted some of the techniques of lively political discussion programming, although within limits. At the other extreme, Abu Dhabi television has changed substantially, in part because of competition with private satellite broadcasters.

The popularity of the satellite channels has been due to the fact that they are freer to present news, ideas, and opinions, and less controlled than the existing government-owned terrestrial broadcasters had been, and that they more closely reflect Arab public opinion.

One informed Arab analyst concludes that Arab satellite TV for the first time has allowed Arabs to see each other through Arab eyes, rather than foreign eyes or their own government's filters, because Arab reporters and commentators were speaking to a region-wide audience. He adds, however, that shouting matches on TV may be only superficial noise and sensationalism and do not guarantee real freedom, accurate information and, critical insights, and those cannot easily be channeled into political action because an accountability process does not exist.[68]

One study concludes that in the past the media were part of the state apparatus but "amazing developments" in Arab media have made it impossible to find a (simple) correlation between the views of the state or ruling party and their media except in a few cases such as Iraq, Syria, Libya, and al-Manar. This is due to competitiveness, the effort to be credible, and democratic pretense. He says al-Jazeera and Abu Dhabi "have stood out with respect to their extensive news coverage and the issues raised in their talk shows on everything relating to the Palestinian cause as a whole. Many of the other satellite channels however are not lagging far behind in this respect. . . . Most of the Arab satellite stations, perhaps with the exception of the Egyptian, Jordanian, Kuwaiti, and Saudi channels, seemed to voice the stand of their peoples."

Some Arab media professionals have been critical of developments. One argues that Arab satellite TV has "combined the worst aspects of American and British television with the worst aspects of Arab political culture; that is, we have adopted the Western style of confrontational, argumentative television entertainment with the Arab tradition of absolutist, heated ideological debate. . . . These are hugely entertaining shouting matches, but they do not have any significant impact on Arab political culture or decision-making by the Arab elites. This is because the media activities in our region are still totally divorced from the political processes. The concept of investigative reporting is totally absent from the Arab mass media . . . the role of the pan-Arab media is to entertain, rather than to promote political accountability."[69]

Another Arab journalist concedes that al-Jazeera is unique in style and content but says it is watched mainly for news and viewers get bored with it and do not view it for long periods of time as they do others, so LBC and Future have the biggest impact because they carry lots of entertainment. MBC and LBC are doing well with advertisers. Even al-Jazeera has taboos: it does not criticize Qatar too much despite the fact that Qatar has problems that should be reported. Also al-Jazeera has trouble getting ads because it is not watched on a sustained basis and because the Saudis have considerable control over advertisers.[70]

In short, the advent of Arab satellite television has clearly caused changes in Arab media in a number of ways and affected Arab politics. Opinions differ about the benefits and drawbacks but the impact has been profound.

NOTES

1. Mohammed El-Nawawy and Adel Iskandar, *Al-Jazeera,* Cambridge, MA: Westview, 2002, pp. 3, 29, 85.

2. Interview with Shaikh Hamad bin Thamar al Thani, TBS no. 7, fall/winter 2001.

3. Nawawy and Iskandar pp. 92–103, 129.

4. Edmund Ghareeb "New Media and the Information revolution in the Arab World: an Assessment," *Middle East Journal,* vol. 54, no. 3, summer 2000, pp. 405ff.

5. Chart adapted from Najib Ghadbian, in *Middle East Review of International Affairs,* vol. 5, no. 2, June 2001, with additional notes from Nawawy and Iskandar op. cit., pp. 100–108.

6. Nawawy and Iskandar, p. 33.

7. Hafiz Mirazi, speech at the Middle East Institute annual conference, Washington D.C., October 19, 2001, and C-Span interview October 14, 2001.

8. *Al-Sharq al-Awsat,* October 14, 2001.

9. Nawawy and Iskandar, p. 56.

10. Ghareeb, op. cit., p. 408.

11. Nawawy and Iskandar, pp. 118–19, 125–26.

12. AFP Report May 10, 2002; *Middle East Week in Review,* vol. 2, issue 7, May 31, 2002.

13. Nawawy and Iskandar, p. 122–25, and by the Associated Press, August 8, 2002 and August 10, 2002, and by Julia Wheeler, BBC News, August 30, 2002.

14. Nawawy and Iskandar, op. cit., pp. 108, 121, 122.

15. TBS issue no. 5, fall/winter 2000, and *Middle East International,* November 10, 2000; Simon Henderson, "The Al Jazeera Effect," Washington Institute on Middle East Policy, Study no. 507, December 8, 2000; Nawawy and Iskandar pp. 116, 118.

16. Interview with Mohammed Jasim al-Ali, in TBS issue no. 7, fall/winter 2001.

17. Nawawy and Iskandar pp. 40, 153–56, 176.

18. Alterman, p. 23; Nawawy and Iskandar, p. 84.

19. Nawawy and Iskandar, pp. 83–88, 140–41; and interview, Ahmad al-Malik, Qatari journalist, Abu Dhabi, January 19, 2003.

20. Alterman, *New Media,* pp. 23–24.

21. Interview with the Deputy Director of al-Jazeera, Doha, May 2001.

22. Ghareeb op. cit., p. 409; Alterman, *New Media,* op. cit., p. 22.

23. Interview, Khalid al-Mansuri, Qatari Foreign Ministry, Doha, May 2001.

24. Naomi Sakr, *Middle East Report,* Spring 1999, p. 6.

25. Nawawy and Iskandar, op. cit., pp. 4, 104, 107, 156; Ghareeb, op. cit., p. 406.

26. Sharon Waxman, *Washington Post,* December 4, 2001, p. C-1.

27. Fuad Ajami, *New York Times Magazine,* November 18, 2001, p. 50.

28. Sharon Waxman, *Washington Post,* December 4, 2001, p. C-1.

29. Nawawy and Iskandar, p. 53.

30. Hafiz Mirazi, talk at the Middle East Institute annual conference, Washington D.C., October 19, 2001; C-Span interview with Hafiz Mirazi, October 14, 2001.

31. Salama Ahmad Salama, al-Ahram, October 2000.

32. Alterman, *New Media,* pp. 23–24.

33. World Press Freedom Review, 1999, Qatar Section.

34. Interview, Hisham Milhem, Washington D.C., May 2001.

35. Ghareeb, op. cit., p. 402; Muhammed I. Ayish, in TBS issue no. 6, Spring/summer 2001; and interviews with Steve Clark and Hany El Konyayyesi, in TBS issue no. 7, fall/winter 2001.

36. Alterman, *New Media,* op. cit., pp. 19–20.

37. Interviews with Ian Ritchie Steve Clark, TBS issue no. 7, fall/winter 2001.

38. Alterman, *New Media,* p. 21.

39. Ghareeb op. cit., p. 403 and Alterman, *New Media,* pp. 27–28; Jon B. Alterman, "New Egyptian Satellite," Washington Institute, Policywatch no. 313, May 5, 1998.

40. Alterman, *New Media,* op. cit., p. 21, and Ghareeb, op. cit., pp. 402–3; Hussein Y. Amin, in TBS issue no. 5, fall/winter 2000.

41. Alterman, *New Media,* pp. 24–25, and Ghareeb, pp. 403–4; Mennawi interview, Cairo, February 9, 2001.

42. Interview with Mona Ziade, *Daily Star,* June 16, 2001; Hisham Milhem interview May 2001.

43. Marwan M. Kraidy, in TBS no. 5, fall/winter 2000.

44. Interview with Ibrahim al-Abid, UAE Information Ministry, June 6, 2000.

45. Alterman, *New Media,* pp. 25–26 and Ghareeb, pp. 410–11; Mennawi interview, Febuary 9, 2001; and Public Affairs Office, U.S. Embassy London, "Profile, Arabic Media London," Summer 2002.

46. Future TV Web site www.futuretvnetwork.com, January 8, 2002.

47. Magda Abu Fadil interview, Lebanese American University, Beirut, June 15, 2001.

48. Magda Abu-Fadl, in *IPI Global Journalist,* 4th Quarter 2000, p. 12; *Middle East International,* July 27, 2001 pp. 9–10; interviews with Arab journalists, Washington D.C. May 2001 and Cairo February 2001.

49. Sana Kamal, *Middle East International,* April 19, 2002, p. 18.

50. Interviews with Jasim al-Azzawy, and Mohamed Dourrachid, of Abu Dhabi TV, TBS issue no. 8 (spring 2002); also *Gulf News,* November 11, 2001.

51. Abdallatif Mennawi interview, February 9, 2001.

52. Interview with Ibrahim al-Abid, Senior Advisor to the UAE Minister of Information, June 6, 2000.

53. Interview with Mohamed Dourrachid, Deputy Director, Abu Dhabi TV, TBS issue no. 8 (spring 2002).

54. Amina Elbendary, *Al-Ahram International Weekly,* June 14–20, 2001, p. 10; *Middle East International,* December 7, 2001.

55. *Gulf News,* November 2, 2002 and November 4, 2002.

56. Interview with Sana'a Mansour, head, Egyptian Satellite Sector, in TBS issue no. 5, fall/winter 2000.

57. Edmund Ghareeb lecture at Georgetown, April 25, 2000; Steve Nugus, "Media Mismanagement," Middle East International, May 8, 1998, p. 9.

58. Abdullah Hidri, "Tunisia" chapter in Kamalipour and Mowlana, Eds., *Mass Media in the Middle East,* Westport CT: Greenwood Press, 1994, pp. 278–79.

59. 1999 World Press Freedom Review, Algeria section.

60. Interview with Hany El Konayyesi, APTN senior editor, in TBS no. 7, fall/winter 2001.

61. U.S. Department of State, *Country Reports on Human Rights Practices, 1996 and 1999,* January 30, 1997 and Febuary 25, 2000, Algeria section; Laid Zaghlami, "Algeria" chapter in Kamalipour and Mowlana, op. cit., pp. 17–19.

62. Nabil H. Dajani, in TBS issue no. 7, fall/winter 2001.

63. "Rift Widening Between Qatar and Gulf Neighbors," *Compass Newswire,* Compass Media Inc., January 15, 1996.

64. *Middle East International,* January 11, 2002.

65. Coalition for Justice in Iraq, bulletin, January 30, 2002 and February 6, 2002.

66. *New York Times,* October 24, 2000.

67. Jon B. Alterman, "New Egyptian Satellite," Washington Institute, Policywatch no. 313, May 5, 1998.

68. Hisham Milhem interview May 2001.

69. Rami G. Khouri, "Arab Satellite TV: News Without Impact," *Jerusalem Post,* May 13, 2001.

70. Interview with Wafa'i Dab, deputy chief editor, *al-Anba* Newspaper, Kuwait, May 5, 2002.

12

Conclusions

This book has examined the mass media in the Arab world, as these media relate to the societies in which they function, and especially to the political process. In the previous chapters I have described in some detail: the structure of the daily newspaper as an institution, and the structure and content of Arab radio and television. I have presented a typology of typical Arab press forms, and asked what conditions have led to the emergence of each subtype, and what conditions are likely to cause perpetuation of the status quo or, alternatively, lead to transformations in the system.

My underlying thesis has been that newspapers, radio, and television respond in many ways to their environment, both in content and in functioning of institutional structure. The Arab news media can only be understood in terms of the economic conditions, cultural milieu, and political realities of the societies they serve. As for content, the readers of an Arab newspaper or listeners to an Arab radio broadcast would agree that most of the media usually carry unmistakable local identification of some kind, reflecting local conditions. The items that presumably have the most political impact, such as commentaries on current events, seem to reflect local conditions most clearly, but often newspaper headlines and even fictional pieces do too.

To be sure, the news media carry out their functions to a large extent the way news media do anywhere in the world. They convey local and international news, information, opinion, entertainment, and advertising to a mass audience. Much of this material originates from the same common sources, and is processed by the same news agencies and other international services as the material used outside of the Arab world. Arab media report on important events at the same time as American media, and to some extent in similar fashion. Advertising and entertainment material also has some international interchangeability. But Arab news media content usually carries the stamp of the originating institution in one way or another, which alert audiences can detect. The message provides them with clues about the origin and control of the medium.

This book, however, does not present a comprehensive qualitative survey of media content. The above observations about content are made on the basis of opinions of experienced consumers of these media and not on the basis of an objective and systematic content analysis of press, radio, and television in all eighteen countries. Such a study has not yet been done, and would be an enormous undertaking. This book, instead, has analyzed the news media as institutions, to see what forms they have taken in the independent Arab states, how the self-governing Arab societies have chosen to control them, and how they relate to the political processes in the Arab world.

Arab media have characteristics that can be found elsewhere in non-Arab developing countries. The electronic media, especially radio, have become true instruments of mass communication, reaching the bulk of the population across barriers of literacy, geography, and economy, while print media still generally reach only elite groups. The commercial side of the media is still relatively weak, and neither the wide circulation newspaper dependent on advertising revenues nor fully commercialized television and radio, U.S.-style, have appeared. But the political side is relatively strong, and the role of government quite prominent.

GOVERNMENT-MEDIA RELATIONS

You have seen that Arab government-media relations are quite complex. The Arab medias do play a role in the political process and are affected by it, but it is clear that the role cannot be described accurately by using one of the theories that have been used to describe other media systems. The one which comes closest to fitting is the authoritarian theory, by which the medias are controlled by the elite who believe they understand truth better than the masses do, and who assume they should use the press, radio, and television to convey information and interpretation downward. That theory has many adherents in the Arab world, where one sees in many places its most common practical consequence the strong influence of government on the media.

There are, however, also manifestations of the libertarian and social responsibility theories, by which the media are supposed to present a variety of viewpoints, a clash of opinions, and some criticism of government.

The extent to which this occurs varies from country to country and over time, and the advent of satellite television has focused new attention on this approach. In any case, the actual performance of the media on the Arab political stage cannot be judged on the basis of the prevailing law or formal structure alone. More important are such factors as the existence of real and open opposition to the government, the legitimacy and actual strength of the ruling group, the stability of the political system, the existence of perceived external threats, the economic base of the media, the regional and international political systems, and the vigor of an independent journalistic tradition in the country. As these vary, so does the behavior of journalists, regardless of the media laws which invariably, in one way or another, proclaim freedom of the press, speech, and information.

Crucial to understanding the dynamics of Arab media structures is a comparison of the four distinct subtypes of organization for the daily press which have emerged in the Arab world. Radio and most television organization is much more uniform throughout the area primarily because their broad reach and their potential for instant mass political impact have persuaded Arab regimes to insist that they be under direct governmental control, particularly since for technical and economic reasons there are usually only one or two broadcasting stations serving the entire country, although satellite television has added an entirely new dimension. Newspapers, which theoretically could be published by many different people but which reach smaller audiences, have been organized in one of four basic systems in the independent Arab countries. A given system emerges at different times and places, depending on certain conditions.

PRESS SUBTYPES AND POLITICAL OPPOSITION

First, a system we have called the mobilization press has emerged in countries where the ruling group is aggressively dedicated to revolutionary change, and it has managed to eliminate all real organized public opposition domestically, but requires active support from the media to help achieve its stated goals and combat its declared enemies. All the newspapers of any political consequence are owned by agents of the ruling group, and control over newspaper content is assured primarily through personnel control, but also on occasions by censorship, legal sanctions, rewards, and indirect means made possible by the existence of a political environment in which the regime is unopposed. There is no public discussion of press freedom.

Secondly, the loyalist press exists in countries where a more traditional political system prevails; all are monarchies except for Palestine, which has been dominated overwhelmingly by one man. No significant organized public opposition exists, but the government, more satisfied with the status quo than intent on change, is content with passive acquiescence from the public and does not require the press to generate public action. The press is generally loyal to the regime and its fundamental policies but newspapers often avoid the most controversial issues rather than engaging them with the zeal of a mobilization type newspaper. There is some criticism of government agencies but not of the top leadership. The loyalist press is privately owned. The government uses several means to obtain its support, including financial inducements and legal sanctions but the primary reason for press loyalty is the consensus that prevails in public debate on important issues: the regime's basic policies are not criticized in public, so the press does not dissent either.

The third system, the diverse press, functions in a political environment where the public expression of a variety of opinions and viewpoints, including criticism of the government, is possible, and where the regime does not intervene to suppress all open dissent. The press is in private hands or owned by political parties which are legal and active. The government may occasionally take action against a newspaper but these interventions are used sparingly and done through the courts, because the government prefers to exercise restraint in dealing with the press.

Finally, the transitional press is a mixed system in which the largest circulation print media are controlled directly by the government but smaller ones are owned by private individuals or parties, and they have some latitude to criticize those in power. The government does try periodically to restrict them but it uses the existing law and the courts to do so, and there is some self-censorship. The question of press freedom is discussed regularly in public and changes in the system are proposed, indicating possible future modification, although the exact direction of change is not clear.

Table 12.1 puts these four systems together into an overall typology and shows the countries in which they are found as of the 1980s. Within these groupings there are some differences. Among mobilization systems, Iraq has had the most mobilized press until 2003, while Syria has had the least, and the Sudan after the 1985 coup seemed to be moving away from this system, but the final outcome depends on how the political system stabilizes.

Diversity among newspapers is a key indicator in determining the nature of the relationship between the government and the press. In all of the Arab countries, at least some of the press reports and supports government policy. But the newspaper reader is better informed about any given subject, and has more of a chance to discern the true facts and make up his own mind without relying on what the government tells him, if there is genuine diversity in the newspapers available to him. Different newspapers will print different versions and interpretations of the story, and taken together, they provide more to choose from. Thus considered as a whole, a diverse press system is likely to be freer than the others even though individual papers may be biased, because the reader has greater access to a spectrum of information and opinions. The essential factor behind a

TABLE 12.1   Typology of Arab Print Media Systems

	Mobilization	Loyalist	Diverse	Transitional
Press characteristics				
Ownership	regime agents	private	private	mixed
Variety	nondiverse	nondiverse	diverse	diverse
View of regime	strong support	support	pro and con	pro and con
Style and tone	active	contentious	passive	diverse
Political conditions				
Ruling group	revolutionary	traditional	various	various
Public debate	none	none	active	active
Public opposition	nonexistent	nonexistent	established	limited
Countries where system prevails (2003)				
	Syria	Bahrain	Lebanon	Algeria
	Libya	Oman	Morocco	Egypt
	The Sudan	Palestine	Kuwait	Jordan
		Qatar	Yemen	Tunisia
		Saudi Arabia	Iraq	
		UAE		

diverse press is the existence of genuine opposition to the ruling group that is able to function openly. If no real public opposition to the regime is permitted in the political system, then it follows that the press speaks with one uniform voice and the individual newspaper reader is less able to make up his own mind about important issues of the day. The existence of public opposition is, in turn, usually related to the existence of representative political parties. The parties must be representative of truly different policies including some not espoused by the regime.

For example, Lebanon has a political system in which several political parties function, and Iraq under Saddam Hussein did also, but the Lebanese parties represent truly contrasting policies and points of view, while the Iraqi parties did not disagree in public on any issues of major consequence; Lebanese press diversity and Saddam's Iraqi press uniformity are to a great extent dependent on this important distinction. It is, on the other hand, also possible to have a diverse press backed by genuine opposition groups rather than parties, as is the case in Kuwait for example, where formal parties do not exist. But the essential requirement is that the opposition must differ substantially and publicly with the policies of the regime. The differences do not have to include every issue of consequence but they must be sufficiently comprehensive so as to provide a distinction between the regime and the out-group on matters of national importance. The more comprehensive the list of differences, the more diverse the press is likely to be. A second important factor in government-press relations is whether the press has developed the status of an independent institution (the so-called Fourth Estate) and the profession of journalism has become a prestigious one.

The Arab print media systems cannot be divided into neat categories, however. The fourfold division, for purposes of analysis, into mobilization, loyalist, diverse, and transitional systems is a rough one. In fact, a kind of spectrum exists from the highly mobilized newspapers in Iraq to the rather diverse and independent press in Lebanon, with the others in between. The Iraqi system under Saddam Hussain was not as mobilized as are totalitarian ones such as in China, and the Lebanese press is not as independent as, say, British newspapers. All of the Arab countries have some elements of an authoritarian press system, in which the ruling elite in the country has considerable influence over newspaper content and the independence of journalists is periodically abridged.

One characteristic of an authoritarian media system is that communication tends to be top-down, with the overwhelmingly predominant flow of messages from the government to the people. Often when editors determine the content of the newspapers, readers are largely ignored, and audience feedback is uncommon. This has been generally true of Arab media, although with the advent of satellite television, it has started to change. Candid discussion and contentious call-in programs on television and radio have become much more common, and newspapers like *al-Ittihad* in Abu Dhabi or *al-Hayat* have expanded their op-ed pages, bringing more reader viewpoints into the discussion. The audience is not as passive as it used to be, although it still tends to be more passive than in the West.

DYNAMICS OF CHANGE

The four basic types of press system which I have identified are not static and permanent, but depend very much on existing conditions.

The diverse type of print media existed in 2003 in only four Arab countries, but it appeared at earlier times in the four countries that now have mobilization systems. The press in those countries also went through a nonpartisan stage, somewhat similar to the loyalist type of press that exists in four Arab countries. The four countries with transitional systems in 2003 belonged to different categories a decade earlier.[1] Thus it is possible for a country to move from any one of the four types to any other, provided conditions are right. One can to a certain extent predict the type of media system by looking at the conditions and key indicators. If there are changes in the status of political parties and opposition groups, in the attitude of the government toward the press, and in the ownership of the newspapers, their role in the political process could be converted into another type.

The type of press system is not merely the accidental byproduct of political realities, however, but is itself an object of political calculations. Rulers know well that if they encourage a freer debate and competition on the political scene, they are encouraging the growth of newspapers some of which will criticize them. So although most Arab governments pay lip-service to a free press, in practice they make attempts to control it. If the regime is determined to make the press a political tool and conditions are just right, it will be able to create a mobilization system out of a loyalist or even a diverse one.

Professional journalists, on the other hand, tend to pull in the other direction and seek more independence from government controls. Backed by powerful enough political factions, they can succeed in gaining at least a measure of freedom. But in the Arab world in the early twenty-first century, with enormous problems of economic development and of foreign policy (the Arab-Israeli conflict) to deal with, it is more difficult for independent-minded journalists to resist the pressure for submergence of press freedom under the regime's demands for national unity needed to face the common problem. In these circumstances it seems easy for people to accept the authoritarian rationale.

RADIO AND TELEVISION: DOMESTIC UNIFORMITY, INTERNATIONAL COMPETITION

Until the 1990s, this rationale had been most forcefully put forward, and most universally accepted, in the case of radio and television. A government monopoly still controls radio in each country in the Arab world and it controls television in every one but Lebanon. Governments insist on controlling the electronic media because of their obvious political importance in communicating with most of the population across the literacy barriers that prevail in the area. The four mobilization states control the electronic media more strictly and they have pushed radio and television development faster in order to use them more, but radio and TV structural forms are more similar in the Arab world than are the forms of press organization. This began to change with the advent of satellite television, which allowed Arab TV to cross political boundaries and reach the entire Arab world. This attracted the attention of audiences and political leaders alike, and on balance, Arab satellite television has been a liberalizing factor.

Paradoxically, in part it has been radio and television, the media most tightly controlled by Arab governments, which gave the Arab public its greatest choice and variety of information and opinion. Prior to 1990, almost all of the Arab electronic media were controlled and restricted by the governments where they were headquartered, and the only way Arab audiences heard news and views other than what was locally approved, was by cross-border radio or, for a few people living in border areas, cross-border television. Thus for several decades, only Arab radio listeners with transistor receivers were able to hear broadcasts of other countries. The close proximity of many countries in the area to each other, and the fact that radio broadcasts did not stop at borders, made it possible for the average Arab to tune in to broadcasts by Arab stations, plus Israel and others, presenting other points of view than his government's. Then after 1990, Arab audiences with access to satellite television have been able to see and hear much more that they had earlier, because of the emergence of the new satellite TV channels in Arabic.

In the twenty-first century, sharp differences remain between Arab print and electronic media. The advent of Arab satellite television during the 1990s gave many Arabs more variety of news and comment, and more quickly, than they had ever had before, and became the preferred medium for those who could afford it. Newspapers could not compete with the electronic media which offer 24/7 coverage, but television depends on visuals and it is impossible to fit all the news into television, so the print media still have a role for in-depth analysis and detailed coverage. The relatively new offshore pan-Arab newspapers in particular have found a niche as somewhat more liberal and broadly-focused media which many readers like because they are different from the local newspapers. However, because of economic circumstances, both satellite television and offshore newspapers face financial constraints which make them dependent on subsidies and the willingness of censors to allow them to circulate, that affects content.

Also, despite satellite television, the information available to Arab audiences on a daily basis still varies considerably from country to country, depending on the nature of the local media system. This local system depends, in turn, on various conditions prevailing in the individual country, as we have seen. Editors and other journalists who are interested in doing a professional job are also consciously and unconsciously influenced by the political environments they work in.

The mass media in the Arab world also participate significantly in the political process, and political and other factors shape the press, radio, and television as institutions. Neither the media nor their environments can be understood properly without reference to the other.

NOTE

1. Tunisia and Jordan were in the loyalist category, Egypt and Algeria were in the mobilization category.

Index

About the Author

WILLIAM A. RUGH was a U.S. Foreign Service Officer from 1964 to 1995, serving in Washington and several Middle Eastern posts, including as Ambassador to Yemen and the United Arab Emirates. From 1995 until 2003 he was President and CEO of AMIDEAST, a private American nonprofit organization promoting cooperation between America and the Middle East. He holds an MA from Johns Hopkins and a PhD from Columbia, and he speaks Arabic.